MEMORY MANAGEMENT IN A MULTIMEDIA WORLD

JOEL POWELL

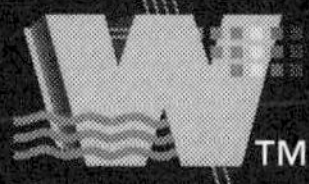

Waite Group Press™
Corte Madera, California

PUBLISHER ◆ MITCHELL WAITE
EDITOR-IN-CHIEF ◆ SCOTT CALAMAR
EDITORIAL DIRECTOR ◆ JOEL FUGAZZOTTO
MANAGING EDITOR ◆ JOHN CRUDO
PRODUCTION DIRECTOR ◆ JULIANNE OSOSKE
CONTENT EDITOR ◆ HARRY HENDERSON
TECHNICAL REVIEWER ◆ RICHARD S. WRIGHT, JR.
DESIGN AND PRODUCTION ◆ SESTINA QUAREQUIO
ILLUSTRATIONS ◆ PAT ROGONDINO
COVER DESIGN ◆ TED MADER + ASSOCIATES

Published by Waite Group Press™, 200 Tamal Plaza, Corte Madera, CA 94925.

Waite Group Press is distributed to bookstores and book wholesalers by Publishers Group West, Box 8843, Emeryville, CA 94662, 1-800-788-3123 (in California 1-510-658-3453).

Printed in the United States of America
94 95 96 97 • 10 9 8 7 6 5 4 3 2 1

Powell, Joel.
Memory management in a multimedia world / Joel Powell.
p. cm.
Includes index.
ISBN: 1-878739-65-4 : $18.95
1. Memory management (Computer science) 2. Multimedia systems.
I . Title.
QA76.9.M45P69 1994
005.4'3--dc20

93-49871
CIP

DEDICATION

For my parents, James T. and Josephine A. Powell.

Joel Powell

ABOUT THE AUTHOR

Joel Powell is a technical writer, programmer, and educator. He currently writes technical documentation for commercial graphic imaging equipment. When he is not teaching or writing, he is usually in front of a personal computer. Joel is an avid C/C++ and Windows programmer. He has also written several training documents for the United States Air Force on ground radar technology and has provided training for over 3,000 students for the U.S.A.F., vocational schools, and private companies. Over 25 countries are represented by his former students. Joel is the co-author of *Falcon 3: The Complete Handbook* (Waite Group Press, 1992) and the author of *Multitask Windows NT* (Waite Group Press, 1993).

TABLE OF CONTENTS

CONTENTS

ACKNOWLEDGMENTS

I would like to thank Mitch Waite for the ideas and inspiration that led me to write this book. Thanks to Scott Calamar, who guided the project during its early stages, and to John Crudo who kept the project (and me) moving from start to finish. Thanks also to Julianne Ososke for managing the production issues.

Special thanks to Harry Henderson, who edited this book for content and clarity. He made a significant contribution as a result. Also, I would like to thank Richard S. Wright, Jr., who edited this book for technical accuracy. Thanks also to the many computer users I bounced ideas off of throughout the project.

Finally, I would like to thank Lori, Dave, and Sarah for their understanding, help, and much needed distractions throughout the project.

Dear Reader:

What is a book? Is it perpetually fated to be inky words on a paper page? Or can a book simply be something that inspires—feeding your head with ideas and creativity regardless of the medium? The latter, I believe. That's why I'm always pushing our books to a higher plane; using new technology to reinvent the medium.

I wrote my first book in 1973, *Projects in Sights, Sounds, and Sensations.* I like to think of it as our first multimedia book. In the years since then, I've learned that people want to experience information, not just passively absorb it—they want interactive MTV in a book. With this in mind, I started my own publishing company and published *Master C,* a book/disk package that turned the PC into a C language instructor. Then we branched out to computer graphics with *Fractal Creations,* which included a color poster, 3-D glasses, and a totally rad fractal generator. Ever since, we've included disks and other goodies with most of our books. *Virtual Reality Creations* is bundled with 3-D Fresnel viewing goggles and *Walkthroughs and Flybys CD* comes with a multimedia CD-ROM. We've made complex multimedia accessible for any PC user with *Ray Tracing Creations, Multimedia Creations, Making Movies on Your PC, Image Lab,* and three books on Fractals.

The Waite Group continues to publish innovative multimedia books on cutting-edge topics, and of course the programming books that make up our heritage. Being a programmer myself, I appreciate clear guidance through a tricky OS, so our books come bundled with disks and CDs loaded with code, utilities, and custom controls.

By 1994, The Waite Group will have published 135 books. Our next step is to develop a new type of book, an interactive, multimedia experience involving the reader on many levels.

With this new book, you'll be trained by a computer-based instructor with infinite patience, run a simulation to visualize the topic, play a game that shows you different aspects of the subject, interact with others on-line, and have instant access to a large database on the subject. For traditionalists, there will be a full-color, paper-based book.

In the meantime, they've wired the White House for hi-tech; the information super highway has been proposed; and computers, communication, entertainment, and information are becoming inseparable. To travel in this Digital Age you'll need guidebooks. The Waite Group offers such guidance for the most important software—your mind.

We hope you enjoy this book. For a color catalog, just fill out and send in the Reader Report Card at the back of the book.

Sincerely,

Mitchell Waite

Mitchell Waite
Publisher

Waite
Group
Press™

INTRODUCTION

The popularity of personal computers continues to grow daily. One reason for this phenomenon is that more people require computer skills in their day-to-day lives. Another reason is that the cost of home computers is reaching the affordable range of most households. The typical system (at the time of this writing) is a 486SX with 4 megabytes of memory. Such a system was beyond the reach of most users as recently as two years ago.

Even though these systems are affordable and well equipped with memory, there still seems to be a common thread between most new (and some experienced) computer users: They cannot manage their memory in a way that is optimal for their systems. Users with newer multimedia devices (such as CD-ROM interfaces, advanced video adapters, etc.) have problems loading the necessary drivers and running their software because of stringent memory requirements.

That's where *Memory Management in a Multimedia World* comes in. This book is written for the user who wants to get the most out of his or her memory. Simply having 2, 4, or even 8 megabytes of memory isn't worth much if your system is not configured to get the most out of it.

This book does not take the approach of giving you a solution to your problems without an explanation. After all, a book full of solutions serves its goal only if it has the solution to your specific problem. This book gives you the information to help you solve your own memory problems and, at the same time, teaches you why memory problems occur in general. With this knowledge, you'll not only be able to solve your memory problems, you may find yourself solving your friends' and co-workers' memory problems as well.

Memory for Your Future Needs

If you are not running into memory problems at this time, you may find that newer applications are becoming increasingly hungry for memory. This book also presents information that will be useful to you in the future. You'll know ahead of time what kind of problems to expect, and more importantly, how to solve them.

Who This Book Is For

This book targets new and experienced users who are looking for solutions and ideas in memory management. If you feel that you should be getting more out of your system's memory, this book is for you. If you are an experienced user with several memory-hungry applications, this book will help you configure your system's memory to get the most out of each application.

How This Book Is Structured

This book has nine chapters that cover a variety of memory and multimedia hardware topics. Some chapters are common to all computer users and other chapters address specific needs such as DOS 5.0, DOS 6, or Windows memory management.

If you are a DOS 5.0 user considering an upgrade to DOS 6.0 or DOS 6.2, you may want to read Chapter 5 to see what DOS 6 has to offer. Likewise, if you are not using a third-party memory manager, you can read Chapter 7 to see how QEMM and 386MAX can manage your memory.

Here is a summary of the chapters in *Memory Management in a Multimedia World.*

- *Chapter 1: An Introduction to PC Memory* introduces you to memory in physical terms and how it is divided in your system. We discuss the two major types of memory: read-only memory (RAM) and random-access memory (ROM). We also discuss how RAM is divided into different sections such as conventional, upper, and extended. This chapter provides a base for the remainder of the book.

- *Chapter 2: Memory and Your Computer* contains procedures you can use to get the current configuration of your system. You can use this information to determine where to start in managing your memory. This chapter also introduces CONFIG.SYS and AUTOEXEC.BAT, the DOS configuration files.
- *Chapter 3: Managing Configuration Files* contains examples for systems that require more than one set of configuration files. Also included are two batch files (STORE.BAT and CHANGE.BAT) which you can use to store and retrieve sets of configuration files. This chapter also contains procedures on creating a boot disk for your system and creating custom startup menus in DOS 6.
- *Chapter 4: DOS 5.0 Memory Management* contains memory configuration information for DOS 5.0 users. Examples are provided for the DOS-supplied memory management tools, such as HIMEM.SYS and EMM386.EXE. This chapter also contains examples on loading device drivers and memory-resident programs into high memory.
- *Chapter 5: DOS 6 Memory Management* contains memory configuration information for DOS 6 users (both versions 6.0 and 6.2). Examples are provided for the DOS-supplied memory management tools, such as HIMEM.SYS and EMM386.EXE. This chapter also contains examples on loading device drivers and memory-resident programs into high memory. You can compare this chapter's example results with the DOS 5.0 chapter if you are considering an upgrade.
- *Chapter 6: Windows Memory Management* contains information on the memory requirements of Microsoft Windows in both standard and 386 enhanced mode. Example configurations are provided that optimize a system running the Windows operating system and Windows applications exclusively. This chapter also contains information on virtual memory and swap files.
- *Chapter 7: Third-Party Memory Management* contains information on two popular third-party memory managers: Quarterdeck's QEMM and Qualitas' 386MAX. Use this chapter to see if you might benefit from one of these products. This chapter also contains information on the memory utilities provided with these memory managers.
- *Chapter 8: The Configuration Files* contains example sets of configuration files you can use as a starting point for your system. Examples are

provided for DOS 5.0 and 6 users. This chapter also contains example configurations for Windows users.

- *Chapter 9: IRQs, DMA, and Other Mysteries* discusses the conflicts that occur when installing new hardware in your PC (SCSI adapter, sound card, etc.). Examples of interrupt (IRQ), direct-memory access (DMA), and input/output ports (I/O) are provided.

Time to Get Started!

It's time to go to work and find the perfect memory configuration for your computer. The first chapter lays the groundwork for the remainder of this book. There is quite a bit of information covered in Chapter 1, so don't be too discouraged if you don't understand it on the first pass. You can always refer back to it while reading the later chapters. Good luck with your memory!

CHAPTER 1

An Introduction to PC Memory

The personal computer and computer software have evolved at a rapid pace over the last decade. Just think. Less than twenty years ago we were excited at the introduction of Pong. This was an interesting computerized version of table tennis we could play at the arcade, or even in the comfort of our homes. Didn't you feel as though you were part of the action?

Then the floodgates opened. The personal computer, or PC, was introduced in the late seventies and we've hardly had time to look back. I still fondly remember my first PC—a TRS-80 with 4K of random-access memory. Sounds impressive doesn't it? At least it did at the time. I fired it up and started to teach myself BASIC programming. Eight hours later my heart was broken as I stared at an ominous message on the screen: OUT OF MEMORY. I couldn't believe it! I found myself back at the store the next day upgrading my system to a whopping 16K, and paying an amount of money I don't even want to discuss.

Here we are in the 1990s, when 16K is a tiny fraction of the memory installed in the average PC. And guess what? Most of us still run into those dreaded messages indicating that our system isn't up to snuff memory-wise. Why does this keep happening to us? The main reason is that software developers continue to push the boundaries of memory. They try to get the most out of the computer's memory so you can get the most out of their product. Multimedia applications are no exception. In fact, they can be some of the most demanding programs on the market.

There is no reason to become discouraged about these memory requirements, however. Armed with some knowledge about PC memory and memory configuration, you can solve many of the problems you run into. Chances are you won't have to purchase additional memory to solve a memory problem. It may just be how you configure your system that makes the difference between running and stumbling.

Before you start to configure your system, it is very helpful to understand what memory is and how your PC utilizes it. That's where this chapter comes in. By the end of this chapter you will have a solid understanding of memory. There is a lot of information in this chapter, so don't be discouraged if you don't understand it on the first pass. You can use this information as a springboard to tackle most of your memory problems. Let's look at a quick overview of the topics we will discuss in this chapter.

TOPICS COVERED

- A Definition of Memory
- Types of Computer Memory
- Memory Packaging
- Computer Numbering Systems
- The 80x86 Microprocessor Family
- Memory Addressing
- Conventional Memory
- Upper Memory
- Expanded Memory
- Extended Memory
- High Memory
- Buying Additional Memory

What Exactly Is Memory?

On a basic level, computer memory is made up of a set of integrated circuits, or "chips." These memory chips store information that is utilized by the microprocessor in different ways. For example, the microprocessor uses memory to store data. This data may be a letter you are typing into a word processor or names and addresses in a database. On the other hand, the microprocessor also uses memory to store programs. Computer programs are made up of instructions, or code, that the microprocessor uses to manipulate the data. Figure 1-1 shows the interaction of the microprocessor, memory, data, and code for a word processor.

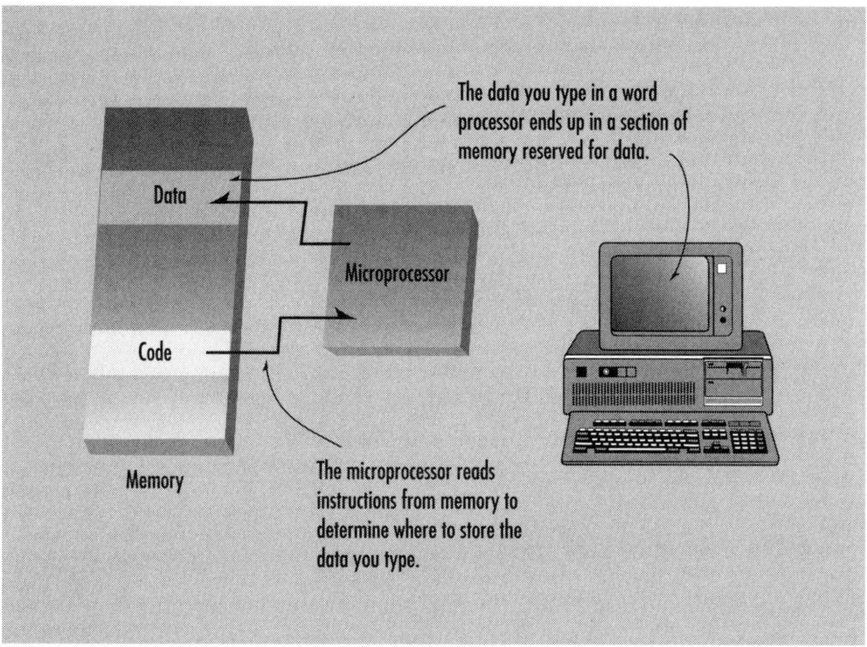

Figure 1-1 A microprocessor using data and code in memory

When you type information into a word processor, the microprocessor uses instructions to interpret your keystrokes and store the data in memory. Without memory the microprocessor is nearly useless. But a microprocessor also depends on being able to find the right instructions in memory. In turn, it uses the instructions to determine where to store the data in memory. Although the figure shows a one-way path between the code or data and microprocessor, this is not always the case. The microprocessor can also read data from memory as well as write data into the code (although the latter is more uncommon).

You can see that the larger a program is, the less memory space is available for data (and vice versa). Programs that are available today require more and more memory. This is why it is important for your system to be optimally configured so that it gets the most out of every byte of memory.

Another important note about Figure 1-1 is that it does not show that memory is used for more than code and data for one program. An operating system (such as MS-DOS) resides in memory also. The operating system plays a big role in how memory is allocated and in the input/output (I/O) between the processor and the various devices attached to your PC. Without the operating system, your computer would not be able to access disk drives, the video display, and other devices. Later in this chapter we will show how memory is divided among the operating system, programs, and I/O.

Our simple example shows only one type of memory. There are actually several kinds of memory in your PC. Let's take a closer look at how PC memory is organized and used.

Types of Computer Memory

A computer requires two basic types of memory to do its job: read-only memory and random-access memory. Although we don't have much control over read-only memory, it is important to understand where it is located and how it comes into play in memory management.

Read-Only Memory (ROM)

Read-only memory, or *ROM*, is a more permanent form of memory. Perhaps the most important ROM chip in your computer is the *basic input/output system*, or *BIOS*. The BIOS is the first program to run on your PC when you turn it on. Without the BIOS, the computer would not even know that there are disk drives or a monitor attached.

You may have noticed a message that your PC displays when you first turn it on. This may give you some indication of who manufactured your BIOS ROM. Two popular BIOS manufacturers are American Megatrends (AMI) and Phoenix. This message comes from the ROM installed in the main board (also called the motherboard) of your PC. If you are comfortable with cracking open your PC, you should be able to find your BIOS ROM or ROMs somewhere on your motherboard. The location of the BIOS ROM varies depending on the manufacturer of the board. If you would rather stay away from the inner workings of your computer, Figure 1-2 shows a typical ROM chip.

A ROM chip has two rows of metal contacts, or leads, on either side of its body. The formation of the pins and body is commonly referred to as "packaging." The packaging for a ROM is a dual in-line package; there are two rows of leads in parallel with each other. The leads, when inserted into the appropriate socket, are the connection to the microprocessor via a bus (a series of foil paths that carry data signals) and associated circuitry. This allows the microprocessor to access (retrieve) specific data within the ROM.

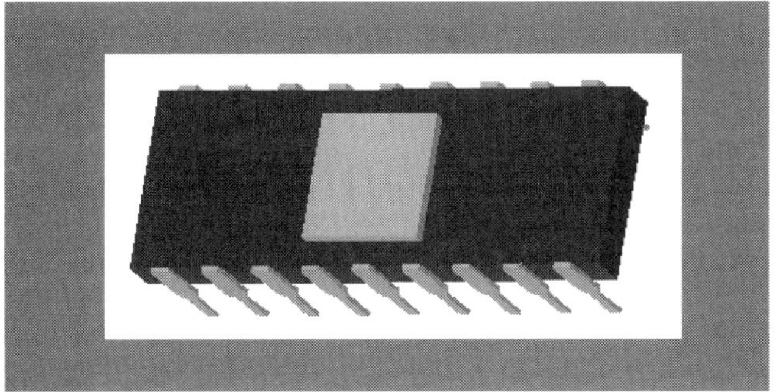

Figure 1-2 A read-only memory (ROM) chip

ROMs Are Not Just for System BIOS

If you explore the inside of your PC, you may see other ROM chips. For example, many motherboards have keyboard ROMs. Expansion boards (such as video adapters and hard disk controllers) also have ROMs. Each of these ROMs has a program that aids in controlling the particular device.

Advantages and Disadvantages of ROM

The main advantage of a ROM chip is that the data is persistent. The chip does not require power to maintain its data. But how does the data get there in the first place? The data is loaded into the ROM by a special piece of equipment. We'll discuss different types of ROMs in a moment.

The disadvantage of ROM is that it cannot be changed (at least by the end-user of the computer). We're stuck with whatever is stored in the ROM. Fortunately, most ROMs are carefully programmed to contain the data that is necessary for the job. Another disadvantage of ROMs is that they are slow. When the microprocessor requests data from ROM memory, the data is not available immediately; it takes time for the chip to respond. A bit later on we'll examine random-access memory, which has a much shorter access time.

Types of ROM

There are three types of ROM used in PCs today. Two are more common, while a third is becoming more popular. The first is EPROM, or *erasable programmable read-only memory.* This type of ROM can be erased and programmed with the aid of special equipment. An EPROM has a window on its top which, if exposed to ultraviolet light, allows data to be erased. Most EPROMs have a label covering the window.

The second type of ROM is EEPROM, or *electrically erasable programmable read-only memory.* The advantage of this ROM is that it does not have to be removed from its socket to be erased and reprogrammed. However, the circuitry in the PC itself normally doesn't support doing so.

The last type of ROM is *flash* EPROM. This type of ROM is becoming more popular, especially in adapter ROMs such as hard drive controllers. By running a special program, a manufacturer can make changes to the flash EPROM while it remains in the PC.

Why Do We Care About ROM?

Our main concern with ROM does not lie in its programming or whether or not it can be erased. You will see later in this chapter that our main concern is where the ROMs (BIOS and adapter) fit in the scheme of memory addresses. The ROMs must coexist with RAM in a system. Now let's examine the type of memory that is the primary focus of this book: *random-access memory.*

Random-Access Memory

The main concern of most PC users is the quantity of *random-access memory,* or RAM. In general, the more RAM you have installed in your PC, the better. However, having tons of RAM doesn't mean much if you do not have your system configured properly. This concern is central to almost every chapter in this book.

RAM has several advantages over ROM. For example, RAM is not read-only; the microprocessor can read and write to RAM. Another advantage is that RAM is faster than ROM. The microprocessor does not have to wait as long after requesting a piece of information from RAM.

The main disadvantage of RAM is that it is *volatile.* This means that it will not retain information if the chip loses power. Many of us have had the experience of entering information into a computer, losing power, and consequently losing the information. That's why we need persistent data storage, such as magnetic disks and tape.

Before digging into the details of how memory is laid out in your PC, let's look at the types of packages that RAM comes in. Figure 1-3 shows the three types of RAM chips.

Dual In-Line Package

The dual in-line package, or DIP, was the most popular RAM chip in early model PCs. If you bought your PC more than a few years ago, chances are you probably have DIP memory chips. The DIP looks like a small rectangular piece

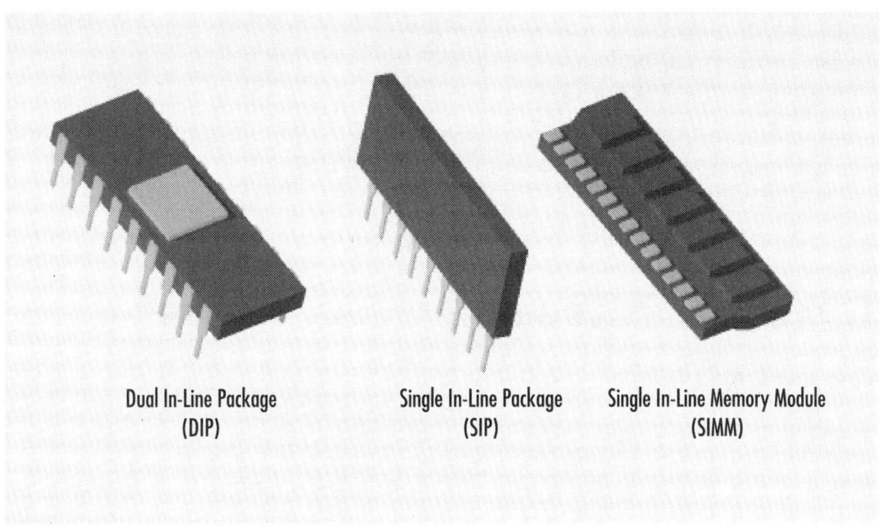

Figure 1-3 RAM packaging—DIP, SIP, and SIMM

of plastic with leads coming out of both sides; the design is similar to the ROM discussed earlier in this chapter.

DIP memory chips are installed in groups of nine chips called *banks.* (We will discuss the significance of nine chips later in this chapter.) The amount of memory installed in your PC is a function of the capacity of the DIP and the number of banks. Different brands and models of computer motherboards can accept varying numbers of DIP banks.

Single In-Line Package

The single in-line package, or SIP, is probably the least popular of the three types of RAM. However, this does not mean that your PC does not use them. A SIP is identified as a thin chip that mounts vertically. Its leads plug into a single-rowed socket on your motherboard.

The SIP replaces an equivalent of nine DIPs with a single chip. Most PCs that employ SIPs allow multiple banks of them. The total memory installed is a function of the capacity of the SIP and the number of banks.

Single In-Line Memory Module

If you run down to your computer store today and buy a PC, the motherboard will most likely contain single in-line memory modules, or SIMMs. A SIMM looks like a small circuit card with three or nine (there's that number again!)

chips mounted on it. Instead of metal leads, the SIMM has an *edge connector* similar to an expansion board in your PC.

Like the SIP, a SIMM replaces nine DIPs with a single package. Most of today's PCs allow up to four, eight, or sixteen SIMMs on the motherboard. Again, the total memory installed is a function of the capacity of the SIP and the number of banks.

Think Like a Computer—Binary and Hexadecimal

Now it's time to consider certain "magic numbers" that keep coming up when we talk about PC memory. In order to understand memory management, it is important to see how computers store data. The data in a computer is numeric; even when data represents a character of the alphabet, the computer stores the character as a number.

Humans are used to the decimal numbering system. We start counting at zero, and when we get to nine we add a digit (a one) and start all over again at ten. Therefore, we have ten numbers in our numbering system, hence the name, *deci*mal.

Computers are digital devices. This means they can keep track of two numbers at a time: zero and one. Inside your computer this is represented as a voltage being present, or not present (or two different levels of voltage).

Although we could continue to discuss memory in terms of the decimal system, this is not usually used in computer documentation. Computer manuals and books normally discuss memory in terms of the hexadecimal numbering system. Another reason we are discussing these numbering systems is to help us understand the differences and capabilities of different microprocessors. Let's take a closer look at the binary and hexadecimal numbering systems.

Do You Speak Binary?

As we mentioned, the binary system consists of two numbers: 0 and 1. Sounds easy doesn't it? The trouble is that we are constantly trying to convert this foreign numbering system back into our familiar decimal system. Let's start with a simple example of counting from 0 to 15. Figure 1-4 shows this process.

The decimal portion of the example is fairly obvious to us; however, the binary example requires some discussion. The first difference is noted when we go from the number 1 to the number 2 (in decimal). Notice that the binary equiv-

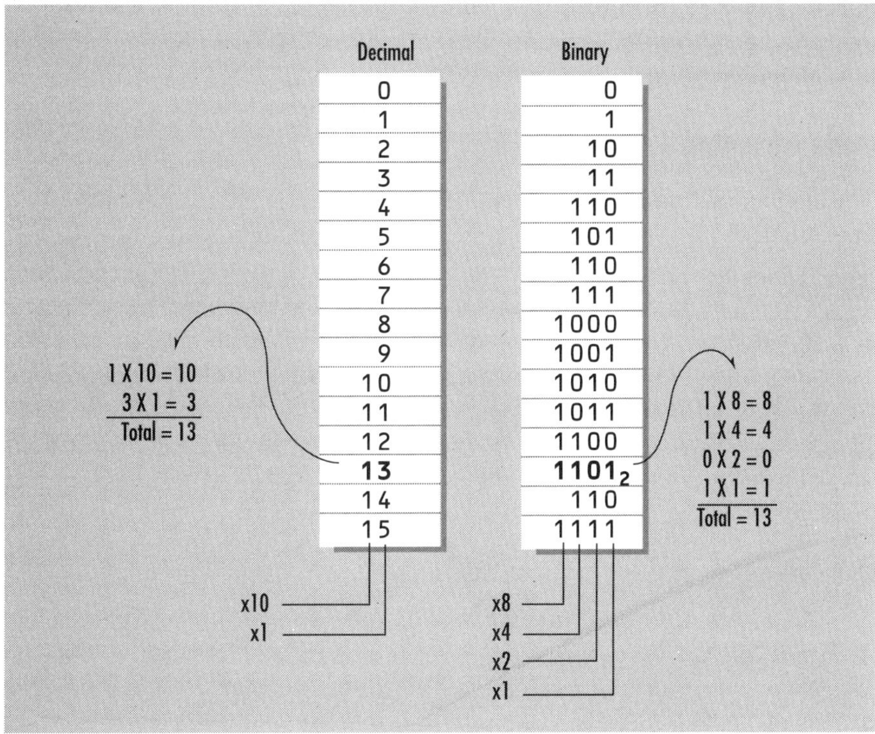

Figure 1-4 An example of the binary numbering system

alent adds a new digit at this point. This is because the binary (or "base 2") numbering system does not have a number 2.

At the bottom of Figure 1-4 you will notice the weights of each digit for both the decimal and binary systems. The rightmost digit of the decimal system is worth 1 and the next digit has a weight, or power, of 10. This process continues for the decimal system, each digit being worth 10 times the previous (1, 10, 100, 1000, and so on). In the binary numbering system, however, subsequent digits are increased by a power of 2 (1, 2, 4, 8, 16, and so on). Binary numbers are often identified by a subscript 2 tacked onto the end of number; for example 1101_2 when the $_2$ indicates base 2, power of 2, or binary.

The example also shows how to find the decimal value of a binary number, in this case 1101_2. We do this by multiplying the digit's weight by the digit itself and adding the values as we move from left to right. For example 1101_2 is (1 x 8) + (1 x 4) + (0 x 2) + (1 x 1). This reduces to 8 + 4 + 0 + 1, or 13 decimal.

Notice that it takes four binary digits to represent the number 13. Because there are only two possible numbers in the binary system, it requires more digits than the decimal system which has ten. Now let's look at another numbering system which fits in with the binary numbering scheme, yet is easier to understand by humans.

Understanding Hexadecimal

The hexadecimal numbering system, also called base 16, has 16 possible digits. In addition to the 0 through 9 that the decimal system uses, it also uses the first six letters of the alphabet (A through F). This numbering system fits well with computer technology because 16 is a power of 2. The number 10 isn't a power of 2, so our familiar numbering system does not fit well with microprocessors.

Let's look at an example comparing the decimal and hexadecimal numbering systems. Figure 1-5 shows this example.

This example shows an arbitrary decimal number, 64,906, and its hexadecimal equivalent, $FD8A_{16}$ (note the subscript 16 denoting the hexadecimal

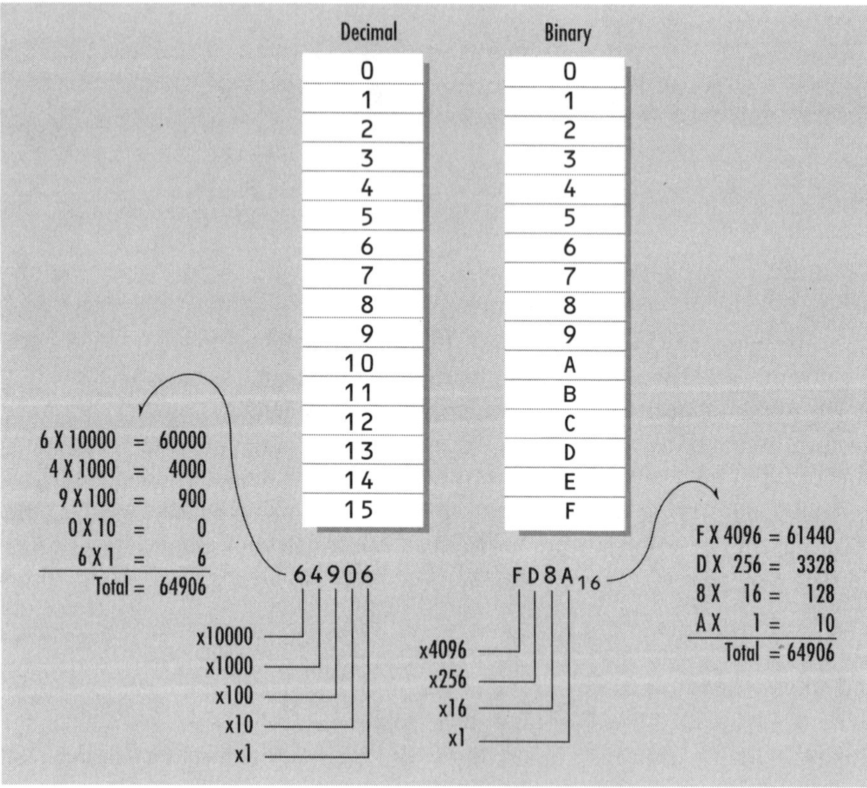

Figure 1-5 An example of the hexadecimal numbering system

number). As with the binary number, we can find the decimal equivalent of the hexadecimal number by multiplying each of the digits by its weight. Each more significant digit of the hexadecimal number is multiplied by 16 (1, 16, 256, 4096, and so on). In this example, we take FD8A and calculate (15 x 4,096) + (13 x 256) + (8 x 16) + (10 x 1), which reduces to 61,440 + 3,328 + 128 + 10, or 64,906.

Do I Have to Be a Binary/Hexadecimal Wizard?

If this is your first exposure to binary and hexadecimal numbering systems, they may seem a little confusing. You do not have to be a wizard at these systems to optimally configure your PC's memory. It just helps to understand the general concept of memory management. Binary helps you understand why some microprocessors can access more memory than others. Hexadecimal will help you understand the memory layout in your own PC and many commands and utilities that work with memory to display it in hexadecimal. You will not have to calculate numbers throughout this book.

Memory and Microprocessors

Different types of processors can use different amounts of memory. Why is that? The reason lies in the *architecture* of the microprocessor itself. Architecture is a fancy way of saying how the processor is designed. The key factors of architecture we will consider are the *data bus, address bus,* and *maximum addressable memory.* These three factors are closely related as you will see in a moment. Let's look at them individually.

Data Bus

The data bus for a microprocessor is measured in lines. Each line in the data bus is capable of carrying one *bit,* or binary digit. The wider the data bus, the more information the processor can move at a time. The processors we will be discussing have an 8-bit, 16-bit, or 32-bit data bus. Table 1-1 shows a comparison of the three bus widths. An 8-bit data bus can carry a *byte* at a time. A byte is 8 bits; this can represent a decimal number range of 0 to 255. Represented in binary this is 00000000_2 to 11111111_2. A 16-bit data bus can carry 2 bytes at a time. This can represent the decimal numbers 0 to 65,535. Finally, the 32-bit data bus can carry 4 bytes. This can represent the decimal numbers 0 through 4,294,967,295.

Data Bus Width	Decimal Range	Hexadecimal Range
8-bit	0 to 255	0h to FFh
16-bit	0 to 65,535	0h to FFFFh
32-bit	0 to 4,294,967,295	0h to FFFFFFFFh

Table 1-1 Numerical ranges of PC data bus widths

Memory Chips and the Infamous "Ninth" Bit

Memory chips do not store a byte individually. Instead each chip is responsible for storing a bit. Eight chips storing a bit each make up an individual byte. When we discussed banks of memory we said that a bank of DIP memory required nine chips. Nine is certainly not a power of two. The truth is that a byte is 8 bits, so we should only need eight chips, right? The ninth bit is there so the processor can test the integrity of the data. This is called *parity.* The parity bit is 1 or 0 based on the number of ones in the byte. If the microprocessor checks the parity bit for a particular byte, and the parity is wrong, a parity error occurs. This usually halts the system. Parity errors are usually caused by faulty memory chips or static electricity.

Address Bus and Maximum Addressable Memory

The width of a microprocessor's address bus determines how much memory can be *addressed.* Every byte in computer memory has an address. Address bus widths for the processors we are concerned with (the Intel 80x86 family) are 20-bit, 24-bit, or 32-bit address buses. Table 1-2 shows a comparison of address bus widths. If you do the conversion, this equates to 1,048,576 bytes for a 20-bit address bus, 16,777,216 bytes for a 24-bit address bus, and a whopping 4,294,967,296 bytes for the 32-bit address bus. Let's look at the significance of these numbers.

Bit, Byte, Kilobyte, Megabyte, and Gigabyte

We've already said that a bit is a single binary digit (0 or 1), and a byte is 8 bits. Now we need to define a few more terms. Kilo is a prefix that we normally relate to one thousand. Well, that's not exactly true when it comes to computers. A kilobyte is not a thousand bytes, it's actually 1,024 bytes. Why not 1,000 bytes? Remember that computers are based on the binary system and 1,024 is a power of 2 while 1,000 is not. The same rule applies to the prefixes mega and giga. Mega normally refers to 1,000,000 in the human world, and giga refers to

Address Bus Width	Amount of Addressable Memory
20-bit	1,048,576 bytes (1 megabyte)
24-bit	16,777,216 bytes (16 megabytes)
32-bit	4,294,967,296 bytes (4 gigabytes)

Table 1-2 Addressable memory for PC address bus widths

1,000,000,000. Table 1-3 shows the decimal equivalents for the prefixes as they relate to computers.

So you can see that if we refer to a kilobyte, we are not saying one thousand bytes. We are actually saying 1,024 bytes. The same goes for mega and giga. If you have a computer with 4 megabytes, you do not have 4,000,000 bytes, you actually have 4,194,304 bytes (4 x 1,048,576).

This all may seem trivial at the moment; however, many people have been confused when a program claims that it needs 600K of memory to run. They check the available memory and find out they have 601,234 bytes available, but the program still claims they don't have enough memory. What is happening? They mistook 600K for 600,000 bytes. It is really 614,400 bytes or 600 x 1,024. Don't let yourself fall into this trap.

Now let's look at the individual processors that are in today's PCs. They are all based on the Intel architecture, although Intel is not the only manufacturer of these processors. This set of processors is known as the 80x86 family.

The 8088 and 8086

The earliest models of IBM and IBM clone computers used the 8088 processor. Although impressive at the time, these processors have severe limitations by today's standards. Newer software (such as Windows, multimedia applications,

Prefix	For a Human	For a Computer
Kilo	1,000	1,024
Mega	1,000,000	1,048,576
Giga	1,000,000,000	1,073,741,824

Table 1-3 Prefixes for humans and computers

games, and graphics intensive programs) require a lot of memory. The 8088 falls short of the requirements for most programs.

You may think the only reason newer microprocessors are superior is that they have the ability to run at faster clock speeds. While speed is certainly an important consideration, another major difference between the processors is that the address bus grew wider as the microprocessor family grew.

The 8088 has a 20-bit data bus. This allows the processor to address up to 1 megabyte of memory, or 1,048,576 bytes. The 8088 also has an 8-bit *external* data bus and a 16-bit *internal* data bus. This means the processor can move information 8 bits at a time external to the processor (that is, between the processor and memory) and 16 bits at a time internal to the processor. This is the primary difference between the 8088 and 8086. Figure 1-6 shows the 8088 and 8086 processor's internal/external data buses and their address buses.

The 8086 processor also has 20 address lines, and as such can address 1 megabyte of memory. It has a 16-bit internal and external data bus. The major drawback to this processor, compared to the 8088, was that it was more expensive. This was the major reason early IBM and IBM clone computers used the 8088.

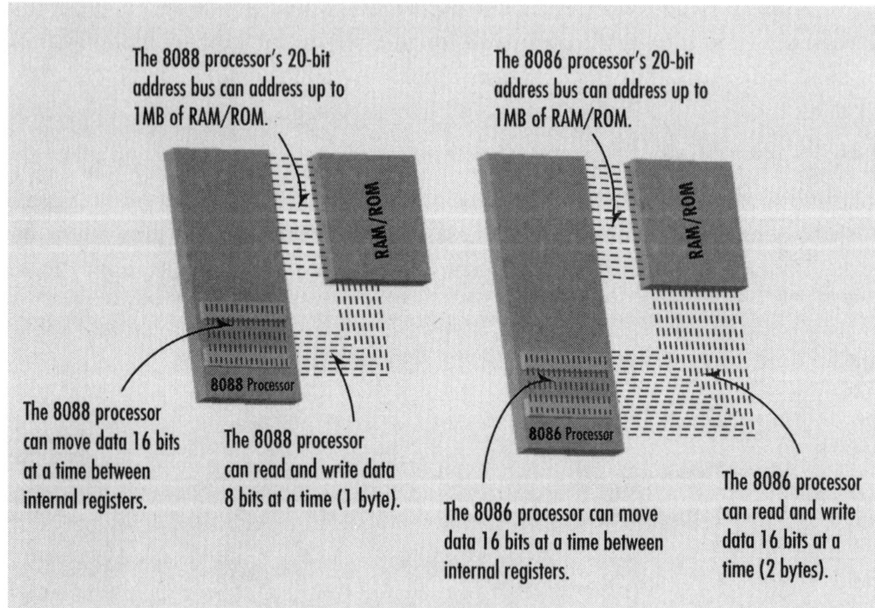

Figure 1-6 The 8088 and 8086 processors—inside and out

The 80286

The next major step in the 80x86 microprocessor family was the 80286, sometimes referred to as a 286. It is superior to the 8088 in three ways. First, the 80286 was built to run at higher clock speeds. Second, the 80286 has a 16-bit internal and external bus width (remember that the 8086 has an 8-bit external data bus). The final, and the most significant change in terms of memory, is that the 80286 has a 24-bit address bus. This wider bus width permitted this processor to address up to 16 megabytes of memory. Figure 1-7 shows the 80286 processor's internal/external data bus and its address bus.

Even though the 80286 could address this huge (at the time) amount of memory, there were still limitations. Thes limitations were not due to the microprocessor architecture. Instead they were limitations of the operating system: DOS. We'll examine the limitations DOS imposed in just a moment.

The 80386SX and 80386DX

The transition from the 80286 to the 80386 was perhaps the most dramatic in terms of addressing memory and moving data. The 80386DX has a 32-bit data bus (internal and external) and a 32-bit address bus. Not only can this processor move 4 bytes of data at a time, it can also address up to 4 gigabytes of memory! This amount of actual physical memory is unheard of in PCs...so far. Perhaps someday we will consider this limitation a problem. Figure 1-8 shows the

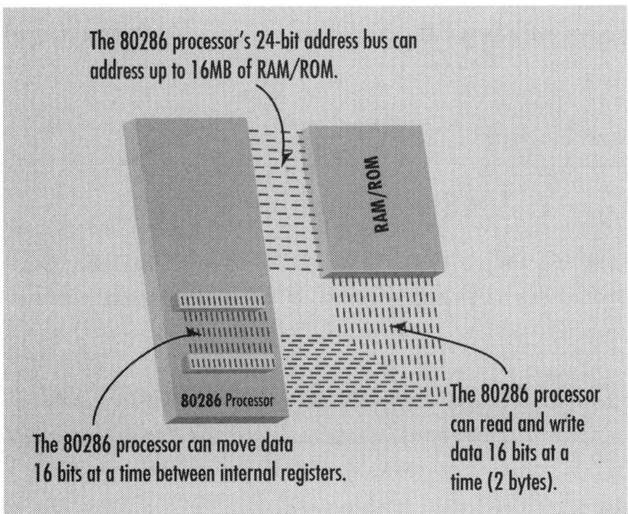

Figure 1-7 The 80286 processor—inside and out

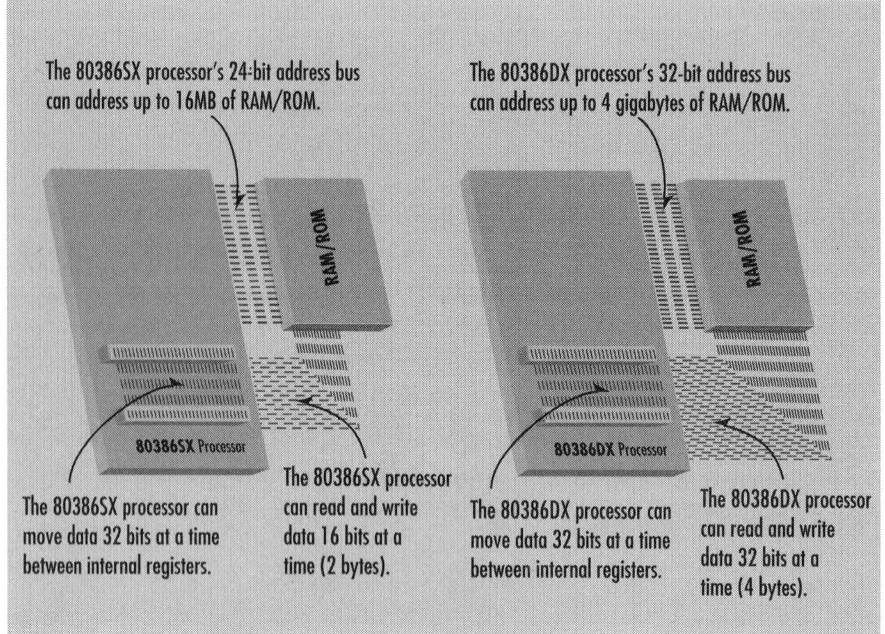

Figure 1-8 The 80386SX and 80386DX processors—inside and out

80386SX and 80386DX processors' internal/external data buses and their address buses.

The 80386SX is scaled down a bit compared to the 80386DX. It has a narrower external data and address bus width. The 80386SX has a 16-bit external data bus width as opposed to the 32-bit data path the 80386DX offers. It also has the same limitation of a 80286 when it comes to addressing memory. This is due to the 24-bit address bus width.

The 80486SX, 80486DX, 80486DX2, and the Pentium

If you go out to buy a new PC today, you will probably have a hard time finding a PC with the processors we've discussed thus far. The minimum, off-the-shelf system today will probably contain an 80486SX processor. In terms of performance and cost new systems range from the 80486SX to the 80486DX (which has an internal numeric coprocessor), to the 80486DX2 (which uses clock-doubling technology for higher speed), and finally to the Pentium (sometimes referred to as a '586). Figure 1-9 shows the 80486 family of processors' internal/external data bus and their address buses.

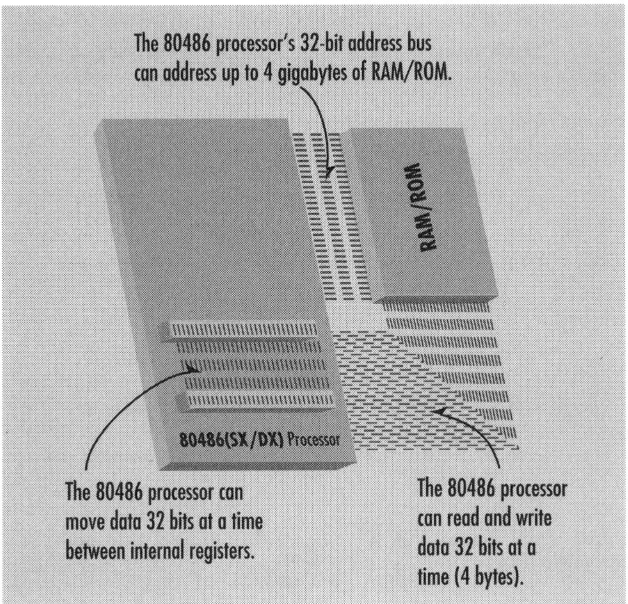

Figure 1-9 The 80486SX and 80486DX processors—inside and out

There is some good news in terms of basic architecture (data bus width and address bus width). For all of these new processors, the architecture is the same as the 80386DX; that is a 32-bit internal and external data bus width, and a 32-bit address width. Table 1-4 shows a summary of the 80x86 microprocessors and their respective data and address bus widths.

DOS and Memory Limitations

As we noted earlier, processor architecture is only one source of memory limitations. The operating system in use also plays an important role. Even with DOS version 6.0, we are still limited by how memory is addressed. Recall that the original IBM PC used an 8088 microprocessor, which had a 20-bit address bus and an internal 16-bit data bus. Because you can't fit 20 bits in a 16-bit area, a special technique had to be used to represent memory addresses. This work around is known as *segment-offset addressing*.

Processor	Internal Data Bus	External Data Bus	Address Bus	Addressable Memory
8086	16-bit	8-bit	20-bit	1 megabyte
8088	16-bit	16-bit	20-bit	1 megabyte
80286	16-bit	16-bit	24-bit	16 megabytes
80386SX	32-bit	16-bit	24-bit	16 megabytes
80386DX	32-bit	32-bit	32-bit	4 gigabytes
80486SX	32-bit	32-bit	32-bit	4 gigabytes
80486DX	32-bit	32-bit	32-bit	4 gigabytes
80486DX2	32-bit	32-bit	32-bit	4 gigabytes
Pentium	64-bit	64-bit	32-bit	4 gigabytes

Table 1-4 The 80x86 family of microprocessors

Segment-Offset Addressing

In order to represent an address in memory, DOS combines two 16-bit values. One 16-bit value is known as the *segment,* the other is the *offset* to the segment. Figure 1-10 shows an example of this technique. Note that there are 16 segments of 64K each. A segment is limited to 64K becuse the offset is 16 bits; 16 bits can address up to 64K.

The 20-bit address is formed by adding the segment (shifted to the left one place) to the offset. The segment value specifies which segment we are addressing and the offset specifies how far into the segment the address is located. For example, Figure 1-10 shows how we can locate a specific byte. The byte is in segment 5000h (the h stands for hex), and the offset is FFF8h. We shift the segment to the left one place and add the offset. This ends up being 50000h + FFF8h = 5FFF8h. This is the physical address of the byte.

Now you can see how we can construct 20-bit addresses with 16-bit values by combining a segment and an offset. Remember each hex digit represents four bits.

How much memory can we address using this scheme? Because we have 16 segments, and each segment is 64K, the total addressable memory is 16 x 64K, or 1,024K. This value also happens to be 1 megabyte. Recall that the 8088 processor can address up to 1 megabyte of memory. So you would think that by

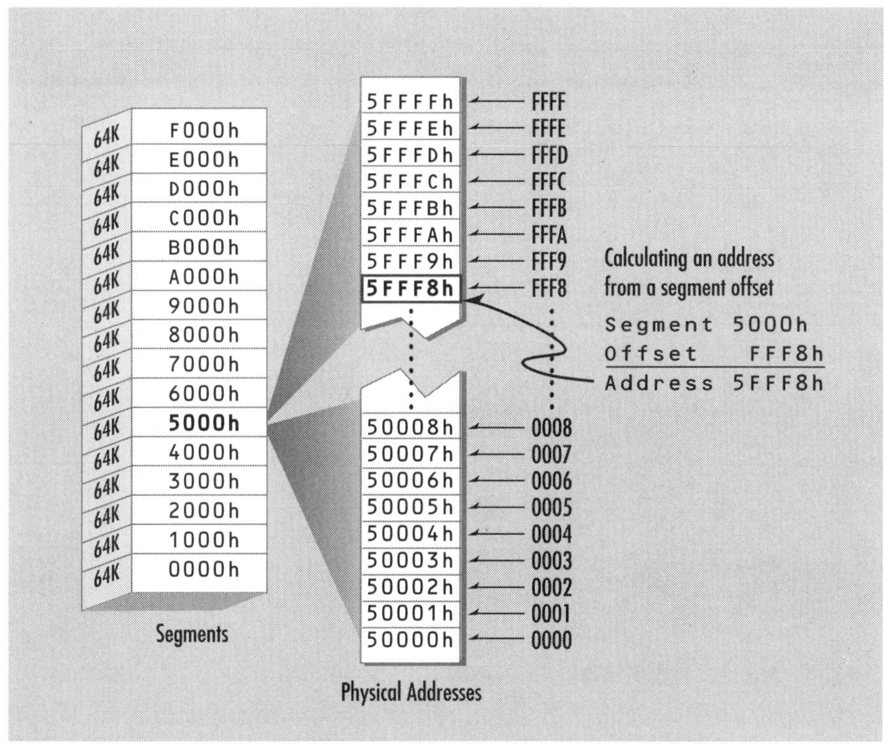

Figure 1-10 Segment-offset memory addressing

using an 8088 and MS-DOS we can use up to 1 megabyte of memory. Right? Unfortunately not.

The Infamous 640K Barrier

DOS programs are limited to using 640K of *conventional memory.* We'll cover what conventional memory is in detail in the next section. In the early days of DOS, an arbitrary decision had to be made. How much of the 1 megabyte of memory addresses can we use for RAM and how much can we use for other purposes? Remember, there are other things in a computer we need to address. Things like ROMs for the system and hard disk controllers, video RAM so we can display messages and graphics to the screen, and so on.

The designers of DOS decided that the breakdown should be 640K for RAM and 384K for ROM, video RAM, and others uses. The 640K plus the 384K adds up to the 1MB value. DOS uses the first ten segments to address the RAM

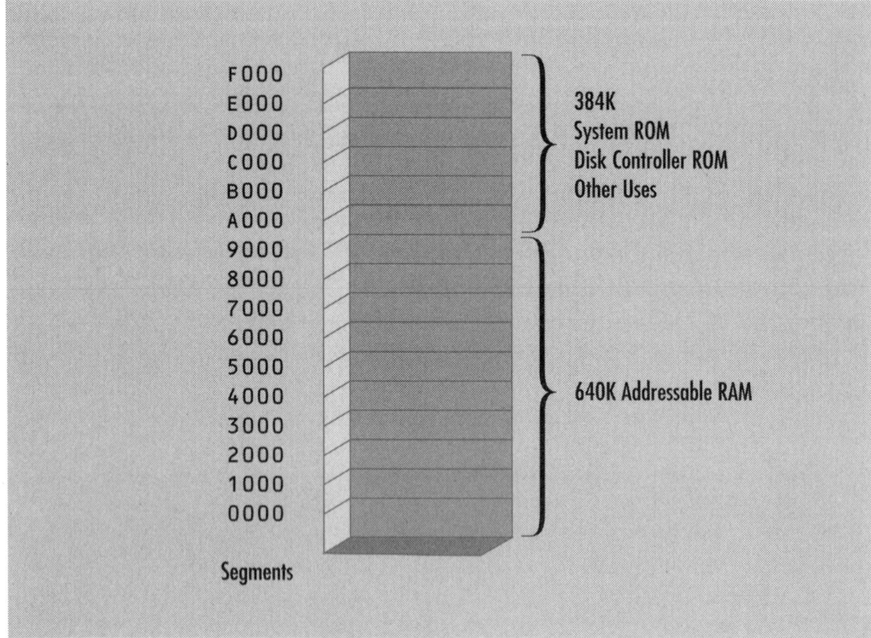

Figure 1-11 The 640K RAM barrier

with which we are most concerned. It uses the remaining six segments for the other areas. Figure 1-11 shows this breakdown.

Now we have these great 80486 computers with 32-bit address and data buses so we should be able to address tons of RAM with no problem; however, this is not the case. DOS continues to use the segment-offset memory addressing scheme in order to be compatible with the older machines. This does not mean we can never use more than 640K of memory. It does, however, mean that we need more than one *type* of memory.

Types of Memory Configurations

Now that we have a background on ROM and RAM memory, types of microprocessors, and DOS limitations, we can get to the main topic: managing our memory. To manage memory effectively, we need to know three things: the amount of memory we have installed, which applications we want to run, and which configuration (or configurations) will allow us to run the applications effectively. You'll answer these questions as you work your way through this book.

Before we do that, however, let's look at five types of memory: conventional, upper, extended, high, and expanded. You'll find that different programs have different requirements when it comes to memory. For example, some programs require a lot of conventional memory, while others require extended or expanded.

Conventional Memory

Conventional memory simply consists of the 640K that we discussed in the previous section. If a PC is equipped with less than 640K, the amount of conventional memory will be less as well. For example, if a PC has 256K of memory installed, it will have 256K conventional memory. All PCs sold today have a full 640K of conventional memory.

Conventional memory is not entirely used for running DOS programs. DOS itself is a program and is loaded in conventional memory. You will learn how to move the majority of DOS into high memory in Chapter 4, *DOS 5.0 Memory Manangement* and Chapter 5, *DOS 6 Memory Management.* This will free up a considerable amount of conventional memory for your own programs. Many of today's programs (multimedia, games, graphics, and so on) require a significant amount of free conventional memory. For now, remember that conventional memory is the first 640K (hex addresses 00000h to 9FFFF).

Upper Memory

Upper memory is probably the most difficult concept to understand, even for experienced PC users. Recall that the upper 384K of memory addresses were reserved for special purposes such as system ROM, hard disk controller ROM, video RAM, and others. Figure 1-12 shows a more detailed description of this area.

Notice that not all the address space in the upper memory area is used. You may be able to use some of these address ranges for RAM and store terminate-and-stay-resident programs or device drivers in this area. Keep in mind that Figure 1-12 is just an example. Your system may have more or less available address space. We will go deeper into this topic in Chapters 4 and 5. For now, keep in mind that address space may be available in upper memory.

It is important to note that utilizing the upper memory addresses requires an 80386 processor or higher. Why? The reason is that a program that ships with DOS 5.0 and DOS 6.0, EMM386.EXE, requires a microprocessor mode called the Virtual 86 mode. How the processor does this is pretty complicated; however, EMM386.EXE does the work for you, providing you have the minimum of an 80386 and the available RAM.

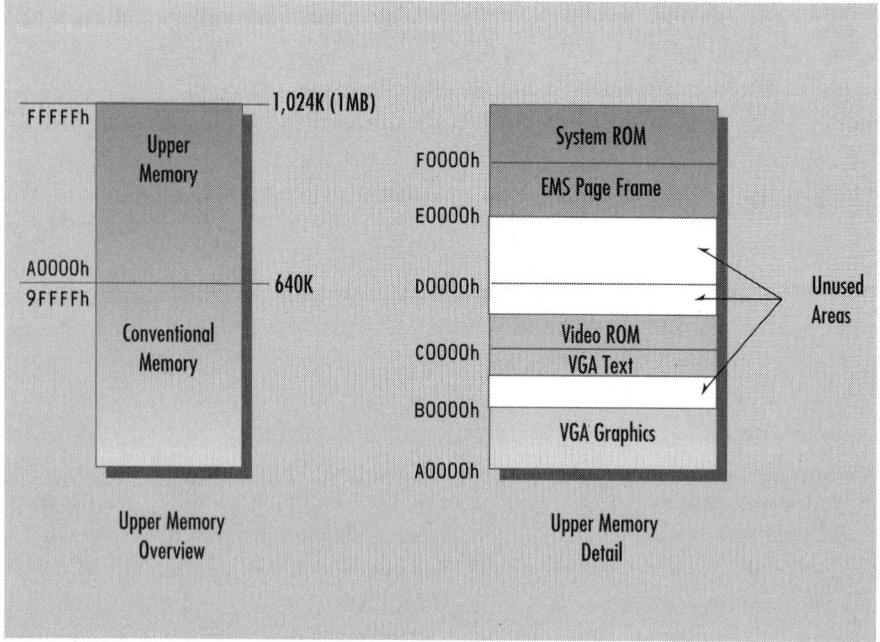

Figure 1-12 The upper memory area

Expanded Memory

Expanded memory came about in the middle of the 1980s when it was determined that many programs required more than the conventional 640K of RAM. The specification for expanded memory was known as *LIM EMS.* This stands for Lotus-Intel-Microsoft expanded memory specification. The first version of LIM EMS was 3.2 (don't ask why). This specification required an expanded memory expansion card and a driver called an *expanded memory manager* (EMM).

Version 3.2 of LIM EMS allowed up to 8 megabytes of RAM on an expanded memory card. The current version of LIM EMS is 4.0, which allows programs to address up to 32MB. It is important to note that a program must be written specifically to take advantage of expanded memory. All the expanded memory in the world won't help if the program never takes advantage of it.

Let's take a look at how a program uses expanded memory. Figure 1-13 shows this process. The figure does not show that an expanded memory manager is loaded, although it is a requirement.

In this expanded memory example, we are using an *EMS page frame* in upper memory at address E0000h. This value is specified when the EMM driver is loaded. The values are usually D0000h or E0000h. The EMS page frame is a

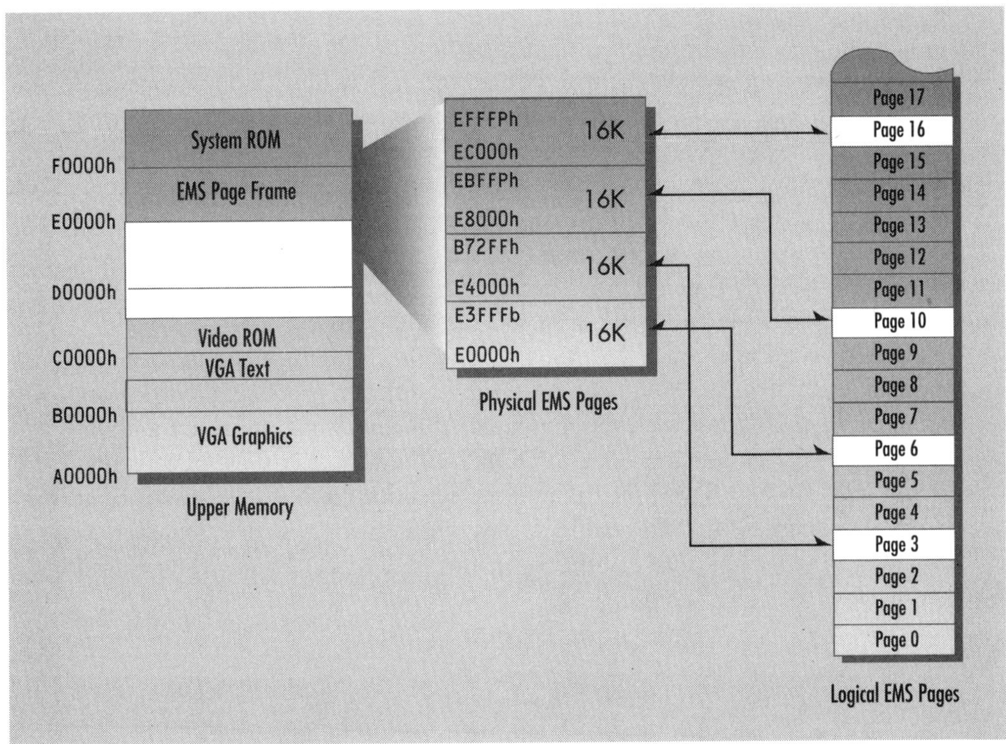

Figure 1-13 How expanded memory works

64K area in upper memory that is divided into four 16K regions called *physical pages.* The actual expanded memory is on the expansion card and is also divided into 16K regions called *logical pages.* A program can swap physical pages to and from the logical pages. Note that the actual expanded memory is outside the normal address space of the microprocessor. The processor can only "see" 64K of expanded memory at one time. That is the four pages that are loaded into the EMS page frame.

You can see that if a program does not take advantage of expanded memory, it has no use. Most computer programs have documentation that states whether or not they use or require expanded memory.

If you have a newer PC, chances are you do not have an expanded memory card. Instead you probably have extended memory which is discussed in the next section. There is no need to go out and buy an expanded memory card in this case. If you have programs that require expanded memory, you can convert extended memory to expanded. This is done using the EMM386.EXE driver (supplied with DOS 5.0 and 6.0) or third-party expanded memory managers.

Extended Memory

The most common memory outside of conventional memory today is extended memory. If you have an 80386/486 with 4 megabytes of RAM, for example, you have 640K conventional, 384K upper, and the rest is extended memory. Like expanded memory, extended memory requires a driver and is subject to an actual program using it. An 8088 microprocessor is incapable of using extended memory because it only has 20 address lines (a limit of 1 megabyte). Figure 1-14 shows that extended memory lies just above the 1-megabyte boundary. This example shows the memory layout for a 2-megabyte system.

How does a PC running DOS get around the 640K barrier and read and write to extended memory? It does so by using a different processor mode known as *protected mode.* In order to utilize extended memory, you must use a driver named HIMEM.SYS (supplied with DOS 5.0 and 6.0), or a third-party equivalent. The HIMEM.SYS driver follows the extended memory specification, or XMS. Like the LIM EMS standard, this specification was put together by Microsoft, Intel, and Lotus. Another company, AST Research, also collaborated on XMS.

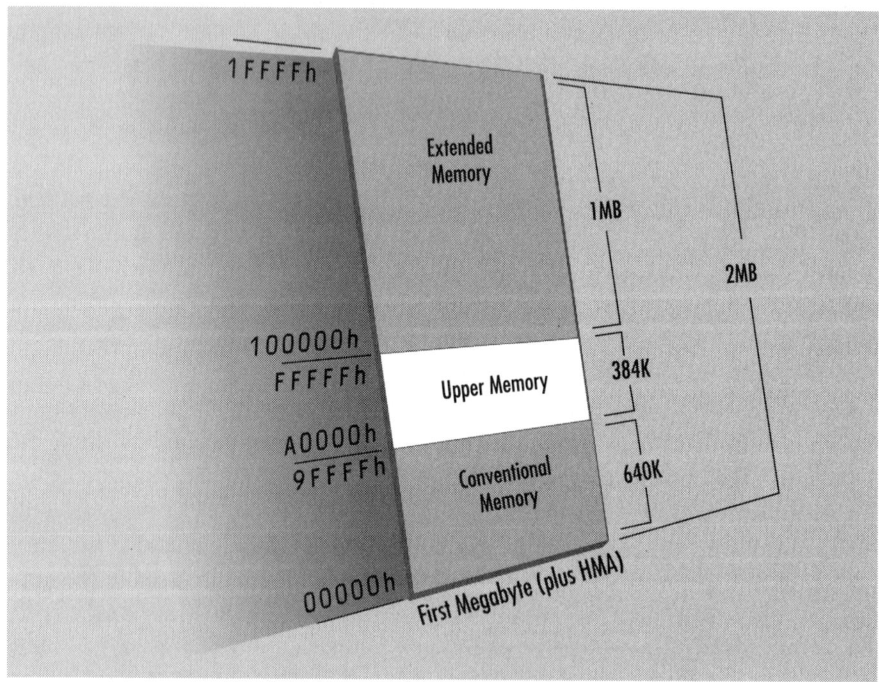

Figure 1-14 Extended memory

The High Memory Area

The last area of memory we are going to discuss is actually in the same address range as extended memory. The high memory area is the first 64K past the 1-megabyte boundary. Actually it falls a little short of 64K, as we'll see in a moment.

Recall that our final segment in the first megabyte is F000h and the maximum offset is FFFFh. By shifting the segment to the left one place and adding the offset, we ended up with FFFFFh. However, if we set the segment value to FFFFh and the offset to FFFFh—and perform the same shift and addition—the result is 10FFEFh. This translates to 1,114,095 decimal. Because the last valid memory address in the first megabyte is 1,048,575, this gives us an additional 65,520 bytes with which to work . This is 16 bytes shy of 64K. This was all done using the 16-bit segment and offset values.

The high memory area is a kind of extension of conventional memory. It is often used to hold a large portion of DOS 5.0 or 6.0 so more conventional memory will be available for applications.

What is the advantage of high memory over extended? The advantage is that the processor does not have to switch to protected mode to access the high memory area. However, you do have to load the HIMEM.SYS driver for this to work. Why? Even though we can construct an address over the 1-megabyte boundary, any address line above 20 is disabled when the processor is in the normal mode (also referred to as *real* mode). Address lines are numbered starting at 0 so you'll commonly hear about address line A0 through A19. In order to access the high memory area, we need the twenty-first address line (or A20). This line is normally disabled in real mode; therefore, HIMEM.SYS is a requirement for the A20 line to function properly.

Buying Additional Memory

Now that we've covered the different types of memory, you may have the urge to go out and buy additional RAM. Keep the following tips in mind when purchasing and installing RAM in your computer.

- Check your motherboard documentation for the type (DIP, SIP, or SIMM) and size (64K, 256K, 1MB, 4MB, etc.) of memory chips your system requires. It also will specify in what increments you can add memory.

- RAM is rated by speed. This is normally measured in nanoseconds. It is best to match the speed of your existing RAM whenever possible.
- If you feel comfortable opening your PC, check to see if there are any open banks (sockets). You may find you will have to discard a bank of lower capacity chips and replace them with higher capacity.
- Watch the prices of RAM closely in computer magazines or at your local computer store. RAM is like the stock exchange, the price fluctuates depending on supply and demand.
- Although installing memory is fairly easy, consult a knowledgeable friend or computer store before attempting it for the first time. The two largest hazards with installing memory are static electricity (memory chips are very sensitive to static) and bent leads. Each chip must be placed securely in its socket. (SIMMs are the easiest to install, because they don't have individual pins.)

Summary

This chapter covered a lot of ground. If this was your first exposure to memory addressing, it may seem confusing to you at this point. Don't let it get you down, however. You do not have to be a "memory address wizard" to configure your PC memory. This information provided a foundation that you can build on as you progress through the rest of this book. We'll remind you of the intricate details where necessary. Here is a summary of the key points we covered in this chapter.

- The purpose of memory is to store data and programs (code).
- The two main types of memory are read-only memory (ROM) and random-access memory (RAM).
- ROMs retain information even when power is removed; however, they cannot be written to without special equipment.
- RAM chips are volatile, meaning they lose information when power is removed. The advantages of RAM are that the microprocessor can read or write data as needed, and RAM is faster than ROM.
- RAM comes in three types of packages: the dual in-line package (DIP), the single in-line package (SIP), and the single in-line memory module (SIMM). SIMMs are the most common in newer PCs.

- Computers store information in the form of zeros and ones. The binary numbering system best represents computer data. The hexadecimal numbering system helps humans represent binary numbers because it is based on a power of two.
- The Intel microprocessor family consists of the 8088, 8086, 80286, 80386SX, 80386DX, 80486SX, 80486DX, 80486DX2, and the Pentium. In addition to clock speed, the major difference among these processors is data and address bus width. A wider data bus carries a larger amount of data at a given time. A wider address bus enables the processor to access larger amounts of memory.
- DOS limits memory addressing to 1 megabyte by using segment-offset addressing.
- There are five types of memory we will refer to in this book: conventional, upper, expanded, extended, and high memory.
- Conventional memory starts at address 0 and runs to the 640K mark. It is used by programs and DOS itself.
- Upper memory is partially reserved for system ROM, video ROM and RAM, and other peripherals (disk drives for example). Unused memory addresses in upper memory may be used by 80386 processors and up with the help of EMM386.EXE.
- Expanded memory is outside the bounds of normal PC memory addresses. It requires an expanded memory card and driver (EMM386.EXE for example) to function properly. Extended memory can also emulate expanded memory.
- Extended memory lies above the 1-megabyte boundary. It requires the HIMEM.SYS driver to function properly.
- The high memory area is the first 65,520 bytes above the 1-megabyte boundary. The advantage of high memory is that the processor can access additional memory without switching from real to protected mode.

These topics will be constantly reinforced as this book progresses. There is no need to memorize this information; it serves as a foundation for subsequent chapters. Let's take a break from theory and get started on your machine. In the next chapter, you will examine your system's current configuration.

Memory and Your Computer

In Chapter 1, *An Introduction to PC Memory,* we discussed types of computer memory, both physical and configured. We also showed how different types of microprocessors are limited to addressing different amounts of memory. In this chapter we will start to explore your computer and its current memory configuration. The information you obtain from this chapter will help you determine why you are able to run some programs, and why others fail.

We will start by finding out the amount of memory you have installed in your computer. However, this is only the beginning. Many computer owners have megabytes of RAM, yet they continue to run into "out of memory" messages frequently. The reason for this is usually related to the configuration of the memory, not the amount of physical memory itself.

We will also cover the configuration files that affect how your computer manages memory: AUTOEXEC.BAT and CONFIG.SYS. It is important to be very familiar with these two files. We will discuss what the information in these files means and whether or not the information affects memory usage.

The first step in finding the optimum memory configuration for your computer is to examine its existing configuration. How you do this depends on the DOS version you are using. We will start with examples from DOS 5.0 followed by examples for DOS 6. If you are a DOS 5.0 user, you can use the DOS 6 information to determine whether or not an upgrade to DOS 6 would be useful to you.

Before we start with your computer's physical memory, let's look at a brief overview of the topics for this chapter.

TOPICS COVERED

Determining the Amount of Physical Memory in Your Computer

The AUTOEXEC.BAT and CONFIG.SYS files

Terminate-and-Stay-Resident-Programs and Device Drivers

Checking Your Current Memory Configuration—DOS 5.0

Checking Your Current Memory Configuration—DOS 6

Using Microsoft Diagnostics to Examine Your System

Determining the Amount of Physical Memory

You may already know how much memory is installed in your computer. If so, you can skip this section. If you don't know how much memory you have, you can find out by using one of the three following methods.

Checking Memory During Startup

Checking the amount of memory in your PC using this method is perhaps the easiest. Most computers perform a memory check when you first power on the system. The computer's BIOS (Basic Input/Output System) displays the memory check information as a running total on your display (usually in the upper-left corner). You can determine your amount of memory by observing the number when the memory check reaches its highest point. The memory amount is usually shown in kilobytes (K). For example, if the memory test displays 2,048K at its highest point, you have 2 megabytes of memory installed. Recall that 1,024 kilobytes (or 1K) equals one megabyte (or 1MB).

If your computer does not display a memory test, it may display a summary at startup. The summary, in addition to other things, displays the base and extended memory. For example, the summary may display: BASE = 640K, EXTENDED = 1,024K. This also would indicate a 2-megabyte system. These

BIOS summaries usually do not include the 384K that resides in the upper memory area addresses.

Keep in mind that different BIOS manufacturers display information in different ways. Some types of BIOS may not display this information at all (although this is rare in today's PCs). If you cannot obtain the information you need, try the next example. By the way, the BIOS memory check will not report memory on an expanded memory expansion board; it only reports memory installed on the main board.

Checking Memory with CMOS Setup

Most newer (80386 and 80486) computers store setup information in a small amount of memory. This memory is usually in a CMOS (complementary metal-oxide semiconductor) chip. In addition to the amount of installed memory, the CMOS memory also stores information such as the disk drive types, time and date, and advanced information.

To see the information stored in CMOS memory, you must enter a setup program (usually at startup). Watch your screen closely when you turn on your system. You may see a message such as "Press F1 to enter Setup," or "Press DEL to enter Setup." You can start the setup program by pressing the appropriate key before the system starts to load DOS (usually a few seconds). The key to enter the CMOS setup program varies from computer to computer. Figure 2-1 shows an example BIOS setup screen for a version of AMI BIOS. The setup screens vary from manufacturer to manufacturer and version to version.

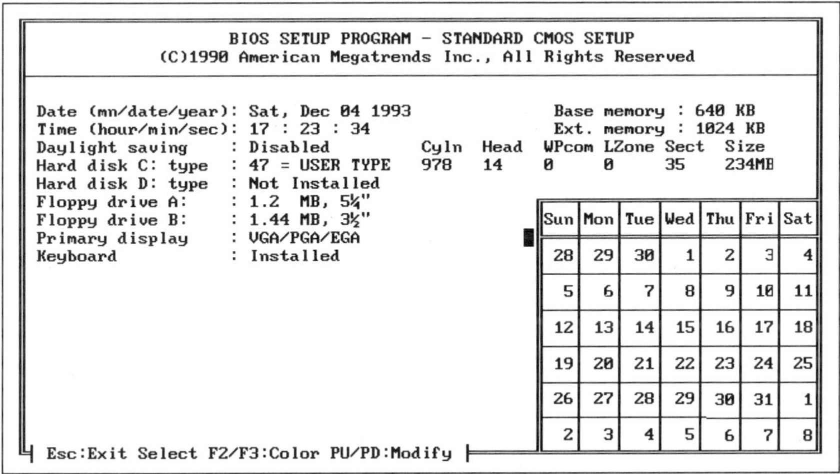

Figure 2-1 Example CMOS setup screen

Once the CMOS setup program is running, you should be able to see a report on the memory installed in your computer. You may or may not have to select a menu option to get the memory information. The CMOS report will not report memory on an expanded memory expansion board; it only reports memory installed on the main board.

CMOS Warning

If you use the CMOS setup to check the amount of memory, be sure that you don't modify any configuration information. Consult your computer documentation before attempting to change CMOS configuration.

Checking Memory by Opening Your Computer

As a last resort, you can open your computer and examine your memory chips. Most chips, DIPs, SIPs, and SIMMs have the capacity stamped on them. For example, a 256K memory chip has a 256 somewhere on the chip; a 1-megabyte chip should have a 1; a 4-megabyte chip has a 4. Remember that DIP memory chips are installed in banks of nine. A SIP or SIMM module only requires one package to a DIP's nine chips.

Again, consult your computer documentation to determine the location and layout of the memory in your computer. Now let's turn our attention to the files that affect how memory is configured.

The Configuration Files

Two text files have a significant effect on how your computer uses memory: AUTOEXEC.BAT and CONFIG.SYS. Both of these files must be located in the root directory of the *boot disk.* The boot disk can be either a floppy disk or a hard disk, although the latter is much more common today.

It is important to understand how your computer uses these files. First of all, the files are read at startup. CONFIG.SYS is read first followed by AUTOEXEC.BAT. Figure 2-2 shows the boot process.

Note that there are other files that are loaded before the system reads CONFIG.SYS and AUTOEXEC.BAT. However, these files do not affect memory management in any way, so we'll concentrate on the files that we can control. The example shows the boot disk as drive C:, and its configuration files are in the root directory, C:\.

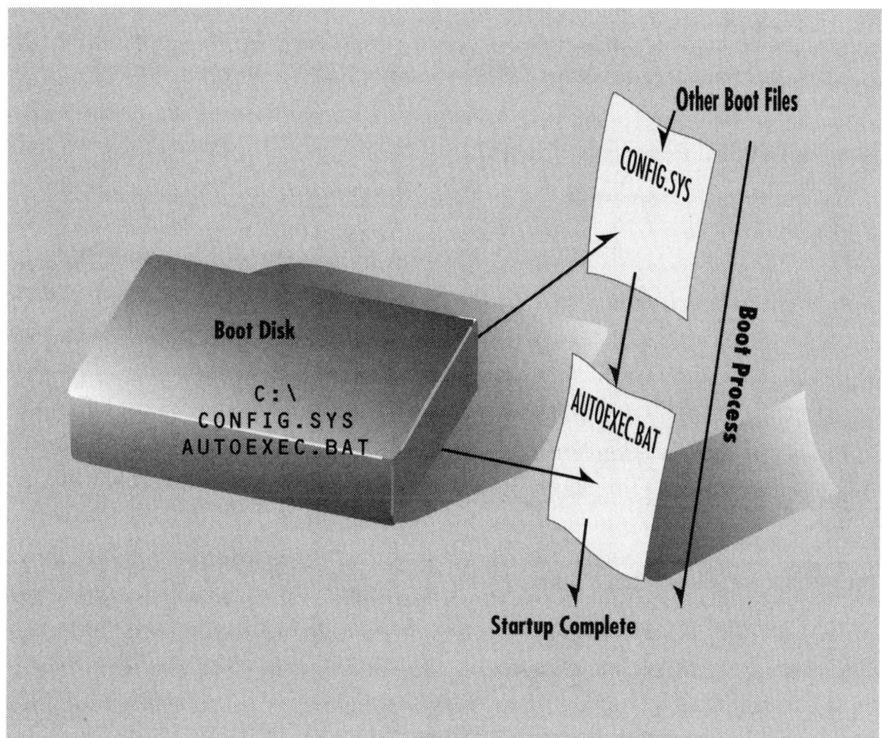

Figure 2-2 The boot process—CONFIG.SYS and AUTOEXEC.BAT

Before we get into the details of memory configuration, let's look at some of the types of entries each of these files contains. Let's start with CONFIG.SYS because it is loaded first.

Viewing and Printing Configuration Files

You can stop at this point and examine your system's configuration files. How you do this depends on which tool (DOS commands, EDIT, Window's Notepad) you are more familiar with. Here are some examples of viewing and printing configuration files using tools supplied with DOS or Windows.

Using DOS Commands to View and Print Configuration Files

To see the contents of your AUTOEXEC.BAT file:

- At the root directory, type **TYPE AUTOEXEC.BAT** and press ENTER.

To print the contents of your CONFIG.SYS file:

- At the root directory, type **PRINT CONFIG.SYS** and press ENTER.

Using the DOS EDIT Program to View and Print Configuration Files

To view or edit the contents of your AUTOEXEC.BAT file:

- At the root directory, type **EDIT AUTOEXEC.BAT** and press ENTER.
- Select File-Exit from the menu to return to the DOS prompt.

To print the contents of your CONFIG.SYS file:

- At the root directory, type **EDIT CONFIG.SYS** and press ENTER.
- Select File-Print from the menu.
- Click on OK or press ENTER to print the complete document.

Using Windows' Notepad to View and Print Configuration Files

To view or edit the contents of your AUTOEXEC.BAT file:

- Start Windows by typing **WIN** and pressing ENTER.
- Open the Accessories program group.
- Start the Notepad application by double-clicking on it (or by highlighting it and pressing ENTER).
- In the Directories box, change to the root directory (C:\).
- In the List of File Types box, select All Files (*.*).
- In the Files box, open the AUTOEXEC.BAT file by double-clicking on the filename (or highlight AUTOEXEC.BAT and press ENTER).
- To exit the Notepad program, select File-Exit from the menu.

To print the contents of your CONFIG.SYS file:

- Load the CONFIG.SYS file using the example above.
- Select File-Print from the menu.

CONFIG.SYS

As we mentioned, CONFIG.SYS is a text file that is read by your computer at startup. This file can contain just a few entries or as many as necessary. In fact, your system will boot even if CONFIG.SYS doesn't exist. In order to configure your memory, however, you must have a CONFIG.SYS file with the proper entries. Let's look at some of the entries a CONFIG.SYS file may contain.

DOS Configuration Commands

Your CONFIG.SYS file may already contain DOS configuration commands such as LASTDRIVE, FILES, BUFFERS, STACKS, and so on. These commands configure your system at startup and this configuration is in effect until the next time you restart (reboot) your computer. Of course, if you don't modify your CONFIG.SYS file, the configuration will be the same the next time you reboot. You can view or edit the CONFIG.SYS file using any DOS TEXT file editor. For example, the EDIT program that comes with DOS 5.0 and DOS 6 is a text editor. Here is a simple example CONFIG.SYS file:

```
FILES = 21                      [DOS command]
BUFFERS = 15                    [DOS command]
DEVICE=C:\DOS\HIMEM.SYS         [Device Driver]
DEVICE=C:\DOS\EMM386.EXE        [Device Driver]
DOS=HIGH,UMB                    [DOS command]
```

CONFIG.SYS and AUTOEXEC.BAT Editing Problems

You must take care when editing CONFIG.SYS and AUTOEXEC.BAT. It is possible to make a change that will prevent your system from booting the next time. You should always prepare a boot disk and keep backup copies of CONFIG.SYS and AUTOEXEC.BAT.

You can create backup copies using the DOS COPY command. For example:

COPY AUTOEXEC.BAT MYAUTO.*

would store a backup of AUTOEXEC.BAT in MYAUTO.BAT.

COPY CONFIG.SYS MYAUTO.*

would store a backup of CONFIG.SYS in MYAUTO.SYS.

Instructions for creating a boot disk are given in Chapter 3, *Managing Configuration Files*.

Device Drivers

Another type of CONFIG.SYS entry is a command that loads a *device driver*. Device drivers establish communication between hardware and software. For example, you can use the EMM386.EXE device driver to simulate expanded memory. Also, most multimedia systems use CD-ROM drives. These drives require device drivers in order to communicate with most multimedia software.

In most cases, the order in which device drivers are loaded doesn't matter. However, you may find in some cases that the order causes problems (certain hardware doesn't work, the system won't reboot, etc.). In these cases you must experiment to find the correct order. With many new computer hardware devices on the market, it's impossible to list all possible configurations. We will discuss this in more depth in Chapters 4 through 7. Now let's look at the AUTOEXEC.BAT file.

AUTOEXEC.BAT

Once the system is configured and device drivers are loaded with CONFIG.SYS, the next step is to read AUTOEXEC.BAT. AUTOEXEC.BAT is a DOS *batch file.* DOS batch files consist of a group of DOS commands in a text file. You can write your own batch files to carry out commands. We will create some batch files in Chapter 3, *Managing Configuration Files,* to help us maintain multiple configurations.

AUTOEXEC.BAT is a special batch file. Because of its name, it is automatically loaded each time you turn on your computer. Like the CONFIG.SYS file, you can edit it using any text editor. Let's look at some example entries in an AUTOEXEC.BAT file along with a description of what each line does:

```
&ECHO OFF               [Don't echo characters to the screen]
CLS                     [Clear the screen]
PROMPT $p$g             [Use the drive/directory prompt]
PATH C:\DOS;C\WINDOWS;  [Set the DOS path]
C:\DOS\DOSKEY           [Load the DOSKEY TSR program]
WIN                     [Start Microsoft Windows]
```

Notice that the AUTOEXEC.BAT file also contains DOS commands. This example also automatically starts Microsoft Windows each time the computer is powered up. In addition to DOS commands, the AUTOEXEC.BAT file also can load *terminate-and-stay-resident* programs, also known as TSRs. These are small utility programs that stay in conventional DOS memory so you can easily access them. One example of a TSR program is DOSKEY. This program stores commands typed in at the DOS command line (see your DOS manual for more information on DOSKEY).

TSRs are important to our discussion because they take up conventional memory by default. Later in this book you will see how to load these programs in upper memory, freeing valuable conventional memory. Now let's look at the memory configuration of your system.

Checking Your Current Configuration

Knowing how your system is currently configured will provide you with a solid starting point on which you can build better and more efficient memory configuration. To examine your configuration you will use the DOS MEM command.

The MEM command is different for DOS 5.0 and DOS 6. If you are running DOS 6, you should skip to the next section. If you are running DOS 5.0, use the following section to examine your current configuration. You may also want to review the DOS 6 section to see some of the benefits that this new revision offers.

Checking Your Configuration with the DOS 5.0 MEM Command

We are going to use the DOS MEM command to see if your system is set up for conventional, extended, expanded, or high memory. In each example, we'll give you an example AUTOEXEC.BAT and CONFIG.SYS file. Keep in mind that the configuration files listed in this chapter may or may not match your files. They are just examples that demonstrate the different types of memory.

Using the DOS 5.0 MEM COMMAND

In order for the DOS 5.0 MEM command to work, you must either have the DOS directory in your PATH, or your DOS directory must be the current working directory. To check your current PATH, type **PATH** and press ENTER. If the PATH shows the DOS directory you can proceed. If the PATH does not contain the DOS directory, change directories by typing **CD\DOS** and pressing ENTER. Also, if you installed your DOS files to a directory name other than DOS, change to that directory name.

DOS versions 4.0 and above automatically set the path to \DOS during installation.

Get Your Current Memory Configuration—DOS 5.0

Perform the following steps to get your current memory configuration:

1. Type **MEM** and press ENTER.
2. Write down the results of the MEM program (or print the screen to your printer if you have one).

The following is an example display output from the DOS 5.0 MEM command. We'll discuss each portion of the information that MEM provides in the sections that follow.

```
  655360 bytes total conventional memory
  655360 bytes available to MS-DOS
  629008 largest executable program size

  655360 bytes total EMS memory
  262144 bytes free EMS memory

1048576  bytes total contiguous extended memory
       0 bytes available contiguous extended memory
 393216  bytes available XMS memory
         MS-DOS resident in High Memory Area
```

Checking Conventional Memory

The first check to make is conventional memory. You will find that many games and multimedia programs are "conventional memory hungry." So it is usually important to free up as much conventional memory as possible.

Here is an example CONFIG.SYS and AUTOEXEC.BAT combination. Note that these files are very simple; they do not load any device drivers or TSRs.

CONFIG.SYS—Conventional Memory Example

```
FILES = 21
BUFFERS = 15
```

AUTOEXEC.BAT

```
@ECHO OFF
CLS
PROMPT $p$g
PATH C:\DOS
```

Now let's look at the end of the output of the MEM program for these example configuration files:

```
  655360 bytes total conventional memory
  655360 bytes available to MS-DOS
  629008 largest executable program size

1048576 bytes total contiguous extended memory
1048576 bytes available contiguous extended memory
```

The important information for conventional memory is contained in the first three lines of MEM's output. We've highlighted these lines with boldface. The first line is the total conventional memory. For this example, the value is 655,360 bytes. This is exactly 640 kilobytes, or 640 x 1,024. The second line is the number of bytes available to DOS; this happens to be the same value.

The third line is the most important to us. This value indicates the largest executable program size. If you have a program that requires more than this amount of conventional memory, the program will not run. This example shows 629,008 bytes. Dividing this number by 1,024 we find that there is a little over 614 kilobytes free.

Compare the MEM output for your computer to the example. Do you have more? If so, that's great. If you have less, don't worry. You will learn how to free up additional conventional memory in Chapter 4, *DOS 5.0 Memory Management,* and Chapter 5, *DOS 6 Memory Management.* For now you are just checking the current memory configuration of your system.

Checking Extended Memory

Now let's check for extended memory. Let's look at the output from the MEM command. Only this time, we are examining *extended* memory. Again, the important lines for our discussion are in boldface.

```
  655360 bytes total conventional memory
  655360 bytes available to MS-DOS
  629008 largest executable program size

1048576 bytes total contiguous extended memory
1048576 bytes available contiguous extended memory
```

Note that the last two lines of MEM output indicate that we have 1,048,576 bytes of extended memory. The first line shows the contiguous (in one piece) extended memory; the second line shows the amount of extended memory that is available. Examine the output from the MEM command for your system. The value may be more or less on your system depending on the amount of memory in your system and whether or not you have converted extended to expanded memory.

Checking Expanded Memory

In order for the MEM command to show expanded memory, you must have either an expanded memory board that conforms to the LIM 4.0 standard, or you must convert a portion of your extended memory to expanded memory.

For our example, we will modify our CONFIG.SYS file to convert some extended memory to expanded memory. Here is the new example CONFIG.SYS file.

CONFIG.SYS—Expanded Memory Example

```
FILES = 21
BUFFERS = 15
DEVICE=C:\DOS\HIMEM.SYS
DEVICE=C:\DOS\EMM386.EXE
```

Note that in this example, we loaded two device drivers. The first driver is HIMEM.SYS which manages extended memory. We need this driver because we are converting extended to expanded memory. The next driver is EMM386.EXE; this driver creates expanded memory from extended. It can perform other functions as well. We'll see much more about EMM386.EXE in Chapter 4, *DOS 5.0 Memory Management,* and Chapter 5, *DOS 6 Memory Management.* Let's see the output of MEM command for this example:

```
655360 bytes total conventional memory
655360 bytes available to MS-DOS
629008 largest executable program size

655360 bytes total EMS memory
262144 bytes free EMS memory
```

Notice that there are now two new lines in the MEM output (actually there are more than two new lines, but we're saving the others for the next section). The first new line indicates that there are 655,360 bytes (640K) of EMS (expanded) memory available. The second line indicates that there are 262,144 bytes (256K) free EMS memory. Why is there only 256K of the EMS memory free? This happens to be the default value when you load EMM386.EXE. 256K is reserved for expanded memory and 384K is used to backfill upper memory. You can add *switches* to override these default values. We'll cover these switches and other information in Chapters 4 and 5.

Also notice that the largest executable program size value is now smaller. This is a result of loading EMM386.EXE.

Check your MEM output to see if you have expanded memory in your system. Not all programs require EMS; whether or not it is important to you depends on the applications you run.

You may also notice the presence of expanded memory when you power up. If EMM386.EXE is in the CONFIG.SYS file, you will see a listing similar to the following on startup:

```
MICROSOFT Expanded Memory Manager 386  Version 4.20.06X
(C) Copyright Microsoft Corporation 1986, 1990

  Available expanded memory . . . . . . . .   256 KB
```

```
  LIM/EMS version . . . . . . . . . . . . . .   4.0
  Total expanded memory pages . . . . . . .     40
  Available expanded memory pages . . . . .     16
  Total handles . . . . . . . . . . . . . .     64
  Active handles  . . . . . . . . . . . . .      1
  Page frame segment  . . . . . . . . . . .   D000 H

EMM386 Active.
```

This listing shows the status of the EMM386.EXE expanded memory manager. In this example 256K of expanded memory is available. This amounts to 16 pages. Recall that an expanded memory page is 16K; therefore 16 x 16K = 256 K. We'll discuss the remaining lines in Chapters 4 and 5.

Checking Upper and High Memory

Our last step in using the DOS 5.0 MEM command is to check for upper and high memory usage. To demonstrate the presence of usable upper and high memory, we must use a new CONFIG.SYS file:

CONFIG.SYS—Upper/High Memory Example

```
FILES = 21
BUFFERS = 15
DEVICE=C:\DOS\HIMEM.SYS
DEVICE=C:\DOS\EMM386.EXE NOEMS
DOS=HIGH,UMB
```

We've modified the fourth line by adding the NOEMS switch to EMM386.EXE. This loads the EMM386.EXE driver without creating EMS memory. We do this because EMM386.EXE is required to access upper and high memory in DOS 5.0.

The fifth line, DOS=HIGH, UMB, performs two jobs. First, it loads DOS into high memory, and second, it allows access to the upper memory blocks (UMB). This could also be expressed in two lines on your system: DOS=HIGH and DOS=UMB.

Let's examine the MEM output for this example:

```
   655360 bytes total conventional memory
   655360 bytes available to MS-DOS
   629024 largest executable program size

1048576 bytes total contiguous extended memory
      0 bytes available contiguous extended memory
  48754 bytes available XMS memory
        MS-DOS resident in High Memory Area
```

Note that the last line of the MEM output indicates that DOS has been relocated from conventional to high memory. But how do we know if the upper memory area is usable? The answer appears at startup, when the EMM386.EXE driver is loaded. Here is an example of the startup message from EMM386.EXE:

```
MICROSOFT Expanded Memory Manager 386  Version 4.20.06X
(C) Copyright Microsoft Corporation 1986, 1990

Expanded memory services unavailable.

  Total upper memory available . . . . . .      95 KB
  Largest Upper Memory Block available  . .     95 KB
  Upper memory starting address . . . . . .   C800 H

EMM386 Active.
```

The first line shows us that expanded memory services are unavailable. This is the reason that no EMS showed up in our MEM command. The second and third lines indicate that there is 95K of high memory available, and it is all in one continuos block. The fourth line shows the starting address (C800h) of the available upper memory. We'll see how to load device drivers and TSRs in upper memory in Chapters 4 and 5.

Now you have seen how to examine your memory configuration using the DOS 5.0 MEM command. Let's look at the new MEM command used with DOS 6.

Checking Your Configuration with the DOS 6 MEM Command

DOS 6 provides a number of memory management enhancements. One of these enhancements is the new design of the MEM program. In DOS 5.0, MEM provides information based on the current configuration of the system. For example, if there is no expanded memory, the MEM output displays nothing about expanded memory. DOS 5.0 MEM also has no way to show the details of the upper memory area.

DOS 6 MEM provides a comprehensive summary of memory configuration. We will examine the MEM output for a system with 8 megabytes of RAM. Note that your system's configuration will most likely vary from these examples.

Get Your Current Memory Configuration—DOS 6

Perform the following steps to get your current memory configuration:

1. Type **MEM** and press ENTER.

Using The DOS 6 MEM COMMAND

In order for the DOS 6 MEM command to work, you must either have your PATH set to your DOS directory, or your DOS directory must be the current working directory. To check your current PATH, type **PATH** and press ENTER. If the PATH shows the DOS directory, you can proceed. If the PATH does not contain the DOS directory, change directories by typing **CD\DOS** and pressing ENTER. Also, if you installed your DOS files to a directory name other than DOS, change to that directory name.

2. Write down the results of the MEM program (or print the screen to your printer if you have one).

The following is an example display output from the DOS 6 MEM command. We'll discuss each portion of the information that MEM provides in the sections that follow.

```
Memory Type          Total =  Used  +  Free
----------------  ------  ------  ------
Conventional        640K     45K    595K
Upper                91K     72K     19K
Adapter RAM/ROM     384K    384K      0K
Extended (XMS)*    7077K   2533K   4544K
----------------  ------  ------  ------
Total memory       8192K   3035K   5157K

Total under 1 MB    731K    118K    613K

Total Expanded (EMS)               7488K (7667712 bytes)
Free Expanded (EMS)*               4784K (4898816 bytes)

* EMM386 is using XMS memory to simulate EMS memory as needed.
  Free EMS memory may change as free XMS memory changes.

Largest executable program size     594K  (608656 bytes)
Largest free upper memory block      19K   (19248 bytes)
MS-DOS is resident in the high memory area.
```

Checking Conventional Memory

The first check we will discuss is conventional memory. As we mentioned in the DOS 5.0 section, many applications require a large amount of conventional memory. Here is an example output from the DOS 6 MEM command (the lines specific to conventional memory are in boldface):

```
Memory Type        Total =   Used  +   Free
----------------   ------    ------    ------
Conventional         640K      45K      595K
Upper                 91K      72K       19K
Adapter RAM/ROM      384K     384K        0K
Extended (XMS)*     7077K    2533K     4544K
----------------   ------    ------    ------
Total memory        8192K    3035K     5157K

Total under 1 MB     731K     118K      613K

Total Expanded (EMS)                    7488K (7667712 bytes)
Free Expanded (EMS)*                    4784K (4898816 bytes)

* EMM386 is using XMS memory to simulate EMS memory as needed.
  Free EMS memory may change as free XMS memory changes.

Largest executable program size         594K  (608656 bytes)
Largest free upper memory block          19K   (19248 bytes)
MS-DOS is resident in the high memory area.
```

Notice that the upper portion of the MEM output has three columns for each memory type: total, used, and free. The key to managing memory is increasing the "free" column as much as possible.

This system has 640K total, 45K is already used, and 595K is free. You may be able to increase the free column by moving TSRs and device drivers into high, expanded, or extended memory. We will show these techniques in Chapter 4, *DOS 5.0 Memory Management,* and Chapter 5, *DOS 6 Memory Management.*

Note that the last line indicates the largest executable program size. Increasing the amount of free conventional memory will directly increase this value.

Checking Extended Memory

The next step is to check the amount of extended memory. This value is important for programs that utilize extended memory. Windows is an example of an application that thrives on extended memory. Let's look at the lines of MEM output that are specific to extended memory.

```
Memory Type        Total =   Used  +   Free
----------------   ------    ------    ------
Conventional         640K      45K      595K
Upper                 91K      72K       19K
Adapter RAM/ROM      384K     384K        0K
Extended (XMS)*     7077K    2533K     4544K
----------------   ------    ------    ------
Total memory        8192K    3035K     5157K

Total under 1 MB     731K     118K      613K
```

```
Total Expanded (EMS)                  7488K (7667712 bytes)
Free Expanded (EMS)*                  4784K (4898816 bytes)

* EMM386 is using XMS memory to simulate EMS memory as needed.
  Free EMS memory may change as free XMS memory changes.

Largest executable program size        594K  (608656 bytes)
Largest free upper memory block         19K   (19248 bytes)
MS-DOS is resident in the high memory area.
```

In this example system, there is a total of 7,077K extended memory, 2,533K is used, and 4,544K is free. Note that the extended (XMS) memory section is marked with an asterisk. Further down the listing you will find a note indicating that EMM386 is using extended (XMS) memory to simulate expanded (EMS) memory. The amount of free EMS will vary depending on the amount of free XMS. In other words, DOS 6 can reconfigure the amount of available EMS/XMS memory on the fly; this is something that DOS 5.0 could not do. Now let's examine expanded memory.

Checking Expanded Memory

By now you've probably got the hang of reading the DOS 6 MEM output. Many applications still require—or at least can take advantage of—expanded memory. Here is an excerpt from the MEM output specific to expanded memory:

```
Total Expanded (EMS)                  7488K (7667712 bytes)
Free Expanded (EMS)*                  4784K (4898816 bytes)
```

This system is reporting 7,488K of total expanded memory (of which 4,784K is free). Note once again that the free expanded memory is marked with an asterisk. This is an indication that this value may change depending on the current needs of the system.

Finally, let's look at the upper and high memory indications from the DOS 6 MEM command.

Checking Upper and High Memory

Recall that the DOS 5.0 MEM command only reported whether or not DOS was loaded into high memory; it did not report the status of high memory. The DOS 6 MEM command reports both as shown in the following listing. The lines specific to upper and high memory are listed in boldface.

```
Memory Type         Total  =  Used   +  Free
----------------   ------    ------    ------
Conventional         640K      45K      595K
Upper                 91K      72K       19K
Adapter RAM/ROM      384K     384K        0K
```

continued on next page

continued from previous page

```
Extended (XMS)*      7077K     2533K     4544K
----------------    ------    ------    ------
Total memory         8192K     3035K     5157K

Total under 1 MB      731K      118K      613K

Total Expanded (EMS)                     7488K (7667712 bytes)
Free Expanded (EMS)*                     4784K (4898816 bytes)

* EMM386 is using XMS memory to simulate EMS memory as needed.
  Free EMS memory may change as free XMS memory changes.

Largest executable program size           594K  (608656 bytes)
Largest free upper memory block            19K   (19248 bytes)
MS-DOS is resident in the high memory area.
```

Note that the last line in the MEM output indicates that DOS is loaded in the high memory area. This is similar to the DOS 5.0 output. However, there are some important additions to the DOS 6 MEM output. These additions report the status of the upper memory area.

The second line of the memory summary indicates the status of the upper memory area. In this example there is 91K total upper memory available, 72K has already been used, and 19K is still free. Note also that the second to the last line indicates the largest free upper memory block. In this case, it is the same as the free amount; however, this does not have to be the case. This line indicates the largest contiguous (in one piece) block of memory.

Now let's look at a hidden treasure supplied with DOS 6 and Windows: Microsoft Diagnostics.

Using Microsoft Diagnostics to Examine Your System

If you are using DOS 6 or Windows, you have a diagnostic utility that you can use to examine your system's memory configuration (along with many other things). This utility is Microsoft Diagnostics, or MSD.

If you are using DOS 5.0 and Windows, MSD.EXE is located in your \WINDOWS directory. If you are using DOS 6, MSD.EXE resides in your \DOS directory.

Starting MSD

Because the DOS installation program adds the \DOS directory to your path (and the Windows setup program adds \WINDOWS to your path), you can

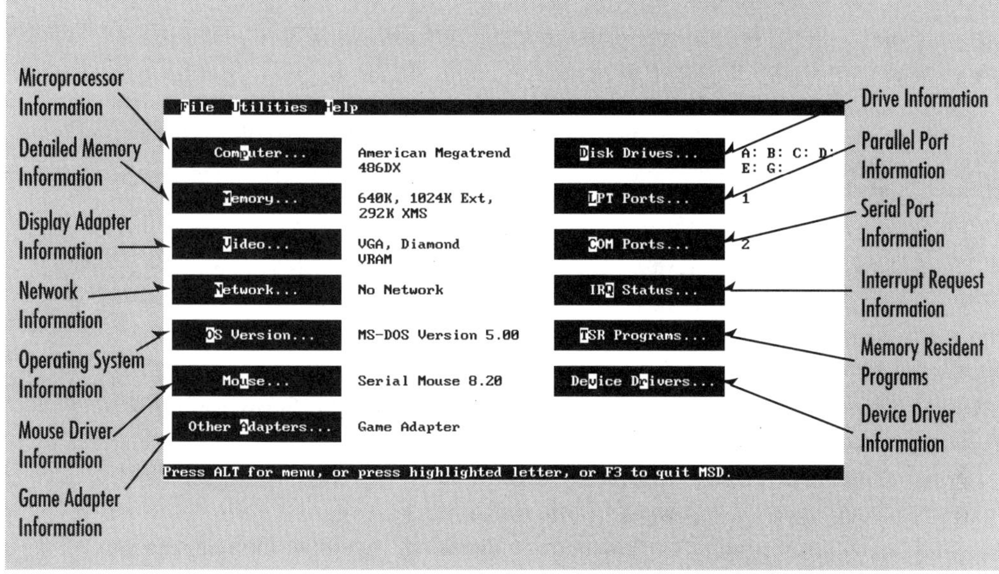

Figure 2-3 Microsoft Diagnostics

start Microsoft Diagnostics by typing **MSD** and pressing ENTER. Figure 2-3 shows the opening screen from Microsoft Diagnostics.

You can see from the main screen of this utility that it covers virtually every area of your system. In addition to providing detailed memory information, MSD also provides the following information:

- Type of microprocessor, BIOS, and keyboard
- Type of video adapter
- Network adapters and drivers
- Operating system version and environment settings
- Mouse driver version, type of mouse, IRQ setting, COM port, COM port address
- Game port
- Disk drive(s)
- Parallel port(s)
- Serial port(s)
- Interrupt request assignments (0 through 15)

- Memory-resident programs
- Device drivers

Each of these above items has an associated screen with detailed information. The File menu gives you quick access to the main configuration files of DOS and Windows (CONFIG.SYS, AUTOEXEC.BAT, WIN.INI, and SYSTEM.INI).

The Utilities menu provides a *Memory Block Display* option; this is a snapshot of your current memory configuration. Also under the Utilities menu is a *Memory Browser* option. You can use this option to search for information in system, video, or adapter ROMs. The *Insert Command* option shows the effects of CONFIG.SYS and AUTOEXEC.BAT entries on your system environment. Finally, the Test Printer option sends test data to your PostScript or non-PostScript printer.

Because our main concern at this point is memory, let's look at the detailed memory screen. Figure 2-4 shows this information.

The top portion of the Memory screen is a legend for the upper memory map (displayed on the left portion of the screen). In this example, ROM fills most of the addresses between C000h and C7FFh. This is video ROM. The top portion of the memory map (addresses F000h to FFFFh) is also ROM. This portion is

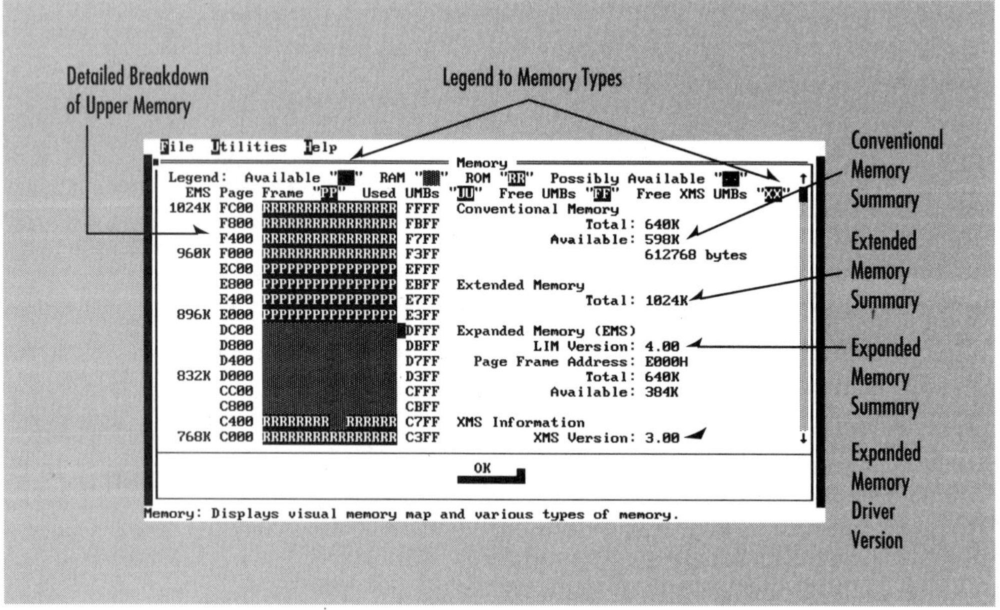

Figure 2-4 Memory screen for Microsoft Diagnostics

system ROM. Notice that a 64K EMS page frame is located in upper memory ranging from address E000h to EFFFh.

The right portion of the Memory screen provides a summary for conventional, extended, and expanded memory. The version of the LIM (EMS) driver and the XMS version and XMS driver are also displayed. You'll have to scroll down to see the XMS driver version.

Try Microsoft Diagnostics to see how your machine is configured. Your screens will probably be different from the above examples. For example, you will not see a page frame area in upper memory if you are not using expanded memory.

Now you have performed a thorough memory checkup on your system. In later chapters, we'll move on to the diagnosis and treatment of your specific memory problems.

Summary

By now you should be familiar with not only the types of memory, but with how your system is currently configured. In the remaining chapters, we will concentrate on adjusting your AUTOEXEC.BAT and CONFIG.SYS to get the most out of your computer and programs. Before we do that, let's review what we covered in this chapter:

- You can determine the amount of physical memory in your system at startup (memory test or BIOS summary), CMOS setup, or by removing your computer's cover and examining the memory chips.
- Your memory configuration is primarily controlled by two configuration files: AUTOEXEC.BAT and CONFIG.SYS. These files must be located in the root directory of the boot disk.
- CONFIG.SYS is the first configuration file loaded by the system, followed by AUTOEXEC.BAT.
- Two items that can consume memory at startup are terminate-and-stay-resident programs (TSRs) and device drivers.
- You can check your memory configuration using the DOS 5.0 or DOS 6 MEM command. The DOS 6 MEM command offers a more comprehensive summary of your system's memory.

Now that you are more familiar with types of memory, configuration files, and your personal computer's configuration, let's examine ways of maintaining different configurations on a single system.

Managing Configuration Files

Now that you have a basic understanding of computer memory and you know how your computer is configured, the next step is learning how to manage configuration files. You may find that one configuration suits your system just fine. However, like many of today's serious PC users, if you run many different types of programs, you may need to use more than one configuration.

Our discussion of managing configuration files consists of two segments: editing configuration files and using multiple configuration files. If you have never modified your CONFIG.SYS or AUTOEXEC.BAT file before, you will need to read this chapter in depth. Doing so will reduce the risk of creating a configuration that prevents your computer from booting. We'll also show you how to make a "bootable disk" to help you recover—just in case a new configuration goes awry.

For the user who runs multimedia programs, complex games, or other memory-intensive programs, we will describe a simple, yet effective way of using more than one set of CONFIG.SYS and AUTOEXEC.BAT files. This will be accomplished using two DOS batch files. One file stores the configuration files with unique filenames, the other file loads a set of configuration files.

Next, we will discuss methods in which you can attempt to combine two or more sets of configuration files. The goal is to get all of your programs to run with a minimal number of configurations.

For DOS 6.0 and 6.2 users, we will cover how to create a custom startup menu. You can use this menu to select a configuration every time you reboot.

Let's look at a brief overview of the topics for this chapter.

TOPICS COVERED

- Creating a Bootable Disk
- Situations Requiring Multiple Configurations
- Using DOS Batch Files to Manage Multiple Configurations
- Combining Multiple Configurations
- Using DOS 6 to Manage Multiple Configurations

The Boot Disk—Don't Modify Files Without It!

One problem that nearly every new computer user experiences when modifying CONFIG.SYS and AUTOEXEC.BAT is a *lockup* during the boot process. A lockup is when your computer just sits there without giving you the DOS prompt or starting a program you specified in AUTOEXEC.BAT.

If a line in the AUTOEXEC.BAT file causes your computer to lock up, you can get around it by pressing CTRL-C during the boot process (but before the offending line in AUTOEXEC.BAT is reached). This should bring up the DOS prompt, where you can start up your text editor, load AUTOEXEC.BAT, and make the necessary changes to correct the problem.

On the other hand, if the offending line is in the CONFIG.SYS file, you cannot press CTRL-C to break into the boot process. Why? When CONFIG.SYS is being executed, the parts of DOS that recognize the CTRL-C combination are not loaded yet; therefore, you cannot break into the boot sequence and make any changes to the file. If you reboot, you continue to lock up at the same point. This is a seemingly hopeless situation. Figure 3-1 shows the boot process and where you can break with CTRL-C.

There is an easy solution to this problem. The solution is to create a "bootable" floppy disk before you start making changes to either CONFIG.SYS or AUTOEXEC.BAT. This way, even if your hard disk configuration files have problems in them, you can always reboot using a bootable floppy disk, change to your hard drive, and edit the offending file(s).

Interrupting the Boot Process in DOS 6

DOS 6.0 and the 6.2 upgrade both provide a way to interrupt the boot process. You can press and release F5 (or press and hold the SHIFT key) while your computer is booting to force the operating system to bypass CONFIG.SYS and AUTOEXEC.BAT. For this reason, DOS 6 users usually will not need a boot disk, although it's still a good idea to make one.

Determining the Boot Drive

Before creating your boot disk you must first determine which floppy drive (if you have more than one) is the boot drive. If your system is equipped with one floppy drive, it is the bootable drive. If you have more than one floppy disk drive, the A: drive is bootable.

If your A: drive is a 5.25" drive, you will need a blank 5.25" disk—or one with discardable information. If your system's A: drive is a 3.5" drive, you will need a blank 3.5" disk. The following procedure will format a disk and make it bootable.

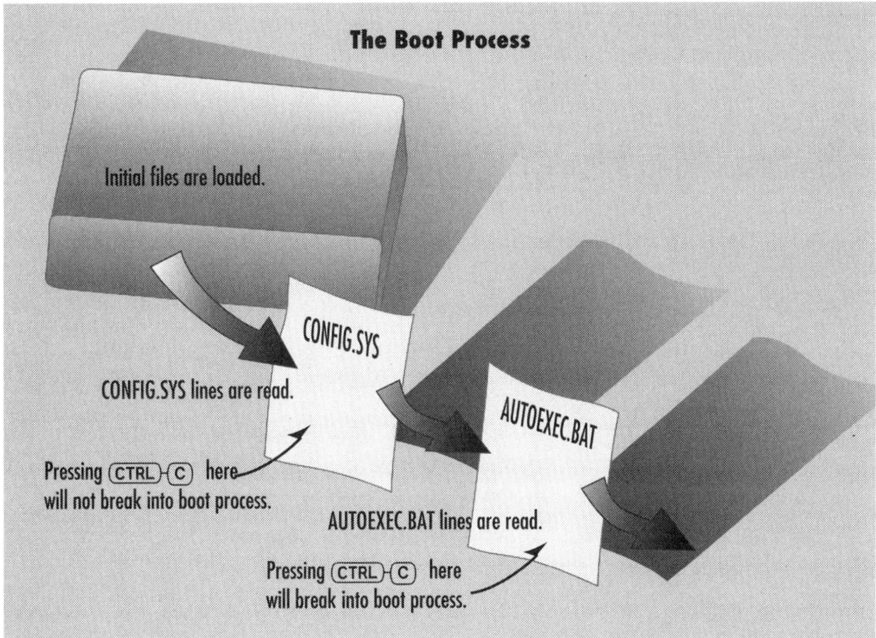

Figure 3-1 Breaking into the boot process

What Makes a Boot Disk Work?

Are you mystified by the difference between a bootable and non-bootable disk? Special files at specific locations on the disk make it bootable. These files are normally hidden files in your root directory. You can't see them with the traditional DOS DIR command.

When you turn your computer on, the BIOS (basic input-output system) provides enough data to give your system the ability to read from disk drives (and various other things). Most systems are configured to boot from a floppy and/or hard drive. The floppy boot drive designation is A:; the hard drive designation is C:.

The BIOS starts reading the operating system (in our case, DOS) from the boot disk. If one of the special files becomes damaged, you will not be able to load the operating system. This is why it is important to have a bootable floppy. It can help you recover from some hard drive configuration problems.

Creating the Bootable Disk

Perform the following steps to create your boot disk:

1. Place the disk (3.5" or 5.25") in your A: drive.
2. At the DOS command line type one of the following lines:

```
FORMAT A: /S         [for 3.5" or 5.25" high-density disk]
FORMAT A: /S /F:720  [for 3.5" low-density disk]
FORMAT A: /S /F:360  [for 5.25" low-density disk]
```

   The /S switch will automatically transfer the system files to the disk following the formatting.

   The /F: switch informs the system of the density of the disk. FORMAT automatically assumes high density; therefore, you only need to use this switch for low-density disk.

3. Press ENTER to confirm the disk format. The system displays the fact that it is formatting and also gives the percentage complete. When the format is complete, the system transfers the boot files automatically as a result of the /S switch. When this process is complete, the system displays the following message:

```
Formatting 1.44M     <-- this line differs depending on disk size/density
Format Complete
System Transferred   <-- this line indicates that the system files are copied

Volume label (11 characters, ENTER for none)?
```

4. Press ENTER to indicate that there is no volume name for the disk (or call it something like BOOT_DISK if you like). The system displays the number of bytes of total disk space, bytes used by the system, and the bytes available on disk.

5. Press ENTER to indicate that you do not want to format another disk.

The remaining steps are optional; however, they serve to make a more functional boot disk by including the PROMPT and PATH DOS commands.

6. Use a text editor to create the following file and save it to your boot disk as AUTOEXEC.BAT:

```
@ECHO OFF
PATH = C:\DOS;
PROMPT = $p$g
@ECHO ON
CLS
```

This will give your boot disk enough information to find a path to your DOS files on your hard disk. It will also provide a DOS prompt that indicates the current directory.

7. Use a text editor to create the following file and save it to your boot disk as CONFIG.SYS:

```
FILES = 21
BUFFERS = 10
```

Alternative AUTOEXEC.BAT/CONFIG.SYS FILES

As an alternative to the minimal AUTOEXEC.BAT/CONFIG.SYS files listed above, you may want to use a set of files that includes more information (such as loading drivers, starting programs, and so on). If this is the case, copy these files from your hard disk to your bootable floppy. Be sure these files work before doing so, however. You do not want to create a boot disk that locks up during the boot process.

8. Check the files on your boot disk by typing **ATTRIB A:**. The system should display lines similar to the following:

```
A  SHR     A:\IO.SYS
A  SHR     A:\MSDOS.SYS
A          A:\COMMAND.COM
A          A:\AUTOEXEC.BAT
A          A:\CONFIG.SYS
```

The first two lines are hidden DOS system files. If we had requested an ordinary directory listing (with DIR) these two files would not have been listed. The third file, COMMAND.COM, is also a necessary DOS system file. The last two files are the AUTOEXEC.BAT and CONFIG.SYS you created and copied over to the bootable disk.

Testing the Bootable Disk

Before you start editing your AUTOEXEC.BAT or CONFIG.SYS files, you should first test the bootable disk. Insert the bootable disk in drive A: and reboot your computer. You should end up at the A:\> prompt when the boot process is complete.

If you are recovering from a condition where your AUTOEXEC.BAT or CONFIG.SYS files on your hard disk are causing a lockup, you can now do the following:

- Place your bootable disk in drive A:.
- Reboot your computer.
- At the A:> prompt, type **C:** and press ENTER.
- Edit the offending file (CONFIG.SYS or AUTOEXEC.BAT).
- Remove your bootable disk from drive A: and reboot to try your hard disk configuration files again.

Not Reading from a Floppy During Boot Process?

If your computer is not reading from your A: drive at startup, it could be that your floppy drives are disabled at boot time by your BIOS system setup. Consult your computer's documentation for specific information.

We will discuss specific configurations of CONFIG.SYS and AUTOEXEC.BAT files in detail later in this book. If you are interested in configuring memory for DOS 5.0 or DOS 6, use Chapter 4 or 5 respectively. If you are a Microsoft Windows user, also use Chapter 6. If you want to see if a third-party memory manager would be useful in your system, or if you're already using one, use Chapter 7.

Multiple Configuration Scenarios

Before we get into the subject of managing multiple configurations, we must first examine some situations that may require them. You may be able to get by with only one memory configuration; or you may have to use two or more configurations for your system.

There are a number of factors that may cause you to create multiple configurations. For example, the software you use plays a big part in memory configuration. What type of memory does it require: conventional, extended, or expanded? How much memory does it require: 512K conventional, 600K conventional, 2MB extended? Knowing your software's memory requirements will help you build a configuration that works.

Another set of factors depends on the hardware you are using. Many types of hardware (CD-ROM drives, sound cards, advanced video cards) require *device drivers.* Hardware device drivers are commonly loaded using a line in the CONFIG.SYS file. Device drivers also require memory. As you install more

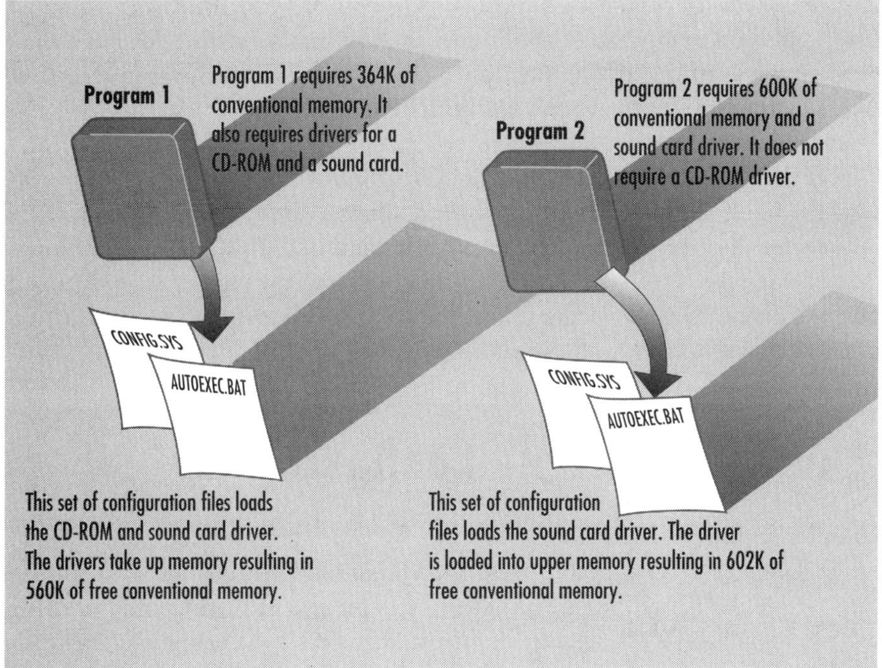

Figure 3-2 A multiple configuration scenario

and more drivers, you have less memory for your programs. Figure 3-2 shows a simplified example of a situation that may require two separate configurations.

The first example in Figure 3-2 shows Program 1 which requires 364K of conventional memory, a CD-ROM drive device driver, and a sound card driver. We are assuming that this system has at least 1 megabyte of memory installed. Because the program does not require much conventional memory, we can load the drivers for the CD-ROM drive and the sound card in conventional memory. After doing so, there is still 560K of conventional memory free, so we can run Program 1. However, we cannot run Program 2 because it requires 600K of conventional memory.

To relieve this situation, we create another CONFIG.SYS (and possibly AUTOEXEC.BAT) that provides a different memory arrangement. Because Program 2 doesn't require a CD-ROM, we can omit loading the driver from the CONFIG.SYS file. We also add some lines to the CONFIG.SYS file that let us put the driver for the sound card into upper memory. This frees up enough conventional memory (602K) to run Program 2.

It's not important to understand what is specifically taking place in the CONFIG.SYS files for this example. We will discuss specific changes you can make in Chapter 4, *DOS 5.0 Memory Management,* Chapter 5, *DOS 6 Memory Management,* and Chapter 6, *Windows Memory Management.* What you should understand at this point is that there may be a need for more than one set of configuration files. In other words, you may require two AUTOEXEC.BAT files and two CONFIG.SYS files.

This example does present a problem though. AUTOEXEC.BAT and CONFIG.SYS must reside in the root directory of the boot disk (in this case your hard disk, or drive C:). Also, we cannot have two files with the same name in the same directory. How can we provide a solution to this problem? We could manually use the DOS RENAME command and give the files temporary names; but this would be time consuming and also prone to errors. The next section provides two simple batch files that can work for you.

Managing Multiple Configurations

In order to use multiple configurations, we must temporarily store a set of AUTOEXEC.BAT and CONFIG.SYS files under different names. That way we can retrieve them later. Figure 3-3 shows this process of storing and retrieving configuration files. We'll show an alternative method for managing multiple configurations in DOS 6 later in this chapter. The following method works for all DOS versions.

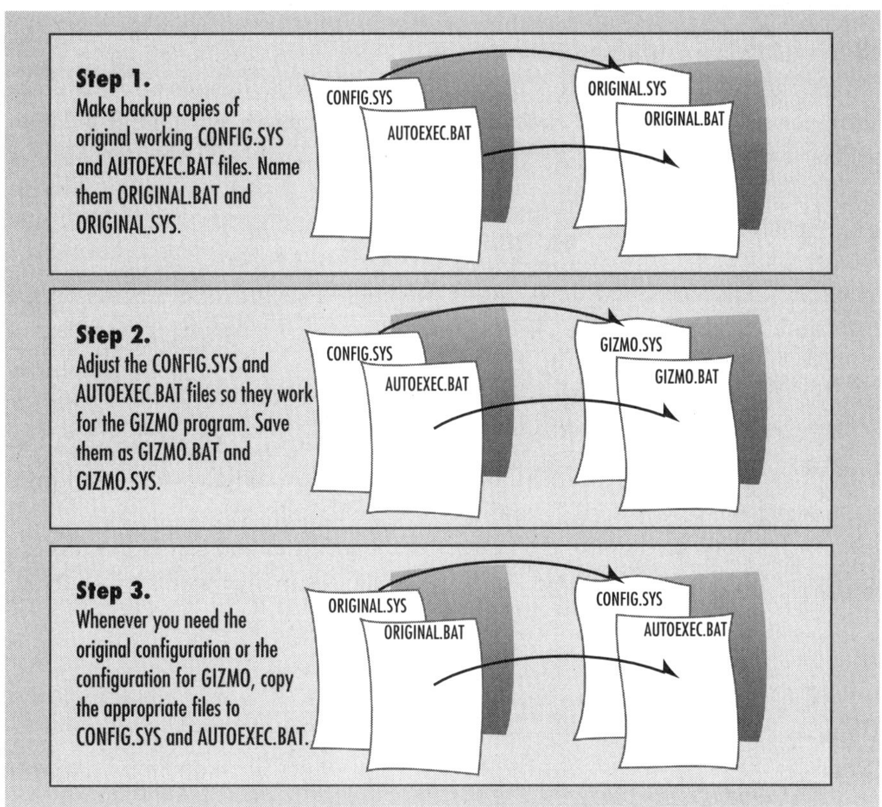

Figure 3-3 Storing and retrieving AUTOEXEC.BAT and CONFIG.SYS files

In this example, we first make a backup of the original CONFIG.SYS and AUTOEXEC.BAT by copying them and using two new filenames: ORIGINAL.SYS (for CONFIG.SYS) and ORIGINAL.BAT (for AUTOEXEC.BAT).

Next, we make changes to the AUTOEXEC.BAT and CONFIG.SYS files in order to run a fictitious program named GIZMO. Once we have a configuration we like, we copy the modified AUTOEXEC.BAT and CONFIG.SYS using two new filenames: GIZMO.SYS and GIZMO.BAT. At this point we have two sets of configuration files. One set represents the original files, the other set represents the files that work with the GIZMO program.

Anytime we want to change back to the original files, all we have to do is copy ORIGINAL.BAT over AUTOEXEC.BAT and copy ORIGINAL.SYS over CONFIG.SYS and reboot. Similarly, when we want to use the GIZMO program again, we copy GIZMO.BAT and GIZMO.SYS over AUTOEXEC.BAT and CONFIG.SYS, and then reboot.

As we mentioned before, copying files manually is tedious and can cause problems; especially if we copy in the wrong direction. To relieve us from this situation we will use two simple DOS batch files: STORE.BAT and CHANGE.BAT.

STORE.BAT—Stores Configuration Files

The first batch file we will cover is STORE.BAT. This file takes a name on the command line and stores the files using that name. For example, if we type:

```
STORE ORIGINAL
```

and press ENTER, AUTOEXEC.BAT is copied to ORIGINAL.BAT and CONFIG.SYS is copied to ORIGINAL.SYS. Because we are copying (not renaming), the original AUTOEXEC.BAT and CONFIG.SYS still exist.

Now let's look at the actual STORE.BAT batch file. You can create this file using any DOS text editor (such as EDIT which is supplied with DOS 5.0 and 6). Listing 3-1 shows STORE.BAT.

Listing 3-1 STORE.BAT

```
CLS
@ECHO OFF
IF "%1" == "" GOTO NONAME
COPY CONFIG.SYS %1.SYS > NUL
COPY AUTOEXEC.BAT %1.BAT > NUL
ECHO The "%1" configuration files have been saved.
GOTO END
:NONAME
ECHO You must supply a name for the new configuration files.
:END
@ECHO ON
```

If you are not familiar with DOS batch files, some of the entries in STORE.BAT may be new to you. We'll examine this file line by line and describe each function. You do not have to totally understand this file to use it. The only requirement is that you type it in a text editor and save it as STORE.BAT.

The first line, CLS, clears the screen. This is not absolutely necessary; however, it provides a cleaner look to the program. The second line (also not a requirement) is @ECHO OFF. This line tells DOS not to echo the remaining lines to the screen and keeps the display uncluttered. This is in effect until an @ECHO ON is issued.

The third line uses a replaceable parameter, %1. This is a place holder that will be filled in when we actually run the program. For example, if we type **STORE ORIGINAL**, the %1 entry is replaced with ORIGINAL when the batch file executes. This line compares the entry to "". This checks to see if you forgot to supply a filename after the word STORE. If so, the line directs execution to a label named NONAME. Note that the NONAME label is defined later in the batch file.

The fourth and fifth lines do most of the work in STORE.BAT. First, the CONFIG.SYS file is copied to %1.SYS. Again the %1 is the replacement parameter. For example, if you type **STORE ORIGINAL**, the CONFIG.SYS file is copied to ORIGINAL.SYS. The next line does the same for AUTOEXEC.BAT. The > NUL on the end of each line keeps the DOS message "1 file(s) copied" from being displayed on the screen.

The sixth line echoes a message to the screen indicating that the files have been saved. For example, our ORIGINAL example would display:

```
The "ORIGINAL" configuration files have been saved.
```

The seventh line directs execution to a point past the error message (NONAME) using GOTO END. Note that the END label is the second to the last line.

The eighth line is the label for the error message. The only way this line is reached is if the filename is not specified on the command line following STORE. In this case, the ninth line echoes the following message as a reminder:

```
You must supply a name for the new configuration files.
```

The remaining lines are the END label and an @ECHO ON command. The latter line tells DOS to start echoing output to the screen again.

Figure 3-4 shows a flowchart for the STORE.BAT batch file. This provides an overview you can compare with Listing 3-1.

Testing STORE.BAT

Once you have typed the lines from Listing 3-1 and saved them as STORE.BAT, you are now ready to test it. Be sure you save STORE.BAT to the root directory. Perform the following steps to test STORE.BAT:

1. Make sure you are in the root directory, type **STORE** and press (ENTER). The screen should clear and you should get the message indicating that you need to supply a filename. This tests the error portion of the batch file.

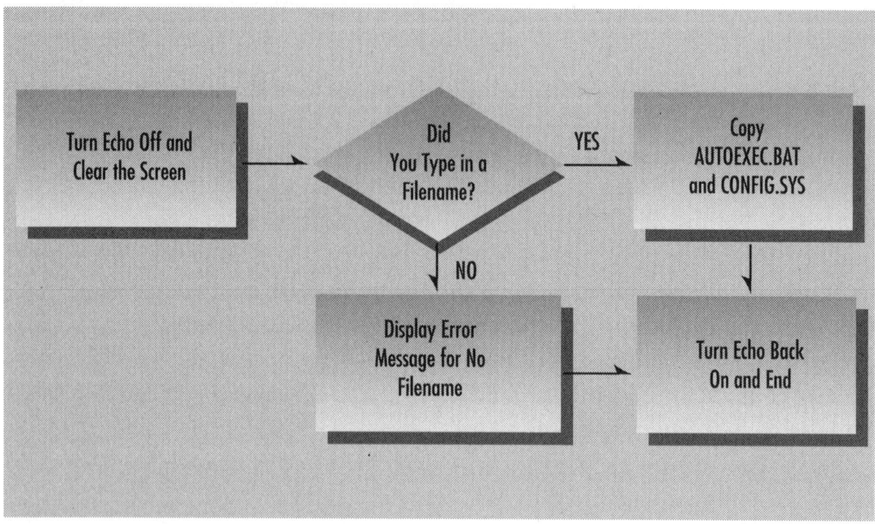

Figure 3-4 STORE.BAT flowchart

2. Type **STORE TEST** and press ENTER. Again, the screen should clear and you should get the message that the files have been saved.
3. Type **DIR** and press ENTER to get the directory contents. You should see TEST.BAT (a copy of AUTOEXEC.BAT) and TEST.SYS (a copy of CONFIG.SYS).
4. Compare TEST.BAT to AUTOEXEC.BAT and TEST.SYS to CONFIG.SYS using the DOS TYPE command. The copies should be identical to the originals.

You can see that STORE.BAT provides a quick way to make a backup of your configuration files. It does have one drawback, however. Make sure you do not use CONFIG, AUTOEXEC, or any other name that may overwrite a BAT or SYS file in the root directory.

Now that we have a way to save the configuration files at any given time, let's look at a batch file that will restore them to CONFIG.SYS and AUTOEXEC.BAT.

CHANGE.BAT—Restores Configuration Files

Our second batch file is CHANGE.BAT. This file takes a name on the command line and restores the files using that name. For example if we type:

```
CHANGE ORIGINAL
```

and press ENTER, ORIGINAL.BAT is copied to AUTOEXEC.BAT and ORIGINAL.SYS is copied to CONFIG.SYS. Because we are copying (not renaming), the original ORIGINAL.BAT and ORIGINAL.SYS files remain intact, where they can be used again later with CHANGE.

Now let's look at the actual CHANGE.BAT batch file. Like STORE.BAT, you can create this file using any DOS text editor (such as EDIT which is supplied with DOS 5.0 and 6). Listing 3-2 shows CHANGE.BAT.

Listing 3-2 CHANGE.BAT

```
CLS
@ECHO OFF
IF "%1" == "" GOTO NONAME
IF NOT EXIST %1.SYS GOTO NOFILES
IF NOT EXIST %1.BAT GOTO NOFILES
COPY %1.SYS CONFIG.SYS > NUL
COPY %1.BAT AUTOEXEC.BAT > NUL
ECHO The "%1" configuration files have been written
ECHO to AUTOEXEC.BAT and CONFIG.SYS.
ECHO Reboot for these files to take effect.
GOTO END
:NOFILES
ECHO The "%1" configuration files do not exist.
GOTO END
:NONAME
ECHO You must supply the name of the configuration files.
:END
@ECHO ON
```

We'll examine this file line by line and describe each function. Again, you do not have to totally understand this file to use it. The only requirement is that you type it in a text editor and save it as CHANGE.BAT

The first line, CLS, clears the screen. The second line is @ECHO OFF telling DOS not to echo the remaining lines to the screen. This is in effect until an @ECHO ON is issued.

Note that STORE.BAT and CHANGE.BAT always work with sets of AUTOEXEC.BAT and CONFIG.SYS files. The third line is the same as the test we performed in STORE.BAT. We are testing to see if you forgot to specify a filename for the configuration files. If so, we GOTO the NONAME label (defined later in the file). This results in the following message being displayed:

```
You must supply the name of the configuration files.
```

The fourth and fifth lines check to see if the configuration files exists. For example, if you type **CHANGE ORIGINAL** and ORIGINAL.BAT or

ORIGINAL.SYS do not exist, we GOTO the NOFILES label. This results in a message similar to the following:

```
The "ORIG" configuration files do not exist.
```

The sixth and seventh lines copy the configuration files over the existing CONFIG.SYS and AUTOEXEC.BAT. This is why it is important that you save your configuration files (using STORE.BAT) before loading new ones with CHANGE.BAT.

The eighth and ninth lines echo two message lines to the screen. For example, if you type **CHANGE ORIGINAL** and press ENTER, the message will appear as:

```
The "ORIGINAL" configuration files have been written
to AUTOEXEC.BAT and CONFIG.SYS.
Reboot for these files to take effect.
```

These messages indicate which set of configuration files are copied and also remind you to reboot your system in order for them to take effect. The remaining lines are the labels and error messages mentioned previously.

Figure 3-5 shows a flowchart for the CHANGE.BAT batch file. This provides an overview you can compare with Listing 3-2.

Testing CHANGE.BAT

Once you have typed the lines from Listing 3-2 and saved them as CHANGE.BAT, you are ready to test it. Be sure you save CHANGE.BAT to the root directory. Perform the following steps to test CHANGE.BAT:

1. If you haven't already done so, use STORE.BAT to store your current configuration files as TEST (type **STORE TEST** and press ENTER).
2. Make sure you are in the root directory, type **CHANGE** and press ENTER. The screen should clear and you should get the message indicating that you need to supply a filename. This tests the NONAME error portion of the batch file.
3. Type **CHANGE XXXX** and press ENTER. The screen should clear and you should get the message indicating that the XXXX configuration files do not exist. This tests the NOFILES error portion of the batch file.
4. Use a text editor and make some changes to AUTOEXEC.BAT and/or CONFIG.SYS and save them. It doesn't really matter what you

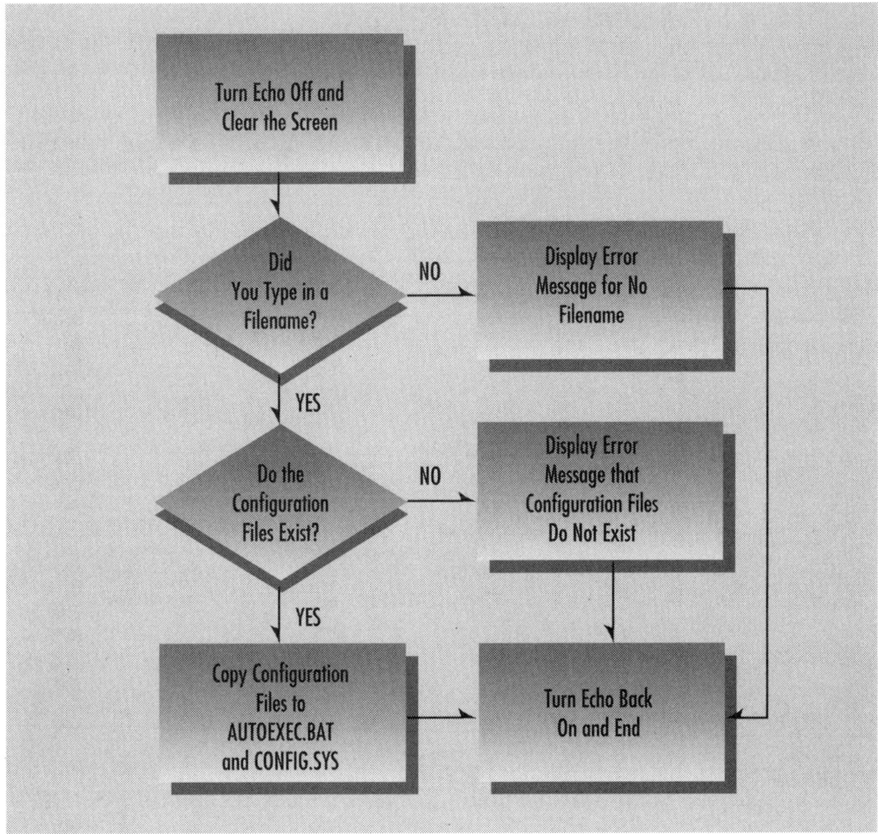

Figure 3-5 CHANGE.BAT flowchart

change since this is just a test. However, DO NOT REBOOT in case your changes may cause a lockup. You made a boot disk didn't you?

5. Now type **CHANGE TEST** and press ENTER. Again, the screen should clear and you should get the message that the files have been written.

6. Examine the contents of your AUTOEXEC.BAT and CONFIG.SYS. files. You should find that the contents have been restored to the original.

You can see that CHANGE.BAT provides a quick way of restoring a set of configuration files.

Using STORE.BAT and CHANGE.BAT

Figure 3-6 shows how you can use STORE.BAT and CHANGE.BAT to manage multiple configuration files. You can use STORE.BAT to save your original configuration files. This way you can always return to a known configuration if you have problems.

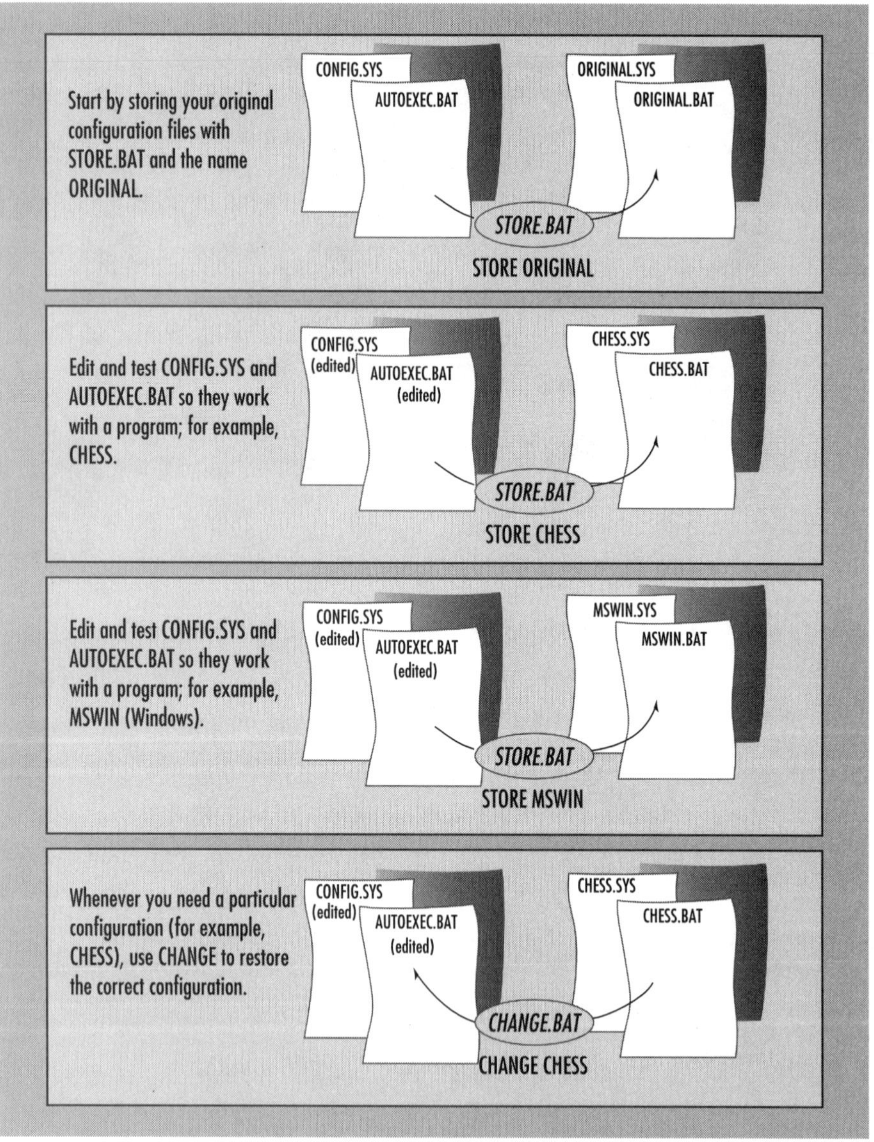

Figure 3-6 Managing multiple configuration files with STORE.BAT and CHANGE.BAT

Next you can edit CONFIG.SYS and AUTOEXEC.BAT so they work with a particular program. Don't worry about what changes to make just yet. We'll cover these topics in the next three chapters. Once you have a configuration that works, save it using a descriptive filename (up to eight characters). Continue to do this for each of your programs. You may also check to see if an existing configuration works with a new program.

Whenever you want to run a particular program, use CHANGE to retrieve the configuration you need. For example, if you used STORE CHESS to save the configuration that works with a chess program, you can retrieve it by typing **CHANGE CHESS.** You then simply reboot by pressing CTRL-ALT-DEL.

Advantages and Disadvantages of STORE.BAT and CHANGE.BAT

For many users, STORE.BAT and CHANGE.BAT provide a simple way to manage multiple configurations. However, there are some advantages and disadvantages.

One advantage of using the batch files is that it is inexpensive. You do not have to purchase a third-party memory manager. Another advantage is you get to know your configurations better—many memory managers are practically automatic and hide the details of memory management from you. You may not want to know the details; it's a matter of personal taste.

On the downside, the batch files make it easy to create a ton of configurations, cluttering your root directory. You may find you have to clean up from time to time. Perhaps the biggest disadvantage to this technique is you must reboot your computer to change configurations. Third-party memory managers reduce the number of configurations; many times you can run everything you need with one configuration. If you run many programs with many different memory requirements, you might consider a third-party memory manager (or at least DOS 6).

Combining Configuration Files

If you find your list of configuration files is getting out of hand, you may want to try combining two or more files and testing the new configuration against your software. For example, you may have a configuration for a flight simulator and a separate configuration for a multimedia application. After some experimentation you may find that you can create one configuration to satisfy both programs' requirements. Once again, you will see the important configuration factors as you progress through the next three chapters. Before we do that however, let's look at a new way of managing multiple configurations in DOS 6.

Multiple Configurations in DOS 6

DOS 6.0 (and the 6.2 upgrade) provides a method by which you can create your own custom menu. Each menu item loads different portions of CONFIG.SYS and AUTOEXEC.BAT. This menu is shown at startup where you can choose a configuration. Keep in mind this only works with DOS 6.

Assembling a custom DOS 6 configuration menu begins in the CONFIG.SYS file. Listing 3-3 shows an example DOS 6 CONFIG.SYS file that creates a start-up menu. Let's examine the new commands.

Listing 3-3 Example CONFIG.SYS for DOS 6 Multiple Configurations

```
[menu]
menuitem=windows, Run Microsoft Windows
menuitem=expanded, Expanded Memory Configuration
menuitem=zeroems, Maximum Extended/No Upper Memory
menucolor=15,7
menudefault=windows,30
numlock=off

[common]
DEVICE=C:\DOS\HIMEM.SYS
BUFFERS=15
FILES=21

[windows]
DEVICE=C:\DOS\EMM386.EXE NOEMS
DOS=HIGH,UMB

[expanded]
DEVICE=C:\DOS\EMM386.EXE RAM
DOS=HIGH,UMB

[zeroems]
DEVICE=C:\DOS\EMM386.EXE NOEMS
DOS=HIGH
```

Creating a Custom Startup Menu with CONFIG.SYS

A multiple configuration CONFIG.SYS file is broken into *blocks*. Each block is prefaced with the name of the block enclosed in bracket characters. For example, [menu] starts the custom menu block. In our example in Listing 3-3, we have five blocks: [menu], [common], [windows], [expanded], and [zeroems]. The first two blocks are predefined DOS 6 blocks. We created the last three blocks to manage three distinct configurations; they are known as configuration blocks. Let's take a closer look at the DOS 6 blocks.

Number	Color	Number	Color
0	Black	8	Gray
1	Blue	9	Bright Blue
2	Green	10	Bright Green
3	Cyan	11	Bright Cyan
4	Red	12	Bright Red
5	Magenta	13	Bright Magenta
6	Brown	14	Yellow
7	White	15	Bright White

Table 3-1 Numeric color values for the menucolor command

DOS 6 Defined Multiple Configuration Blocks

For multiple configurations, the first block must be a [menu] block. The [menu] block contains commands that assemble the menu. Here is a list of the commands that can be used in a [menu] block.

- menuitem—This command creates a menu item for the custom menu. You type this command, followed by an equal sign, a configuration block, and menu text. For example, *menuitem=windows, Run Microsoft Windows* would create a menu item that displays *Run Microsoft Windows* on startup. The games entry directs the CONFIG.SYS file to the [windows] configuration block.
- menudefault—This command determines which menu item is the default. You type this command, followed by an equal sign, a menu item, and a timeout value. For example, *menudefault=windows, 30* would make the *Run Microsoft Windows* option as the default. If the user does not select a menu item in 30 seconds, the menu times out and the system starts the *Run Microsoft Windows* configuration automatically.
- menucolor—This command sets the screen colors for the menu. You type this command, followed by and equal sign, a text color (numeric), and a screen background color (in numeric form). Table 3-1 shows the numeric color values for the menucolor command. For example, our

menu colors in Listing 3-3 are 15,7; this results in a text color of bright white, and a background of white (it actually looks like light gray).

- submenu—This command lets you create a menu tree. To use this command, type **submenu**, followed by an equal sign, followed by a configuration block (which contains the menu submenu), and the menu text. For example, *submenu=cdrom, CD-ROM Configurations* would create a menu item named CD-ROM configurations. If the user selects this item, another menu will appear. You would have to create another menu definition block in this case named cdrom.
- numlock—This command determines whether or not the NUM LOCK key is active on startup. To enable Num Lock on startup, type **numlock=yes**. To disable NUM LOCK, type **numlock=no**.

The [common] Configuration Block

If you have CONFIG.SYS lines that are common to all configurations, place them in a [common] block. For example, our CONFIG.SYS file in Listing 3-3 shows HIMEM.SYS, BUFFERS, and FILE entries. This indicates that all configurations use these lines.

User-Defined Multiple Configuration Blocks

For each menu item you must define a configuration block. For example, our Run Microsoft Windows menu item requires a block named [windows]. In this case, we created the block. Added lines load EMM386.EXE with the NOEMS switch and DOS=HIGH, UMB (DOS in high memory), and provides access to the upper memory blocks. Remember to define a configuration block for every menu item. If you fail to do this, you will get an error on startup indicating the offending CONFIG.SYS line.

The Menu

Before we look at the AUTOEXEC.BAT file for multiple configuration, let's look at the menu that CONFIG.SYS creates. Listing 3-4 shows the menu that results from the CONFIG.SYS file in Listing 3-3. It also shows which blocks are executed when a particular menu item is chosen.

Listing 3-4 DOS 6 Configuration Menu

```
MS-DOS 6 Startup Menu
=====================

   1. Run Microsoft Windows             (executes [common] and [windows])
   2. Expanded Memory Configuration     (executes [common] and [expanded])
```

```
   3. Maximum Extended/No Upper Memory  (executes [common] and [noems])

 Enter a choice: 1       Time Remaining: 29



 F5=Bypass startup files   F8=Confirm each CONFIG.SYS line [N]
```

Notice that the default menu selection is number 1 *(Run Microsoft Windows)*. Also, the timeout value has started to count down toward zero. If it reaches zero before the user interacts, the default menu selection is executed.

The bottom portion of the menu screen identifies two function keys. F5 will bypass the startup files altogether. F8 toggles a setting that determines whether or not you want to confirm each CONFIG.SYS line. This is useful when creating your menu for the first time. You can make sure that the line you intend to execute is being executed.

Setting Up AUTOEXEC.BAT for Multiple Configurations

Now that we have constructed the menu in CONFIG.SYS, we have to break up AUTOEXEC.BAT in a similar manner. Listing 3-5 shows our AUTOEXEC.BAT which works together with the CONFIG.SYS file in Listing 3-3.

Listing 3-5 Example AUTOEXEC.BAT for DOS 6 Multiple Configurations

```
@ECHO OFF
CLS
PROMPT $p$g
C:\MOUSE\MOUSE

goto %config%

:windows
PATH C:\WINDOWS;C:\DOS;
LOADHIGH C:\DOS\SMARTDRV.EXE
win
goto end

:expanded
PATH C:\DOS;C:\123
LOADHIGH C:\DOS\SMARTDRV.EXE
goto end

:zeroems
PATH C:\DOS;C:\WP51;C:\MYFILES
C:\DOS\SMARTDRV.EXE
goto end

:end
```

Common AUTOEXEC.BAT Entries

The first four lines of our example AUTOEXEC.BAT are common entries. Note that you do not have to use a command to indicate this. So, in this case, the screen echo is turned off (@ECHO OFF), the screen is cleared (CLS), the prompt is set (PROMPT pg), and the mouse driver is loaded (C:\MOUSE\MOUSE) for each configuration.

Activating the Custom AUTOEXEC.BAT Lines

Immediately following the common AUTOEXEC.BAT lines, you must place a *goto* command as follows: *goto %config%.* This redirects the execution to the appropriate block. Each custom configuration block in the CONFIG.SYS must also have a block in AUTOEXEC.BAT. However, instead of surrounding the block name with brackets, you add a colon prefix to the block name, for example, *:WINDOWS.*

Skipping Other Custom Configuration Blocks

To ensure that AUTOEXEC.BAT lines for other configurations are not executed, we must jump around them using a *goto* command. To do this, we add an *:end* label to the end of AUTOEXEC.BAT. Also, at the end of each custom section, we jump to the end of the file with *goto :end.* This bypasses the unwanted configuration lines.

Before we get into the specifics of DOS 5, DOS 6, and Windows memory management, let's summarize the management of configuration files.

Summary

This chapter introduced you to the possible need for multiple system configurations. It also demonstrated that you must be careful when editing your configuration files. Knowing *how* to make changes to your files is nearly as important as *what* you change. Here is a summary of the key points we covered in this chapter:

- Always make a bootable floppy disk before editing AUTOEXEC.BAT or CONFIG.SYS on your hard drive. Even if you cause a lockup, you can recover with your bootable disk.

- It may be necessary to have more than one set of configuration files for your system. Both the hardware and software you use can result in the need for multiple configurations.
- You can use two simple batch files from this chapter to manage configuration files. Use STORE.BAT to store your configurations that are known to work for particular programs. Use CHANGE.BAT to retrieve a particular configuration when you need it. Remember that you need to reboot your computer whenever you change configurations.
- Always try combining different configurations to reduce the total number of SYS and BAT files. Some users may get away with using one configuration for all their programs.
- If you are a DOS 6 user, you can create custom startup menus. These menus let you select a custom configuration every time you reboot your computer.

At this point you've seen memory architecture, examined your own configuration, and you've seen how to manage multiple memory configurations. Now it's time to get to the nuts and bolts of memory management. The next chapter discusses memory management for DOS 5.0. If you are a DOS 6 user, you can skip to Chapter 5, *DOS 6 Memory Management.*

DOS 5.0 Memory Management

By now you should understand the types of PC memory and how your system is configured. You also have learned a simple way to manage multiple sets of configuration files using CHANGE.BAT and STORE.BAT. Now we will examine the DOS 5.0 commands and drivers that you can use to optimize the memory in your system. If you are already using DOS 6, skip to the next chapter.

This chapter will start out with modifications that you can make to your CONFIG.SYS file to increase the amount of free conventional memory. The amount of free conventional memory is very important to most PC users; especially those who use non-Windows multimedia applications.

This chapter will also build an example configuration, one step at a time. In each step we will describe exactly what is taking place along with what you will gain (or lose) by performing the step. You can modify your own configuration files along the way (using STORE.BAT to store them), or you can read the entire chapter and develop your configurations on paper before creating them.

We will concentrate on memory management as it relates to DOS applications in this chapter. You will find information that specifically relates to DOS 5.0. If you are using DOS 5.0 and Windows, you will want to read this chapter and Chapter 6, *Windows Memory Management.* It is important to understand the DOS commands and device drivers before proceeding to the Windows chapter. If you are already familiar with DOS 5.0 memory techniques, you can use this chapter as a review.

Let's start with an overview of the topics we will discuss in this chapter.

DOS 5.0 TOPICS COVERED

Getting Detailed Memory Information Using the DOS 5.0 MEM Command

Managing Extended Memory Using HIMEM.SYS

Loading DOS in High Memory Using the DOS= Command

Simulating Expanded Memory Using the EMM386.EXE Driver

Providing Access to Upper Memory Using the EMM386.EXE Driver

Loading Programs in Upper Memory Using the LOADHIGH Command

Loading Device Drivers in Upper Memory Using the DEVICEHIGH Command

Loading Drivers High

Creating a RAM Disk Using the RAMDRIVE.SYS Driver

Creating a Disk Cache Using the SMARTDRV.SYS Driver

Solving Multimedia Memory Problems with DOS 5.0

Memory Management Using DOS 5.0

This section will explore memory management as it relates to DOS 5.0. We will start with a more in-depth look at the MEM command followed by a step-by-step procedure of memory configuration commands and drivers. In each step of the procedure, we will introduce a new feature to the configuration files. We will show what the feature does and describe its options, if any. As we progress, we will show the memory layout in graphical form so you can see what is taking place and how it affects your system.

A 4-Megabyte System Example

We are using a system with 4 megabytes of memory for the examples in this chapter. You will see differences in the MEM output if your system has more or less memory than 4MB.

Switch	Example	Purpose
/P or /PROGRAM	MEM /P or MEM /PROGRAM	Provides the status of programs loaded in memory.
/D or /DEBUG	MEM /D or MEM /DEBUG	Provides the status of programs and drivers loaded in memory.
/C or /CLASSIFY	MEM /C or MEM /CLASSIFY	Provides a list of programs classified by memory usage.

Table 4-1 MEM command line switches

Getting Your Memory Configuration Using MEM in DOS 5.0

In Chapter 2, *Memory and Your Computer,* you used the DOS MEM command to find out the general details of your current memory configuration. We will now demonstrate how you can use the MEM command to gain more detailed memory information. This is done by using a *switch* on the command line when you type **MEM**. A switch is nothing more than a few additional characters on the command line that specify the behavior of the command or program in some way. Table 4-1 shows the possible MEM switches and what they accomplish.

MEM Requires a PATH to Your DOS Directory

MEM was installed to your DOS directory when you installed DOS itself. In order to run MEM from any directory other than DOS, you must have a path to DOS in your AUTOEXEC.BAT file. This may be in combination with other paths. For example: PATH=C:\WINDOWS;C:\DOS; provides a path to both the WINDOWS directory and the DOS directory. The DOS 5.0 installation program automatically adds the PATH statement to your AUTOEXEC.BAT file. It should be there now unless you manually deleted it.

Up until now, we used the MEM command by itself, which produced a memory summary similar to the one shown in Listing 4-1.

Listing 4-1 Sample MEM Output (No Switches)

```
655360 bytes total conventional memory
655360 bytes available to MS-DOS
629024 largest executable program size
```

continued on next page

continued from previous page

```
3145728 bytes total contiguous extended memory
      0 bytes available contiguous extended memory
2632704 bytes available XMS memory
        MS-DOS resident in High Memory Area
```

Now let's look at some sample output produced by each of the DOS MEM switches. The examples use the same memory configuration that produced the previous output.

MEM /PROGRAM—Listing Programs in Memory

The first switch is the /PROGRAM or /P switch which will provide a list of the programs currently in memory. Each entry in the listing provides the program's address (in hexadecimal), the name of the program, its size (also in hexadecimal), and a type. Listing 4-2 shows an example output for MEM /P. We've omitted the memory summary from the listing.

The first several lines refer to memory which the system itself uses. You usually won't have to be concerned with this section of memory. The system always requires it, so don't worry about freeing up the memory for your programs. We will, however, take a closer look at some of these entries later in this chapter.

Listing 4-2 MEM /P Output

```
Address     Name        Size      Type
-------     --------    ------    ------
000000                  000400    Interrupt Vector
000400                  000100    ROM Communication Area
000500                  000200    DOS Communication Area

000700      IO          000AC0    System Data

0011C0      MSDOS       0013F0    System Data

0025B0      IO          0035A0    System Data
              HIMEM     0004A0     DEVICE=
              EMM386    0020D0     DEVICE=
                        0003C0     FILES=
                        000100     FCBS=
                        000200     BUFFERS=
                        0001C0     LASTDRIVE=
                        000740     STACKS=
005B60      MSDOS       000040    System Program

005BB0      COMMAND     000940    Program
006500      MSDOS       000040    -- Free --
006550      COMMAND     000100    Environment
006660      MEM         000050    Environment
0066C0      MEM         0176F0    Program
```

```
01DDC0      MSDOS       082220      -- Free --
09FFF0      SYSTEM      028010      System Program

0C8010      IO          003410      System Data
              SMARTDRV  003400       DEVICE=
0CB430      MSDOS       000050      -- Free --
0CB490      DOSKEY      001020      Program
0CC4C0      MSDOS       013B30      -- Free --
```

Let's break the MEM output in Listing 4-2 into pieces. The first line starts at the bottom of memory (00000h) and is 400h bytes. This is the area in which DOS stores *interrupt vectors.* Interrupt vectors are a collection of addresses that DOS uses internally. We do not have to worry about them in memory management. They'll always be there no matter how we manage our memory.

The same goes for the next few lines. For example, the ROM communication area is at address 000400h. Again, these are addresses that DOS uses internally. This is followed by the DOS communication area at address 000500h.

The next two lines, IO and MSDOS, are the hidden files that are required on a boot disk: IO.SYS and MSDOS.SYS. Up to this point we haven't had much control over the system memory; however, we haven't been taking up much conventional memory yet either (just 0025B0h bytes or 9,648 bytes).

The block of lines that begins at address 0025B0h is at the point where we have some level of control. This is the *DOS environment block* where DOS stores information such as FILES= and BUFFERS= from the CONFIG.SYS file. The more files and buffers we specify in the CONFIG.SYS file, the more space is allocated to this environment block. The lines that are in boldface indicate that we have some level of control over this memory.

Now we have reached the point where programs are located in memory. If you examine the listing, you will see a DOS TSR program at address CB490h. This is DOSKEY, a utility supplied with DOS that saves command line entries. Notice that it takes up 1020h bytes, or 4,128 bytes. At this point, you can start to make decisions about managing your own memory. We'll examine more about addresses and programs in memory as this chapter progresses. Now let's look at a more detailed listing from the MEM command: the /D switch.

MEM /DEBUG—Listing Programs and Device Drivers in Memory

By typing **MEM /DEBUG** or **MEM /D** we can get a more detailed memory listing. An example of this is shown in Listing 4-3. Information added to the MEM output as result of the /DEBUG is listed in boldface. The listing is very similar to MEM /P; however, it also lists specific information regarding device drivers. This information is usually not necessary in memory management, so we'll use MEM /P or MEM /C in this chapter's examples.

Listing 4-3 MEM /D Output

```
Address     Name          Size     Type
-------     --------      ------   ------
000000                    000400   Interrupt Vector
000400                    000100   ROM Communication Area
000500                    000200   DOS Communication Area

000700      IO            000AC0   System Data
                CON                  System Device Driver
                AUX                  System Device Driver
                PRN                  System Device Driver
                CLOCK$               System Device Driver
                A: - D:              System Device Driver
                COM1                 System Device Driver
                LPT1                 System Device Driver
                LPT2                 System Device Driver
                LPT3                 System Device Driver
                COM2                 System Device Driver
                COM3                 System Device Driver
                COM4                 System Device Driver

0011C0      MSDOS         0013F0   System Data

0025B0      IO            0035A0   System Data
              HIMEM       0004A0    DEVICE=
                XMSXXXX0             Installed Device Driver
              EMM386      0020D0    DEVICE=
                $MMXXXX0             Installed Device Driver
                          0003C0    FILES=
                          000100    FCBS=
                          000200    BUFFERS=
                          0001C0    LASTDRIVE=
                          000740    STACKS=
005B60      MSDOS         000040   System Program

005BB0      COMMAND       000940   Program
006500      MSDOS         000040   -- Free --
006550      COMMAND       000100   Environment
006660      MEM           000050   Environment
0066C0      MEM           0176F0   Program
01DDC0      MSDOS         082220   -- Free --
09FFF0      SYSTEM        028010   System Program

0C8010      IO            003410   System Data
              SMARTDRV    003400    DEVICE=
                SMARTAAR             Installed Device Driver
0CB430      MSDOS         000050   -- Free --
0CB490      DOSKEY        001020   Program
0CC4C0      MSDOS         013B30   -- Free --
```

Let's look at the last switch for the MEM command: the /CLASSIFY switch.

MEM /C—Program Classification

By typing **MEM /CLASSIFY**, or **MEM /C**, we can get a listing that provides a memory summary in terms of classification. Listing 4-4 shows example output from MEM /C.

Note that this listing breaks the memory into conventional memory (0 to 640K) and upper memory (640K to 1MB). This version of the MEM command can be very useful when setting up your system's memory. It gives you the program's sizes in decimal and hex. Note that the decimal section also lists the size in bytes and in kilobytes (bytes/1,024).

Listing 4-4 MEM /C Output

```
Conventional Memory :

  Name               Size in Decimal        Size in Hex
-------------      ---------------------  -------------
  MSDOS              13760      ( 13.4K)      35C0
  HIMEM               1184      (  1.2K)       4A0
  EMM386              8400      (  8.2K)      20D0
  COMMAND             2624      (  2.6K)       A40
  FREE                  64      (  0.1K)        40
  FREE              629120      (614.4K)     99980

Total  FREE :       629184      (614.4K)

Upper Memory :

  Name               Size in Decimal        Size in Hex
-------------      ---------------------  -------------
  SYSTEM            163840      (160.0K)     28000
  SMARTDRV           13312      ( 13.0K)      3400
  DOSKEY              4128      (  4.0K)      1020
  FREE                  80      (  0.1K)        50
  FREE               80688      ( 78.8K)     13B30

Total  FREE :        80768      ( 78.9K)

Total bytes available to programs (Conventional+Upper) :     709952   (693.3K)
Largest executable program size :                            629024   (614.3K)
Largest available upper memory block :                        80688   ( 78.8K)

   3145728 bytes total contiguous extended memory
         0 bytes available contiguous extended memory
   2632704 bytes available XMS memory
           MS-DOS resident in High Memory Area
```

We will see the effects of modifying configuration files (CONFIG.SYS and AUTOEXEC.BAT) using MEM /C later in this chapter. For now, remember that the MEM /C command always provides a good summary of your system's memory configuration in a format that's easier for most people to read.

A Bare-Bones Configuration

In order to build a set of working configuration files, we will start with a simple, minimal configuration. This way you can see the effects of each step in the process. For each example, we will show the MEM output and a graphic indicating the effects of each change. Listing 4-5 shows the contents of the AUTOEXEC.BAT and CONFIG.SYS files for this minimal configuration.

Listing 4-5 Minimal AUTOEXEC.BAT and CONFIG.SYS

```
Contents of AUTOEXEC.BAT
------------------------
@ECHO OFF
CLS
PROMPT $p$g
PATH=C:\DOS;

Contents of CONFIG.SYS
----------------------
FILES=21
BUFFERS=15
```

The AUTOEXEC.BAT file in this example has an ECHO OFF command followed by a CLS (clear screen). It also has the PROMPT command and a path to DOS. None of these commands take up any memory with the exception of the PATH statement (which is part of the DOS environment block). However, DOS automatically reserves 256 bytes of environment space; so we might as well use it to store a path to the DOS directory.

Remove CLS and &ECHO OFF When Troubleshooting Memory

It's a good idea to remove the CLS and &ECHO OFF commands from your AUTOEXEC.BAT when troubleshooting memory problems. These commands prevent DOS from displaying important information during the boot process.

Now that we've seen what is in the configuration files, let's look at the output from the MEM command for this minimal configuration. Listing 4-6 shows the MEM /C output.

Listing 4-6 MEM /C—Minimal Configuration

```
Conventional Memory :

  Name                Size in Decimal       Size in Hex
-------------       ---------------------  -------------
  MSDOS              58080       ( 56.7K)       E2E0
  COMMAND             4704       (  4.6K)       1260
  FREE                  64       (  0.1K)         40
  FREE              592352       (578.5K)      909E0

Total  FREE :       592416       (578.5K)

Total bytes available to programs :                592416    (578.5K)
Largest executable program size :                  592256    (578.4K)

   3145728 bytes total contiguous extended memory
   3145728 bytes available contiguous extended memory
```

Note that this output from MEM /C does not show any usage of upper memory. This is because we do not have the necessary drivers to access upper memory yet.

There are four entries in the Conventional Memory section in Listing 4-6. The first line is MS-DOS itself which takes up 58,080 bytes, or about 56.7K. The second line is COMMAND; this is the command interpreter of DOS. Its purpose is to interpret command line internal DOS commands (such as DIR, COPY, and so on). It is using 4,704 bytes, or around 4.6K.

The last two entries in the Conventional Memory section are both labeled FREE. This indicates free conventional memory. It is broken into two entries because the free memory is actually in two different areas of memory. In other words, they are not in a contiguous (all in one piece) block of memory.

If you do the math, you'll find that the Total FREE section is the sum of the two FREE sections of memory. However, adding the size of MS-DOS, COMMAND, and the FREE sections doesn't quite add up to 640K. This is due to a few dead spots in memory. When a program requests and gets memory, it's usually based on a boundary that is rounded up. Therefore, sometimes there are small areas of memory that are not used.

The next two lines of the MEM /C output indicate that there are 592,416 bytes available to programs and 592,256 bytes of memory for executable programs. This disparity is because the system BIOS uses a small amount of memory. It's not much of a factor, however, because the amount is so small (160 bytes).

The last two lines show the total amount of contiguous extended memory and the total amount of extended memory available. Extended memory is not used in our configuration files; therefore, the entire 3 megabytes (3,415,728 bytes) are in one piece and available. Remember, our example system has 4 megabytes total.

Unless a program manages this memory through the use of a *DOS extender*, this memory is useless at this point. A DOS extender is a method that programmers use to write programs that exceed the normal 640K boundary of DOS.

Now let's look at a graphic that represents the memory for this minimal configuration. Figure 4-1 shows this graphic.

The left side of Figure 4-1 shows the entire range of the 4-megabyte example system. The right side shows an enlarged depiction of the first megabyte (conventional and upper memory) and the high memory area (HMA). Recall that the HMA is the first 64K of extended memory. Upper memory and the HMA do not come into play in this example.

Notice that the COMMAND program and MS-DOS are loaded in conventional memory. There are also small pieces of conventional memory (at its lowest point) used for system purposes. Also note that the illustration of COMMAND and MS-DOS is not to exact scale.

Remember that most DOS programs (especially multimedia programs) require as much conventional memory as you can supply. We'll continue with our example configurations one step at a time, with the ultimate goal being max-

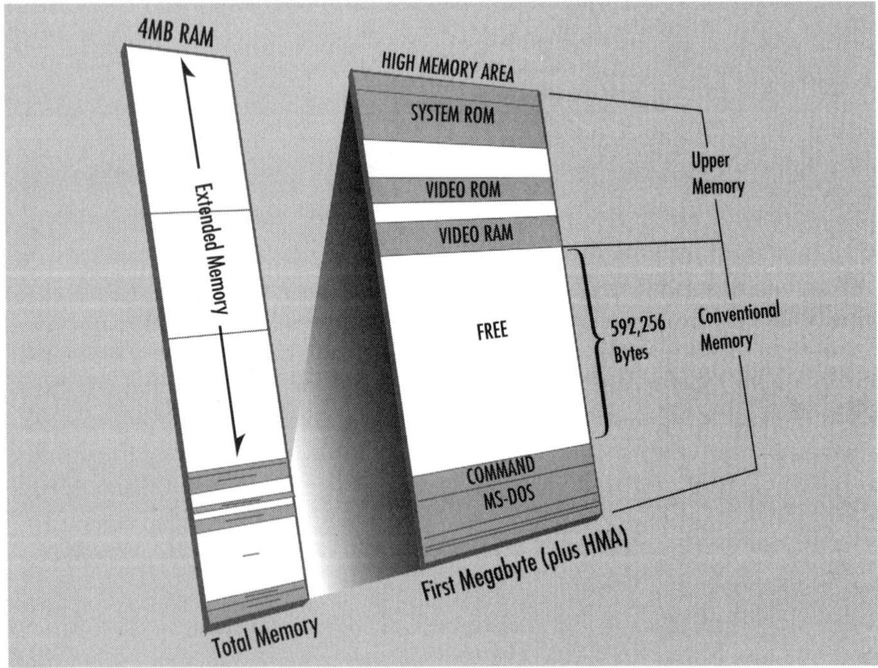

Figure 4-1 Memory configuration for the Minimal example

imized conventional memory. Let's expand on this example by loading the DOS-supplied extended memory driver, HIMEM.SYS.

Adding HIMEM.SYS—Extended Memory Driver

Our next set of configuration files adds the DOS extended memory driver, HIMEM.SYS. The version of HIMEM.SYS supplied with DOS 5.0 is compatible with the XMS specification version 2.0. Do not confuse this with the version of the driver itself. We will see how to check the version level of HIMEM.SYS in a moment.

The bottom line is, you always want to use the most recent version of HIMEM.SYS that you have available. If you buy a copy of Microsoft Windows (which also contains a copy of HIMEM.SYS) compare the versions by examining the time and date stamp on the file. The most recent date will be the newest version.

Now, let's look at our new configuration file. This time we only modified CONFIG.SYS, so it's the only file in the listing. Listing 4-7 shows the new CONFIG.SYS adding the HIMEM.SYS driver.

Listing 4-7 Modified CONFIG.SYS—Adding the HIMEM.SYS Driver

```
Contents of CONFIG.SYS
----------------------
FILES=21
BUFFERS=15
DEVICE=C:\DOS\HIMEM.SYS
```

Note that one line in the CONFIG.SYS file is all that is required to load the HIMEM.SYS driver. This line consists of the DEVICE= statement followed by the full pathname and filename of the driver. You must supply the pathname in this case. Since the system loads the CONFIG.SYS before the AUTOEXEC.BAT file, the PATH statement in AUTOEXEC.BAT has no effect yet.

When the HIMEM.SYS driver is successfully loaded on power up, you will see a message similar to the following:

```
HIMEM: DOS XMS Driver, Version 2.77 - 02/27/91
XMS Specification Version 2.0
Copyright 1988-1991 Microsoft Corp.

Installed A20 handler number 1.
64K High Memory Area is available.
```

This message indicates the version of the driver on the first line (in this case, version 2.77, although your system may differ). The fourth line indicates that a handler for the A20 address line has been installed. Recall that we cannot address the high memory area without a 21st address line. Because the first twenty address lines are A0 through A19, A20 becomes the twenty-first.

Now let's see the effects on the MEM output when we added the new driver and reboot the computer. Remember you must always reboot after making a change to CONFIG.SYS. Listing 4-8 shows the new MEM output (as usual, new or changed material is shown in boldface).

Listing 4-8 MEM /C—After Loading HIMEM.SYS

```
Conventional Memory :

  Name              Size in Decimal        Size in Hex
-------------     ---------------------   -------------
  MSDOS              58080        ( 56.7K)       E2E0
  HIMEM               3200        (  3.1K)        C80
  COMMAND             4704        (  4.6K)       1260
  FREE                  64        (  0.1K)         40
  FREE              589136        (575.3K)      8FD50

Total  FREE :       589200        (575.4K)

Total bytes available to programs :               589200    (575.4K)
Largest executable program size :                 589040    (575.2K)
```

Notice that the HIMEM driver now appears in the Conventional Memory section of the MEM output. It is 3,200 bytes in size. This reduces the amount of conventional memory available by a similar amount.

It may seem like we're going in the wrong direction, but don't despair. There is a method to this madness, as you will see later in this chapter. The main thing the HIMEM.SYS driver buys us is access to the HMA. We just aren't taking advantage of it yet.

Let's look at a graphic to see the addition of the HIMEM.SYS driver. Figure 4-2 shows this addition. We've omitted the overview of the entire 4-megabyte range because nothing has changed there for this example.

Adding EMM386.EXE—Expanded Memory Driver

In addition to the HIMEM.SYS driver, DOS also supplies an expanded memory driver, EMM386.EXE. This driver performs more than one function. EMM386.EXE can do the following:

- Simulate expanded memory using extended memory.
- Provide access to the upper memory blocks (UMB).

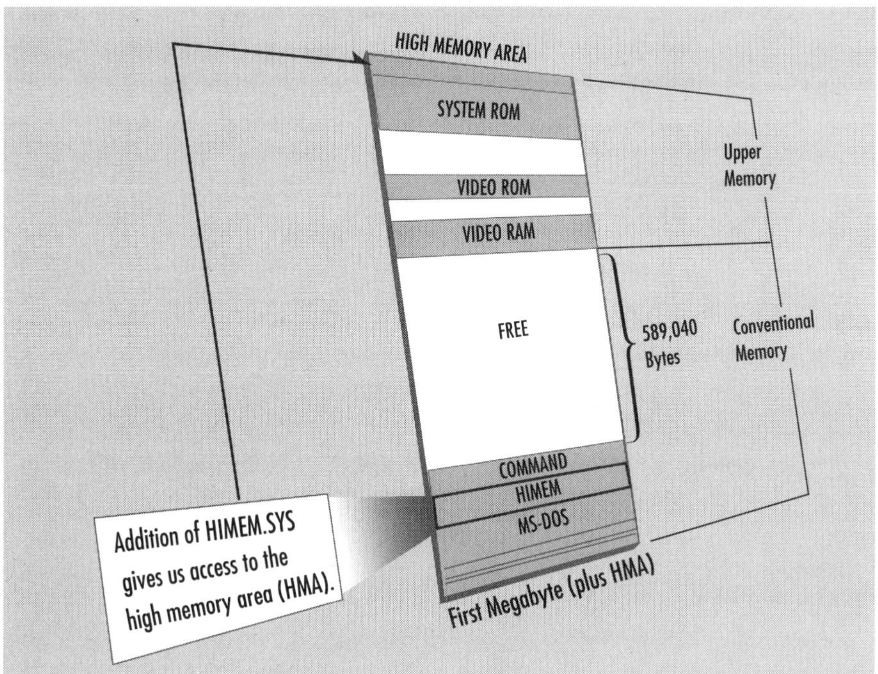

Figure 4-2 Memory configuration—added HIMEM.SYS

- Combine expanded memory simulation with UMB access.

Using EMM386.EXE in CONFIG.SYS

When you add a line for EMM386.EXE in your CONFIG.SYS file, you can specify a number of options in the form of switches. For example, you can specify the amount of expanded memory (in kilobytes) you want to simulate. Here is an example:

```
DEVICE=C:\DOS\EMM386.EXE 512
```

This would allocate 512K bytes of expanded memory. Of course, as a result, the amount of free extended memory would decrease. There are also switches to set the page frame, include or exclude particular addresses, and do other things. However, these switches are usually not required. Consult your DOS manual for more information on these switches.

Two switches are important to our discussion on memory management: RAM and NOEMS. We will look at three examples of EMM386.EXE usage. The first

Switch	Example	Expanded Memory?	UMB Access?
None	C:\DOS\EMM386.EXE	YES	NO
RAM	C:\DOS\EMM386.EXE RAM	YES	YES
NOEMS	C:\DOS\EMM386.EXE NOEMS	NO	YES

Table 4-2 EMM386.EXE with RAM, NOEMS, or no switches

is with no switches, the second is with the RAM switch, and the third is with the NOEMS switch. Table 4-2 shows the effects of these switches on expanded memory simulations and UMB access.

You can see in Table 4-2 that the switch you use affects whether you require simulated expanded memory, access to the UMBs, or both. Let's look at the three examples. We'll start out using no switches.

EMM386.EXE with No Switch

This example loads EMM386.EXE with no switch. According to our table, which should simulate expanded memory without access to the UMBs. Listing 4-9 shows the new CONFIG.SYS for this example. Once again, the AUTOEXEC.BAT file remains unchanged.

Listing 4-9 Modified CONFIG.SYS—Added EMM386.EXE (No Switches)

```
Contents of CONFIG.SYS
----------------------
FILES=21
BUFFERS=15
DEVICE=C:\DOS\HIMEM.SYS
DEVICE=C:\DOS\EMM386.EXE
```

Note that this example CONFIG.SYS file also loads the HIMEM.SYS driver, which is required by EMM386.EXE. You cannot load the expanded memory driver without first loading the extended memory driver.

During the boot process, the system will display the following message to indicate that the expanded memory driver is installed correctly. This is in addition to the message from HIMEM.SYS.

```
MICROSOFT Expanded Memory Manager 386  Version 4.20.06X
(C) Copyright Microsoft Corporation 1986, 1990

EMM386 successfully installed.
```

```
  Available expanded memory . . . . . . . .  256 KB

  LIM/EMS version . . . . . . . . . . . . .  4.0
  Total expanded memory pages . . . . . . .  40
  Available expanded memory pages . . . . .  16
  Total handles . . . . . . . . . . . . . .  64
  Active handles  . . . . . . . . . . . . .  1
  Page frame segment  . . . . . . . . . . .  D000 H

EMM386 Active.
```

This message provides quite a bit of information. The lines that are important for our purposes are in boldface. For example, the first line following the copyright message indicates that EMM386 has been successfully installed. The next line indicates that we have 256K of expanded memory available. This is the default if you do not specify an amount on the EMM386.EXE line. There is actually 640K of expanded memory in this case; 256K of expanded memory and 384K of memory which *backfills* the upper memory area. We'll discuss backfilling later in this chapter.

We have 16 pages of expanded memory available. Recall that an expanded memory page is 16 kilobytes. Therefore 16 x 16K equals 256K.

The second to last line indicates the page frame segment. This is a 64K section of upper memory where programs that utilize expanded memory can keep up to four pages at a time.

Now let's look at the MEM /C output for this example. Listing 4-10 provides this information.

Listing 4-10 MEM /C—After Loading EMM386.EXE (No Switches)

```
Conventional Memory :

  Name                Size in Decimal       Size in Hex
-------------     ---------------------   -------------
  MSDOS              58080        ( 56.7K)       E2E0
  HIMEM               3200        (  3.1K)        C80
  EMM386              8400        (  8.2K)       20D0
  COMMAND             4704        (  4.6K)       1260
  FREE                  64        (  0.1K)         40
  FREE              580720        (567.1K)      8DC70

Total  FREE :       580784        (567.2K)

Total bytes available to programs :                              580784   (567.2K)
Largest executable program size :                                580624   (567.0K)

    655360 bytes total EMS memory
```

continued on next page

continued from previous page

```
  262144 bytes free EMS memory

 3145728 bytes total contiguous extended memory
       0 bytes available contiguous extended memory
 2719744 bytes available XMS memory
         64Kb High Memory Area available
```

Note in the listing that the EMM386 driver now resides in conventional memory. As a result, our free conventional memory is shrinking even more. But we'll correct that soon.

Also note that there are two new lines in the middle of the MEM output. One line indicates 640K (655,360 bytes) total EMS memory. The other indicates 256K (262,144 bytes) of free EMS memory. Remember that 384K of the expanded memory is upper memory backfill. This is the default for EMM386.EXE.

Because we have converted existing extended memory to expanded memory, the total available extended memory (XMS) has decreased. Also, the contiguous bytes available has dropped to zero. This is not cause for alarm, however. It simply means that the extended memory manager has control of the XMS memory (indicated by the second to last line).

To help solidify what happened here, let's look at another graphic. Figure 4-3 shows the memory configuration with EMM386 installed.

As you can see by the illustration, the EMM386 driver takes up space in conventional memory. Once again this reduces the amount of conventional memory. At this point we have MS-DOS, HIMEM, EMM386, and the COMMAND interpreter loaded in conventional memory. This is in addition to the conventional memory that the system always requires.

Because we did not specify a switch on the EMM386.EXE line, we end up creating expanded memory. This results in a 64K page frame being located in upper memory. By default, the address of the EMS page frame is D0000h. The 64K page frame is divided into four pages, each being 16K. The contents of the page frames can be any available page from the expanded memory. The left side of Figure 4-3 shows a section of extended memory converted to expanded memory.

Programs must be specifically written to make use of expanded memory. If all of the programs you run do not utilize expanded memory, there is no point in configuring any simulation of EMS from extended memory (and some programs, especially Windows, can use all of the extended memory they can get).

There is a drawback to using EMM386.EXE without any switches. True, this configuration provides expanded memory; however, it does not provide access to the upper memory blocks, or UMBs. Let's look at an example that starts to open up access to the UMBs.

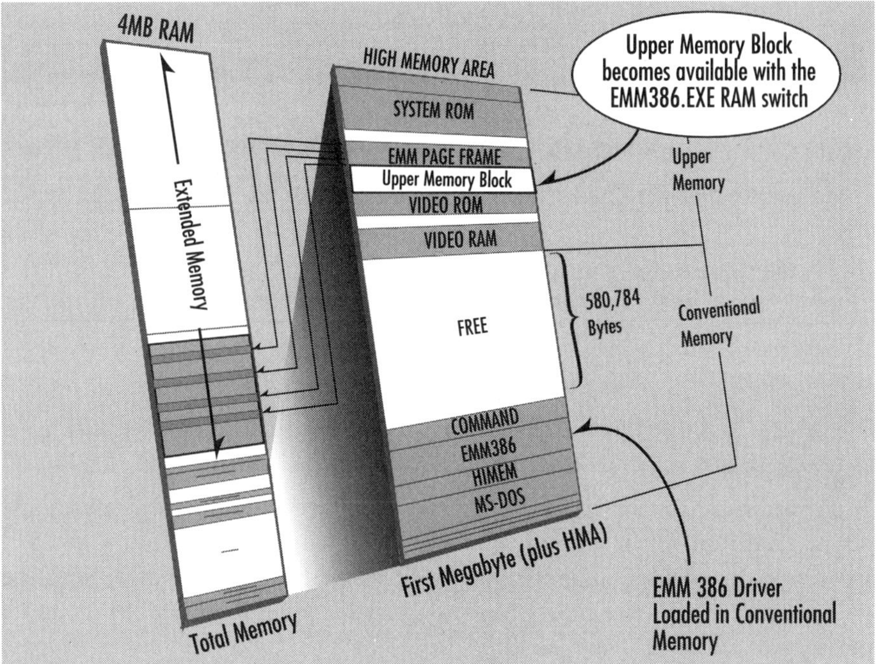

Figure 4-3 Memory configuration—EMM386.EXE loaded with no switches

EMM386.EXE with the RAM Switch

Our next example will modify the CONFIG.SYS line that loads EMM386.EXE by adding the RAM switch. The configuration files are identical except for this line. Using the RAM switch simulates expanded memory and also provides access to the UMBs. Here is the new line:

```
DEVICE=C:\DOS\EMM386.EXE RAM
```

Note the addition of the RAM switch. This switch, unlike the switches used with the MEM command, do not require the forward slash character (/). The first notice of this change appears during the boot process. Here is the message that EMM386.EXE displays:

```
MICROSOFT Expanded Memory Manager 386  Version 4.20.06X
(C) Copyright Microsoft Corporation 1986, 1990

EMM386 successfully installed.
```

continued on next page

continued from previous page

```
  Available expanded memory . . . . . . . .  256 KB

  LIM/EMS version . . . . . . . . . . . . .  4.0
  Total expanded memory pages . . . . . . .  40
  Available expanded memory pages . . . . .  16
  Total handles . . . . . . . . . . . . . .  64
  Active handles  . . . . . . . . . . . . .  1
  Page frame segment  . . . . . . . . . . .  D000 H

  Total upper memory available  . . . . . .    31 KB
  Largest Upper Memory Block available  . .    31 KB
  Upper memory starting address . . . . . .  C800 H

EMM386 Active.
```

Notice that in addition to the expanded memory information, EMM386.EXE also displays information regarding upper memory. In this example, there are 31 kilobytes of upper memory available. We can use this memory to load some device drivers and memory-resident programs. However, this will require an additional step, as we'll see in a moment. Simply loading EMM386.EXE with the RAM switch doesn't move programs to upper memory. It simply makes upper memory *available.*

The last new line in the EMM386.EXE output shows the address (it's actually the segment address) of the start of *available* upper memory. Recall that upper memory actually starts at A0000h, but this area is normally reserved for video RAM.

Let's see the effects of EMM386.EXE RAM on the MEM /C output. This is shown in Listing 4-11.

Listing 4-11 MEM /C—After Loading EMM386.EXE with the RAM Switch

```
Conventional Memory :

  Name              Size in Decimal        Size in Hex
-------------    ---------------------   -------------
  MSDOS             58080       ( 56.7K)       E2E0
  HIMEM              3200       (  3.1K)        C80
  EMM386             8400       (  8.2K)       20D0
  COMMAND            4704       (  4.6K)       1260
  FREE                 64       (  0.1K)         40
  FREE             580720       (567.1K)      8DC70

Total  FREE :      580784       (567.2K)

Total bytes available to programs :                            580784   (567.2K)
Largest executable program size :                              580624   (567.0K)
```

```
 655360 bytes total EMS memory
 262144 bytes free EMS memory

3145728 bytes total contiguous extended memory
      0 bytes available contiguous extended memory
2686976 bytes available XMS memory
        64Kb High Memory Area available
```

Note that the only major change is a drop in extended memory. This is because EMM386.EXE used some of this memory to represent the upper memory blocks. This is known as *backfilling* memory.

Figure 4-4 shows an illustration for the EMM386.EXE RAM configuration. Note that the upper memory block is now available. The starting address is C8000h. This is just above the video ROM addresses in the first megabyte of memory.

The RAM switch is good for situations where you want both expanded memory and access to the upper memory area. If you do not need expanded memory, or you need more upper memory, the next situation is for you.

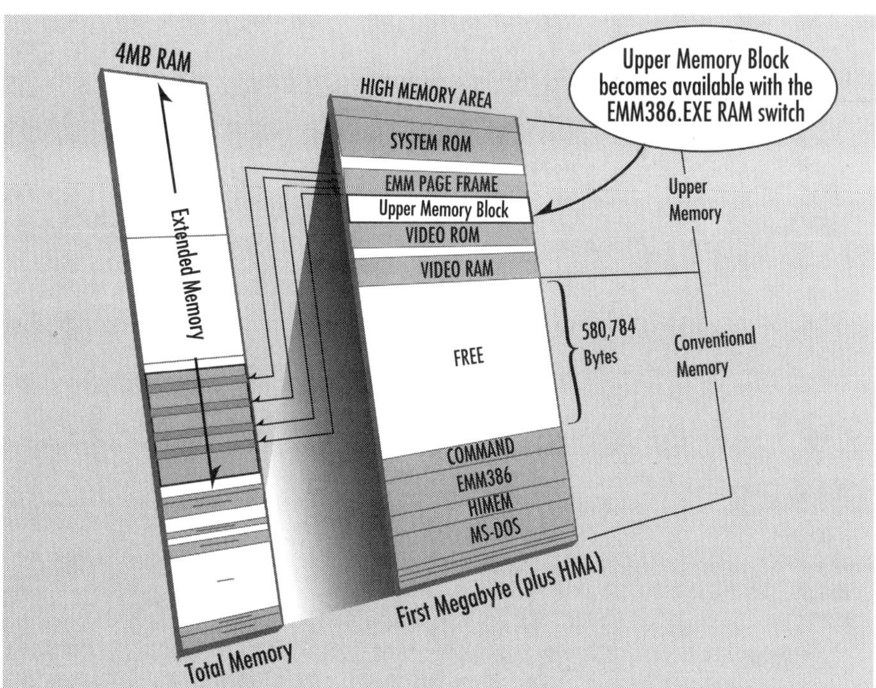

Figure 4-4 Memory configuration—EMM386.EXE loaded with the RAM switch

EMM386.EXE with the NOEMS Switch

Next, we modify the CONFIG.SYS file so the EMM386.EXE driver is loaded using the NOEMS switch. As you might have guessed, this switch means no expanded memory services. However, it does provide access to the upper memory blocks. It also provides a greater amount of upper memory for you to load device drivers or memory-resident programs. Here is the modified EMM386.EXE line:

```
DEVICE=C:\DOS\EMM386.EXE NOEMS
```

Note the addition of the NOEMS switch. As with the RAM switch the first noticeable change appears during the boot process. Here is the new message that EMM386.EXE displays:

```
MICROSOFT Expanded Memory Manager 386  Version 4.20.06X
(C) Copyright Microsoft Corporation 1986, 1990

EMM386 successfully installed.

Expanded memory services unavailable.

  Total upper memory available . . . . . .     95 KB
  Largest Upper Memory Block available . .     95 KB
  Upper memory starting address . . . . . .  C800 H

EMM386 Active.
```

The message from EMM386.EXE is considerably smaller when using the NOEMS switch. This is primarily due to the fact that there is no expanded memory information. This information has been replaced by a line indicating that EMS is unavailable. Also notice that the amount of upper memory has increased to 95K. We'll see why this occurred in a moment. First let's look at the MEM output which is shown in Listing 4-12.

Listing 4-12 MEM /C—After Loading EMM386.EXE with the NOEMS Switch

```
Conventional Memory :

  Name              Size in Decimal       Size in Hex
-------------     ---------------------  -------------
  MSDOS             58080        ( 56.7K)       E2E0
  HIMEM              3200        (  3.1K)        C80
  EMM386             8400        (  8.2K)       20D0
  COMMAND            4704        (  4.6K)       1260
  FREE                 64        (  0.1K)         40
  FREE             580720        (567.1K)      8DC70

Total  FREE :      580784        (567.2K)
```

```
Total bytes available to programs :                          580784   (567.2K)
Largest executable program size :                            580624   (567.0K)

   3145728 bytes total contiguous extended memory
         0 bytes available contiguous extended memory
   2894848 bytes available XMS memory
           64Kb High Memory Area available
```

The new MEM /C output has two distinct changes. First, the expanded memory lines are gone because we are no longer simulating expanded memory. Second, the available extended memory increased. It actually decreased in order to backfill the additional upper memory, but at the same time it increased even more because we are no longer simulating expanded memory.

Let's look at a graphic that illustrates the increase in upper memory. Figure 4-5 shows the memory configuration for the EMM386.EXE NOEMS switch.

You can see from the figure that the increase in available upper memory is a result of the absence of the EMM page frame. Recall that the EMM page frame is always 64K. Our first two examples (with the page frame) had 31K of upper memory available. Now that the page frame is gone, we have 95K (64K + 31K) of upper memory available.

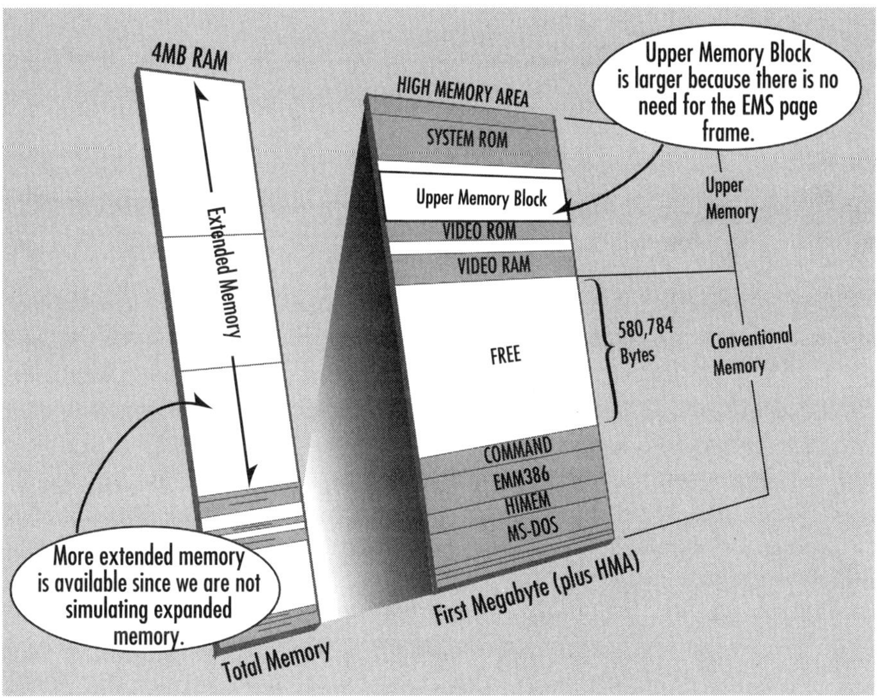

Figure 4-5 Memory configuration—EMM386.EXE loaded with the NOEMS switch

We still have only 580,784 free bytes of conventional memory because we are not loading any programs or drivers in upper memory. Before we do that, however, let's burden the system with an additional device driver and a memory-resident program.

Loading a Device Driver and a TSR in Lower Memory

Let's tax the system a little more to demonstrate how device drivers and terminate-and-stay-resident programs consume more of our precious conventional memory. In a multimedia system, you usually have to load drivers for devices such as sound cards, CD-ROMs, and even some video cards. In this example, we'll use the DOS program DOSKEY and a disk caching driver called SMARTDrive. Listing 4-13 shows the new configuration files.

Listing 4-13 AUTOEXEC.BAT and CONFIG.SYS—Loading Drivers and TSRs

```
Contents of AUTOEXEC.BAT
------------------------
@ECHO OFF
CLS
PROMPT $p$g
PATH=A:\DOS;
C:\DOS\DOSKEY

Contents of CONFIG.SYS
------------------------
FILES=21
BUFFERS=15
DEVICE=C:\DOS\HIMEM.SYS
DEVICE=C:\DOS\EMM386.EXE NOEMS
DEVICE=C:\DOS\SMARTDRV.SYS
```

Note that the SMARTDrive driver (SMARTDRV.SYS) and the memory resident program (DOSKEY) are loaded by the CONFIG.SYS and AUTOEXEC.BAT file respectively. It's not important what they do at this time. We are using them in this case to demonstrate that drivers and memory-resident programs consume memory. You can find information about DOSKEY in your DOS documentation. We'll discuss SMARTDRV.SYS later in this chapter.

To prove that the driver and program are consuming additional conventional memory, let's use the MEM program once again. Listing 4-14 shows the MEM output after these items are loaded.

Listing 4-14 MEM /C—After Loading a Device Driver and TSR

```
Conventional Memory :

  Name                Size in Decimal        Size in Hex
-------------       ---------------------  -------------
  MSDOS               58080      ( 56.7K)        E2E0
  HIMEM                3200      (  3.1K)         C80
  EMM386               8400      (  8.2K)        20D0
  SMARTDRV            13312      ( 13.0K)        3400
  COMMAND              4704      (  4.6K)        1260
  DOSKEY               4128      (  4.0K)        1020
  FREE                   64      (  0.1K)          40
  FREE                   80      (  0.1K)          50
  FREE               563152      (550.0K)       897D0

Total  FREE :        563296      (550.1K)

Total bytes available to programs :                          563296   (550.1K)
Largest executable program size :                            563152   (550.0K)

   3145728 bytes total contiguous extended memory
         0 bytes available contiguous extended memory
   2632704 bytes available XMS memory
           64Kb High Memory Area available
```

Note that our conventional memory list is growing longer as our free conventional memory is shrinking. We are down to 563,152 bytes of conventional memory. This is a common problem to multimedia PC users and PC users in general. Figure 4-6 shows the memory layout with DOSKEY and SMARTDRV in conventional memory.

This figure shows that conventional memory is shrinking as we load more and more programs and drivers. The time has finally come to reverse this trend! Let's start by relocating part of DOS to high memory.

Adding the DOS Command to CONFIG.SYS

DOS 5.0 was the first DOS version to provide a command that relocates a significant amount of the DOS code into the high memory area. The command is also named DOS. Simply adding this command to your CONFIG.SYS file frees up a significant amount of conventional memory. Listing 4-15 shows the CONFIG.SYS file with the DOS command set to HIGH. You can also use DOS=LOW, but because that is the default, it is never necessary.

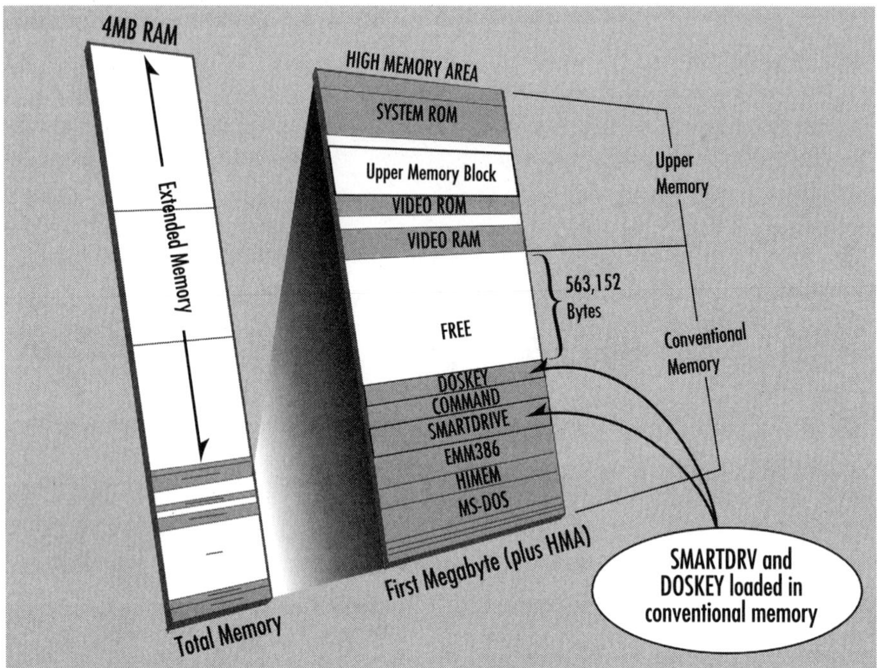

Figure 4-6 Memory configuration—DOSKEY and SMARTDRV.SYS in conventional memory

Listing 4-15 CONFIG.SYS—Adding DOS=HIGH

```
Contents of CONFIG.SYS
------------------------
FILES=21
BUFFERS=15
DEVICE=C:\DOS\HIMEM.SYS
DOS=HIGH
DEVICE=C:\DOS\EMM386.EXE NOEMS
DEVICE=C:\DOS\SMARTDRV.SYS
```

Notice that the DOS=HIGH line is placed after the HIMEM.SYS driver in CONFIG.SYS. This is necessary because it's the HIMEM.SYS driver that gives us access to the HMA. It does not, however, have to be the line immediately following HIMEM.SYS. Any location following the extended memory driver is fine.

Now for the moment of truth. Let's check the memory status using MEM. Listing 4-16 shows the MEM output after using the DOS=HIGH command.

Listing 4-16 MEM/C—After DOS=HIGH

```
Conventional Memory :

  Name                 Size in Decimal       Size in Hex
-------------       ---------------------   -------------
  MSDOS               13744       ( 13.4K)       35B0
  HIMEM                1184       (  1.2K)        4A0
  EMM386               8400       (  8.2K)       20D0
  SMARTDRV            13312       ( 13.0K)       3400
  COMMAND              2624       (  2.6K)        A40
  DOSKEY               4128       (  4.0K)       1020
  FREE                   64       (  0.1K)         40
  FREE                   80       (  0.1K)         50
  FREE               611568       (597.2K)      954F0

Total  FREE :        611712       (597.4K)

Total bytes available to programs :                     611712   (597.4K)
Largest executable program size :                       611568   (597.2K)

   3145728 bytes total contiguous extended memory
         0 bytes available contiguous extended memory
   2632704 bytes available XMS memory
           MS-DOS resident in High Memory Area
```

This MEM output shows a great gain in conventional memory, all due to one line in the CONFIG.SYS file. Notice that three programs have been reduced in size significantly. They are MSDOS, HIMEM, and COMMAND. This resulted in approximately 47K of DOS being moved into the HMA. Also note that the summary at the bottom of the MEM output indicates that DOS has been moved to the HMA. Figure 4-7 shows these results.

Notice that the MS-DOS, HIMEM, and COMMAND programs were reduced in size in conventional memory. They now reside in the HMA providing us with more conventional memory for our memory hungry programs. Now let's get greedy and squeeze out even more conventional memory.

Loading Programs and Device Drivers in Upper Memory

Recall that we loaded HIMEM.SYS to provide an extended memory manager and also to gain access to the HMA. Then we loaded EMM386 (using the RAM or NOEMS switch) to gain access to the upper memory block. We also loaded a device driver (SMARTDRV.SYS) and a memory-resident program into conventional memory. Now let's move the driver and program into upper memory.

In order to gain complete access to upper memory, we must add a line to the CONFIG.SYS file. This line is DOS=UMB. After this line is executed, we can

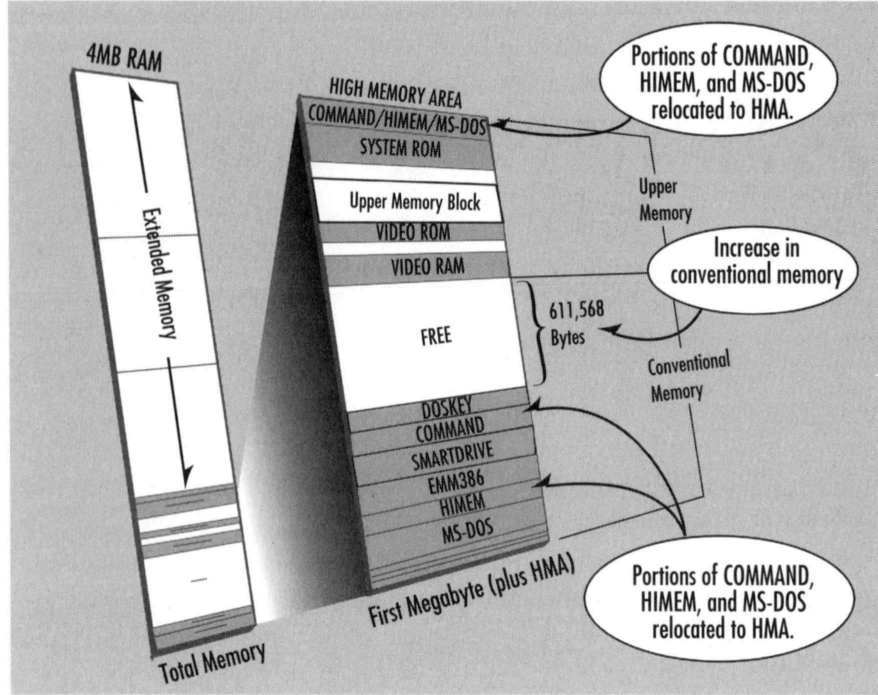

Figure 4-7 Memory configuration—DOS loaded in the HMA

load device drivers into upper memory using DEVICEHIGH= instead of DEVICE=. We can also load memory-resident programs into high memory using LOADHIGH. Let's look at the CONFIG.SYS and AUTOEXEC.BAT files which perform this action. Listing 4-17 shows these configuration files.

Listing 4-17 Loading Device Drivers and Memory-Resident Programs High

```
Contents of CONFIG.SYS
------------------------
FILES=21
BUFFERS=15
DEVICE=C:\DOS\HIMEM.SYS
DEVICE=C:\DOS\EMM386.EXE NOEMS
DOS=HIGH, UMB
DEVICEHIGH=C:\DOS\SMARTDRV.SYS

Contents of AUTOEXEC.BAT
------------------------
@ECHO OFF
CLS
PROMPT $p$g
PATH=C:\DOS;
LOADHIGH C:\DOS\DOSKEY
```

> **A Shortcut for LOADHIGH**
>
> You can use LH in place of LOADHIGH in your AUTOEXEC.BAT file. You cannot, however, abbreviate DEVICEHIGH in CONFIG.SYS.

The first step in loading drivers and programs high is in the CONFIG.SYS file. This is done by using the line: DOS=HIGH, UMB. In this case, we are combining DOS=HIGH and DOS=UMB into one line. This is perfectly legal. However, if you use UMB, you must place it after the line that loads the EMM386.EXE driver. This is because the expanded memory driver is required to access the upper memory blocks.

To load the device driver high, we use DEVICEHIGH, instead of the usual DEVICE command. To load the memory-resident program high, we place LOADHIGH on the line preceding the program name; in this case, it's DOSKEY.

Let's look at the MEM /P (instead of MEM /C) output to check two things. First, we'll see another gain in conventional memory. Second, we can check to see if the driver and program are actually loaded high. Listing 4-18 shows the MEM /P output.

Listing 4-18 MEM /P—Loading SMARTDRV.SYS and DOSKEY High

```
Address     Name        Size      Type
-------     --------    ------    ------
000000                  000400    Interrupt Vector
000400                  000100    ROM Communication Area
000500                  000200    DOS Communication Area

000700      IO          000AC0    System Data

0011C0      MSDOS       0013F0    System Data

0025B0      IO          0035A0    System Data
              HIMEM     0004A0     DEVICE=
              EMM386    0020D0     DEVICE=
                        0003C0     FILES=
                        000100     FCBS=
                        000200     BUFFERS=
                        0001C0     LASTDRIVE=
                        000740     STACKS=
005B60      MSDOS       000040    System Program

005BB0      COMMAND     000940    Program
006500      MSDOS       000040    -- Free --
006550      COMMAND     000100    Environment
006660      MEM         000050    Environment
0066C0      MEM         0176F0    Program
01DDC0      MSDOS       082220    -- Free --
```

continued on next page

continued from previous page

```
09FFF0       SYSTEM       028010     System Program

0C8010       IO           003410     System Data
               SMARTDRV   003400      DEVICE=
0CB430       MSDOS        000050     -- Free --
0CB490       DOSKEY       001020     Program
0CC4C0       MSDOS        013B30     -- Free --


   655360 bytes total conventional memory
   655360 bytes available to MS-DOS
   629024 largest executable program size

  3145728 bytes total contiguous extended memory
        0 bytes available contiguous extended memory
  2632704 bytes available XMS memory
          MS-DOS resident in High Memory Area
```

As you can see in the MEM output, we now have even more conventional memory available. We've increased this amount by 17,456 bytes (around 17K) by loading SMARTDRV.SYS and DOSKEY in upper memory.

The MEM /P output also provides verification that the program and driver were actually loaded into upper memory. We can determine this by checking the starting address. For example, SMARTDRV's starting address is 0C8010h. Recall that the starting address for upper memory in this example is C8000. Any value below this address is in conventional memory. Any value above this address is in upper memory.

Let's look at an illustration that shows the results of this example. Figure 4-8 shows the results of the usage of LOADHIGH and DEVICEHIGH.

You can see in Figure 4-8 that relocating DOSKEY (with LOADHIGH) and SMARTDRV (with DEVICEHIGH) to upper memory has removed them from conventional memory. This resulted in an increase of more than 17K of free conventional memory.

Loading Multimedia Drivers HIGH

You can use LOADHIGH and DEVICEHIGH to relocate the multimedia drivers (sound, CD-ROM, video, and so on) on your system as well. However, you may run into some drivers that do not behave properly when loaded high. If this occurs, try rearranging your CONFIG.SYS and AUTOEXEC.BAT to find a solution that works. As a last resort, you can always load the offending driver in low (conventional memory). As always, make a backup of your configuration files before trying something new.

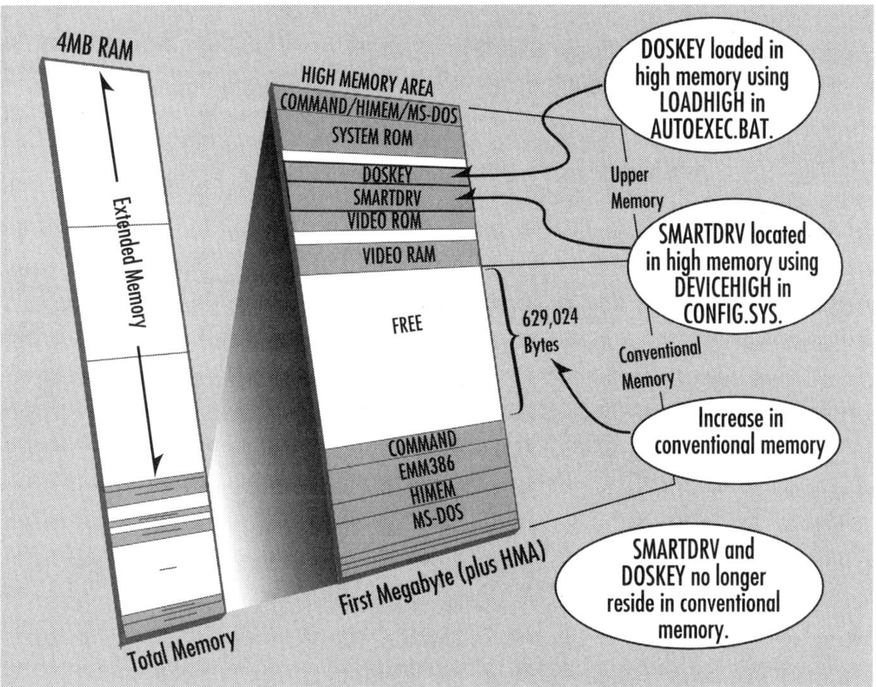

Figure 4-8 Memory configuration—after LOADHIGH and DEVICEHIGH

Now that we have covered the DOS 5.0 memory configuration topics, let's look at a few more features that can improve the performance of your system.

Creating a RAM Disk with the RAMDRIVE.SYS Driver

You can create a simulated disk drive in RAM by using the RAMDRIVE.SYS device driver. This driver is supplied with DOS 5.0. A RAM disk is useful for storing temporary data that you will only use during the current time your computer is turned on. As soon as you turn your computer off, the RAM disk is gone.

Many programs use temporary files. If your programs allow you to specify where the temporary files are stored, you can direct them to the RAM disk. A RAM disk is much faster than a hard disk. Typical RAM access times are normally measured in microseconds, or millionths of a second. Typical hard disk access times are normally measured in milliseconds, or thousandths of a second.

There is a downside when creating a RAM disk, however. It takes up memory. You can install an MS-DOS RAM disk in conventional, extended, or expanded memory. Because our goal in memory management is to free up as much conventional memory as possible, we don't want to put our RAM disk there. Let's look at an example of creating a RAM disk in extended memory.

The bottom line is: If you do not see an improvement when adding a RAM disk, remove it.

Creating an Extended Memory RAM Disk

In order to create a RAM disk, we must install the RAMDRIVE.SYS device driver in the CONFIG.SYS file. This requires the DEVICE or DEVICEHIGH command, the path to the driver, the driver name, and some options. Listing 4-19 shows an example CONFIG.SYS file loading the RAMDRIVE.SYS into upper memory, and the RAM disk itself into extended memory.

Listing 4-19 CONFIG.SYS—Creating a RAM Disk in Extended Memory

```
FILES=21
BUFFERS=15
DEVICE=C:\DOS\HIMEM.SYS
DEVICE=C:\DOS\EMM386.EXE NOEMS
DOS=HIGH, UMB
DEVICEHIGH=C:\DOS\RAMDRIVE.SYS 512 /e
```

Notice that we're loading the RAMDRIVE.SYS driver into upper memory using DEVICEHIGH. This requires that both HIMEM.SYS and EMM386.EXE (with either the RAM or NOEMS switch) are loaded. In order to place the RAMDISK in extended memory, we need at least the HIMEM.SYS driver. These lines must be before the RAMDRIVE line.

Now let's look at the RAMDRIVE line in Listing 4-19. We must specify the entire path because the AUTOEXEC.BAT file has not executed yet. Following the driver name is the size we want for a RAM disk, in kilobytes. In this case, we are using 512 so we will create a 512K RAM disk. The last portion of the line, /e, tells DOS to place the RAM disk in extended memory.

The drive letter will be one letter past the existing drives. For example, if your last disk drive is C:, the RAM disk will be D:. Here is a typical output during the boot process:

```
Microsoft RAMDrive version 3.06 virtual disk D:
    Disk size: 512K
    Sector size: 512 bytes
    Allocation unit: 1 sectors
    Directory entries: 64
```

Notice that the RAM drive is labeled drive D:. The second line indicates that the disk size is indeed 512K. The remaining lines indicate the sector size, allocation unit, and directory entries. You usually don't have to worry about these values. You can modify them with additional options in the CONFIG.SYS file, but this is almost never necessary. Consult your DOS manual about additional options for RAMDRIVE.SYS.

Now let's look at the MEM output for this CONFIG.SYS file. In this example, we are not loading any programs in the AUTOEXEC.BAT file. Listing 4-20 shows the MEM /C output after installing the RAM disk.

Listing 4-20 MEM /C—512K RAM Drive Installed (Extended)

```
Conventional Memory :

  Name                Size in Decimal       Size in Hex
-------------       ---------------------  -------------
  MSDOS               13760      ( 13.4K)       35C0
  HIMEM                1184      (  1.2K)        4A0
  EMM386               8400      (  8.2K)       20D0
  COMMAND              2624      (  2.6K)        A40
  FREE                   64      (  0.1K)         40
  FREE               629120      (614.4K)      99980

Total  FREE :        629184      (614.4K)

Upper Memory :

  Name                Size in Decimal       Size in Hex
-------------       ---------------------  -------------
  SYSTEM             163840      (160.0K)      28000
  RAMDRIVE             1184      (  1.2K)        4A0
  FREE                97056      ( 94.8K)      17B20

Total  FREE :         97056      ( 94.8K)

Total bytes available to programs (Conventional+Upper) :      726240   (709.2K)
Largest executable program size :                             629024   (614.3K)
Largest available upper memory block :                         97056   ( 94.8K)

   3145728 bytes total contiguous extended memory
         0 bytes available contiguous extended memory
   2370560 bytes available XMS memory
           MS-DOS resident in High Memory Area
```

Notice that we have not affected conventional memory in any way. The RAMDRIVE.SYS device driver is located in upper memory. We can see the effect of the RAM disk on extended memory by looking at the bytes available for XMS memory. This has dropped to accommodate the RAM disk.

Now we have a RAM disk, named drive D:. We can direct our programs that store temporary data to this drive. Just remember, if you turn off your computer, drive D: vanishes. So only use a RAM disk for temporary data.

That is an example of creating the RAM disk in extended memory. Let's create the same drive in expanded memory.

Creating an Expanded Memory RAM Disk

Creating a RAM disk in expanded memory is nearly the same as creating the extended memory version. However, we first must ensure that the correct amount of expanded memory is available. We take care of that when we load EMM386.EXE in the CONFIG.SYS file. Listing 4-21 shows the CONFIG.SYS file for this example.

Listing 4-21 CONFIG.SYS—Creating a RAM Disk in Expanded Memory

```
FILES=21
BUFFERS=15
DEVICE=C:\DOS\HIMEM.SYS
DEVICE=C:\DOS\EMM386.EXE 512 RAM
DOS=HIGH, UMB
DEVICEHIGH=C:\DOS\RAMDRIVE.SYS 512 /a
```

Notice the differences between this and the expanded memory driver. First, we added the number 512 to the EMM386.EXE line. This creates 512K of expanded memory, which we'll need to place the RAM disk. We're also using the RAM switch; this simulates expanded memory and provides access to the upper memory blocks, where we'll store RAMDRIVE.SYS.

We've also replaced the /e switch with /a on the RAMDRIVE.SYS line. The /a switch tells DOS to create the RAM disk in expanded memory. When we reboot to install the RAM disk, DOS displays the following message:

```
Microsoft RAMDrive version 3.06 virtual disk D:
    Disk size: 512K
    Sector size: 512 bytes
    Allocation unit: 1 sectors
    Directory entries: 64
```

This is no different from the extended memory RAM disk example. The new drive is still labeled D: and the size is 512K. There is no indication from RAMDRIVE of where the disk is located in memory.

Now let's look at the MEM output for this CONFIG.SYS file. Once again, we are not loading any programs in the AUTOEXEC.BAT file. Listing 4-22 shows the MEM /C output after installing the RAM disk in expanded memory.

Listing 4-22 MEM /C—512K RAM Drive Installed (Expanded)

```
Conventional Memory :

  Name                Size in Decimal       Size in Hex
-------------       ---------------------  -------------
  MSDOS               13760       ( 13.4K)      35C0
  HIMEM                1184       (  1.2K)       4A0
  EMM386               8400       (  8.2K)      20D0
  COMMAND              2624       (  2.6K)       A40
  FREE                   64       (  0.1K)        40
  FREE               629120       (614.4K)     99980

Total  FREE :        629184       (614.4K)

Upper Memory :

  Name                Size in Decimal       Size in Hex
-------------       ---------------------  -------------
  SYSTEM             163840       (160.0K)     28000
  RAMDRIVE             1232       (  1.2K)       4D0
  FREE                31472       ( 30.7K)      7AF0

Total  FREE :         31472       ( 30.7K)

Total bytes available to programs (Conventional+Upper) :      660656   (645.2K)
Largest executable program size :                             629024   (614.3K)
Largest available upper memory block :                         31472   ( 30.7K)

    917504 bytes total EMS memory
         0 bytes free EMS memory

   3145728 bytes total contiguous extended memory
         0 bytes available contiguous extended memory
   2424832 bytes available XMS memory
           MS-DOS resident in High Memory Area
```

Once again, notice that we have not affected conventional memory in any way. The RAMDRIVE.SYS device driver is located in upper memory. We can see the effect of the RAM disk on extended memory in two places. First, there are 917,504 bytes of total EMS (expanded) memory. This is 896K of expanded memory; 512K that we requested and 384K to backfill upper memory. This drops immediately to 0 free EMS because we are using upper memory and the 512K for the RAM disk. Also, the XMS (extended) memory has dropped to accommodate the EMS memory, and ultimately the RAM disk.

You may be wondering: Why go through all the trouble of creating expanded memory for the RAM disk when you can simply place it in extended memory? The answer is: Always place your RAM disk in extended memory if you have it. If you have an expanded memory board (and no extended memory available), however, you must use the /a switch to place your RAM disk there.

Disk Caching with the SMARTDRV.SYS Driver

The SMARTDRV.SYS driver (also supplied with DOS 5.0) creates a disk *cache* (pronounced cash). A disk cache is useful for programs that repeatedly request the same information from disk. The majority of programs do this to some degree.

The SMARTDrive disk cache keeps track of when the disk is read and what data is being read into memory. The cache keeps data in memory if it is being requested frequently. This way, the next time a program tries to read the data from disk, the disk cache intercepts the read and provides the data directly from memory. As we mentioned in the discussion of RAMDRIVE.SYS, memory access is much faster than disk access.

Disk caches are most useful for programs that request the same data frequently. Examples of these are word processors, database applications, and multimedia applications.

The overall performance increase depends on the size of the disk cache and how often similar data is requested. In other words, if your programs never request the same data twice (or more times), a disk cache is of no use.

A Note to Windows 3.1 and DOS 6 Users

If you are running DOS 6 and/or Windows 3.1, you will want to use the SMARTDRV.EXE driver instead of SMARTDRV.SYS. It is totally compatible with DOS 5.0. Always check the versions of HIMEM.SYS, EMM386.EXE, RAMDRIVE.SYS, and SMARTDRV.SYS/.EXE to see if you are loading the newest driver in your configuration files. To do this, check the date of the drivers in your \DOS and \WINDOWS directories.

SMARTDRV.SYS is loaded in your CONFIG.SYS file, andSMARTDRV.EXE is loaded in your AUTOEXEC.BAT file. Refer to Chapter 5, *DOS 6 Memory Management,* for the DOS 6 version of SMARTDRV.EXE. Refer to Chapter 6, *Windows Memory Management,* for the Windows 3.1 version of SMARTDRV.EXE.

As with a RAM disk, you can create a SMARTDrive disk cache in either extended or expanded memory. Unlike the RAM disk, you cannot create a disk cache in conventional memory (you wouldn't want to anyway). Let's look at an extended memory SMARTDrive disk cache.

Creating an Extended Memory SMARTDrive Disk Cache

In order to create a disk cache using SMARTDRV.SYS, we must load its driver in the CONFIG.SYS file. This consists of the DEVICE or DEVICEHIGH command followed by the full path to the driver, the driver name, and some options. Listing 4-23 shows the CONFIG.SYS file for our example extended memory disk cache.

Listing 4-23 CONFIG.SYS—SMARTDrive Disk Cache (Extended)

```
FILES=21
BUFFERS=15
DEVICE=C:\DOS\HIMEM.SYS
DEVICE=C:\DOS\EMM386.EXE NOEMS
DOS=HIGH, UMB
DEVICEHIGH=C:\DOS\SMARTDRV.SYS 2048 1024
```

In this example, we are using the DEVICEHIGH command. This loads the SMARTDRV.SYS device driver into upper memory. We are also installing HIMEM.SYS and EMM386.EXE (with the NOEMS switch) to gain access to upper memory.

The next portion of the line is the path to the driver followed by the driver name itself. We then include two options: the maximum size of the disk cache in kilobytes (2,048), and the minimum cache size in kilobytes (1,024). Programs, such as Windows, can adjust the size of the disk cache between these two amounts.

The defaults for SMARTDRV.SYS (if we omit the size parameters) are 256 and 0. In other words, the command DEVICEHIGH=C:\DOS\SMARTDRV.SYS, would create a maximum disk cache size of 256K bytes and a minimum of 0 bytes.

If you do not specify a location (extended or expanded memory), DOS automatically creates the disk cache in extended memory.

After adding this line to our CONFIG.SYS file, let's reboot and observe the message during the boot process. We are not loading any programs in the AUTOEXEC.BAT file for this example. Here is the message from SMARTDRV during the boot process:

```
Microsoft SMARTDrive Disk Cache version 3.13
    Cache size: 2048K in Extended Memory
    Room for 107 tracks of 38 sectors each
    Minimum cache size will be 1024K
```

You can see from the second line of the message that we have created a 2,048K disk cache in extended memory. The last line indicates that the minimum cache size is 1,024K. This reflects our request in the CONFIG.SYS file.

How large should your SMARTDrive disk cache be? This depends on many factors, such as the types of programs you use and the amount of memory installed in your PC. You can use trial and error to find the optimum setting for your system. You can always use STORE.BAT and CHANGE.BAT (listed in Chapter 3, *Managing Configuration Files*) to store your configuration files while you are testing. Do not use the majority of your extended memory for a SMARTDrive cache if you know your programs need a lot of extended memory. Refer to Chapter 6, *Windows Memory Management* for recommended settings.

To see the effect of SMARTDrive on our 4-megabyte test system, let's use the MEM command to view the status of memory. Listing 4-24 shows the MEM /C output for our extended memory disk cache.

Listing 4-24 MEM /C—2,048K/1,024K Extended Memory Disk Cache

```
Conventional Memory :

  Name                 Size in Decimal          Size in Hex
-------------       ---------------------      -------------
  MSDOS                13760        ( 13.4K)        35C0
  HIMEM                 1184        (  1.2K)         4A0
  EMM386                8400        (  8.2K)        20D0
  COMMAND               2624        (  2.6K)         A40
  FREE                    64        (  0.1K)          40
  FREE                629120        (614.4K)       99980

Total  FREE :         629184        (614.4K)

Upper Memory :

  Name                 Size in Decimal          Size in Hex
-------------       ---------------------      -------------
  SYSTEM              163840        (160.0K)       28000
  SMARTDRV             16256        ( 15.9K)        3F80
  FREE                 81984        ( 80.1K)       14040

Total  FREE :          81984        ( 80.1K)

Total bytes available to programs (Conventional+Upper) :       711168    (694.5K)
Largest executable program size :                              629024    (614.3K)
Largest available upper memory block :                          81984    ( 80.1K)

   3145728 bytes total contiguous extended memory
         0 bytes available contiguous extended memory
    797696 bytes available XMS memory
           MS-DOS resident in High Memory Area
```

As with the RAMDRIVE.SYS driver, using the DEVICEHIGH command allowed us to create our disk cache without affecting conventional memory in any way.

The largest change in the MEM output is the effect the SMARTDrive disk cache has on extended memory. In this case, it has dropped to 797,696 bytes (779K). Of course, this amount could increase to 1,803K (1,024K + 779K) if necessary because we specified a minimum cache size of 1,024K.

Now let's see how to create the SMARTDrive disk cache in expanded memory. As with the RAMDRIVE.SYS driver, you should always create the disk cache in extended memory if you have it available. An expanded memory disk cache should only be used if you have an expanded memory card (and no free extended memory), as on some 80286 systems.

Creating an Expanded Memory SMARTDrive Disk Cache

To create an expanded memory disk cache using SMARTDRV.SYS, we also load this driver in the CONFIG.SYS file. This consists of the DEVICE or DEVICEHIGH command followed by the full path to the driver, the driver name, and the maximum/minimum size options. We also use a switch to tell DOS to create the disk cache in expanded memory. Listing 4-25 shows the CONFIG.SYS file for our example expanded memory disk cache.

Listing 4-25 CONFIG.SYS—SMARTDrive Disk Cache (Expanded)

```
FILES=21
BUFFERS=15
DEVICE=C:\DOS\HIMEM.SYS
DEVICE=C:\DOS\EMM386.EXE 2048 RAM
DOS=HIGH, UMB
DEVICEHIGH=C:\DOS\SMARTDRV.SYS 2048 1024 /a
```

Because we are using a system with extended memory only, we are simulating expanded memory using EMM386.EXE and its RAM option. Recall the RAM option both simulates expanded memory and allows access to the upper memory blocks. We also are specifying the amount of expanded memory we want to simulate, in this case 2,048K. The only time you should load a SMARTDrive in expanded memory is when you have an expanded memory adapter card. However, we will simulate expanded memory for purposes of illustration.

As with the extended memory disk cache example, we are using the DEVICEHIGH command. This loads the SMARTDRV.SYS device driver into upper memory.

The next portion of the line is the path to the driver followed by the driver name itself. We then include two options: the maximum size of the disk cache in kilobytes (2,048) and the minimum cache size in kilobytes (1,024). Programs can adjust the size of the disk cache between these two amounts.

For this example, we are using the /a switch on the SMARTDRV line. This tells DOS to create the disk cache in expanded memory.

After adding this line to our CONFIG.SYS file, let's reboot and observe the message during the boot process. We are not loading any programs in the AUTOEXEC.BAT file for this example. Here is the message from SMARTDRV during the boot process:

```
Microsoft SMARTDrive Disk Cache version 3.13
    Cache size: 2048K in Expanded Memory
    Room for 107 tracks of 38 sectors each
    Minimum cache size will be 1024K
```

Note that the message is identical to the extended memory example with the exception of the second line. This time SMARTDrive informs us that the disk cache resides in expanded memory.

Now let's check the effects of SMARTDrive for our expanded memory disk cache. Listing 4-26 shows the MEM /C output for our expanded memory disk cache.

Listing 4-26 MEM /C—2,048K/1,024K Extended Memory Disk Cache

```
Conventional Memory :

  Name             Size in Decimal         Size in Hex
-------------    ---------------------   -------------
  MSDOS            13760      ( 13.4K)        35C0
  HIMEM             1184      (  1.2K)         4A0
  EMM386            8400      (  8.2K)        20D0
  COMMAND           2624      (  2.6K)         A40
  FREE                64      (  0.1K)          40
  FREE            629120      (614.4K)       99980

Total  FREE :     629184      (614.4K)

Upper Memory :

  Name             Size in Decimal         Size in Hex
-------------    ---------------------   -------------
  SYSTEM          163840      (160.0K)       28000
  SMARTDRV         16640      ( 16.3K)        4100
  FREE             16064      ( 15.7K)        3EC0

Total  FREE :      16064      ( 15.7K)
```

```
Total bytes available to programs (Conventional+Upper) :       645248   (630.1K)
Largest executable program size :                              629024   (614.3K)
Largest available upper memory block :                          16064   ( 15.7K)

   2490368 bytes total EMS memory
         0 bytes free EMS memory

   3145728 bytes total contiguous extended memory
         0 bytes available contiguous extended memory
    851968 bytes available XMS memory
           MS-DOS resident in High Memory Area
```

As with the extended memory disk cache example, using the DEVICEHIGH command allowed us to create our expanded memory disk cache without affecting conventional memory.

Note that the SMARTDRV.SYS device driver is loaded into upper memory. Also, MEM reports that we have created 2,490,368 bytes (2,432K) of expanded memory, but none of it is available. 2,048K is used for the disk cache and 384K is used to backfill upper memory.

Remember to put your disk cache in extended memory if it is available. Only create an expanded memory disk cache if you have a true expanded-memory expansion board.

Solving Memory Problems In DOS 5.0

Although DOS 5.0 lacks some of the tools of DOS 6 and third-party memory managers, you can usually find a combination (or combinations) to get the job done. This section explores the practical aspects of DOS 5.0 memory management, multimedia devices, and multimedia software. We'll present some real-world problems that PC users encounter followed by solutions using DOS 5.0.

There are two major factors that ultimately determine how difficult it will be to configure your system. The first factor is hardware. Basically, the more extra hardware (SCSI adapters, sound cards, etc.) you have installed in your system, the more troublesome configuring your system becomes. Hardware conflicts are covered in Chapter 9, *IRQs, DMA, and Other Mysteries.* However, some hardware devices require drivers which take up memory.

The other major factor affecting your configurations is the type and complexity of your software collection. For example, if you run nothing but Windows programs, configuring the system is easy. However, if you have DOS applications, Windows applications, and DOS applications that require expanded memory, you'll have a bit of work to do to find the optimum configuration.

Let's look at four situations of multimedia and nonmultimedia systems. Each of these systems has a problem with memory configuration. We'll use the drivers (HIMEM.SYS, EMM386.EXE, etc.) supplied with DOS 5.0 to provide solutions to these problems. Each situation starts with an overview of the problem system, its configuration files, and the objective of the user. This is followed by a solution and a new set of configuration files. Let's start with a nonmultimedia system.

Problem #1—The Memory Hungry Game Predicament

Our first user, Steve, has a system that has seemed adequate in recent years. However, he recently purchased a new hot game that introduced a problem he has not seen before. After going through the obligatory installation ritual, he types in the filename that starts the program. Instead of seeing what he hoped to be a colorful graphic opening screen he receives an ugly message: NOT ENOUGH MEMORY. Of course, most programs are friendlier than this.

Steve consults the game's documentation which indicates that the program requires 595K of free conventional memory. He types the MEM command and finds out he only has 561K free. It appears that Steve is about 34K short of what is required to run this game. Before we start to consider a solution, let's take a closer look at Steve's system. Listing 4-27 shows the configuration files.

System Description

- 80386DX
- 2 Megabytes of RAM
- Serial Mouse

Listing 4-27 Problem #1—Configuration Files

```
AUTOEXEC.BAT contents
---------------------
&ECHO OFF
CLS
PATH C:\DOS;C:\MYFILES;
C:\MOUSE\MOUSE

CONFIG.SYS contents
---------------------
FILES=20
BUFFERS=10
DEVICE=C:\DOS\HIMEM.SYS
```

Solving the Problem

The first thing that should jump out at you is that Steve is loading HIMEM.SYS. Although this provides extended memory support, he is not taking advantage of something else HIMEM.SYS offers: access to high memory. The first thing he needs to do is add a DOS=HIGH after the HIMEM.SYS line.

The previous change alone would free up enough memory to run the game; however, he could go further and provide access to upper memory (with EMM386.EXE). This would allow him to relocate the mouse driver in high memory (using LOADHIGH). Even though we have to load the EMM386.EXE driver into conventional memory, the relocation of the mouse driver more than makes up for it.

The solution files for Steve's system are shown in Listing 4-28. The additions and modifications are shown in boldface. He is using the NOEMS switch with EMM386.EXE because he does not use programs which require expanded memory. Not only can Steve load his game now, in the future he will be able to load other resident programs and device drivers in upper memory. This should keep his conventional memory at a high enough level.

Listing 4-28 Solution #1—Configuration Files

```
AUTOEXEC.BAT contents
---------------------
&ECHO OFF
CLS
PATH C:\DOS;C:\MYFILES;
LOADHIGH C:\MOUSE\MOUSE

CONFIG.SYS contents
---------------------
FILES=20
BUFFERS=10
DEVICE=C:\DOS\HIMEM.SYS
DEVICE=C:\DOS\EMM386.EXE NOEMS
DOS=HIGH,UMB
```

Problem #2—The EMS Versus XMS Dilemma

Our next candidate for a memory checkup is Melissa. Melissa has been fortunate enough to receive a computer "hand-me-down." It's not an outdated system by any means; however, she wants to run certain kinds of programs and is having no luck. Her two favorite applications are quite different in their memory needs. One program requires extended memory and the other requires expanded memory.

Melissa also likes memory-resident utilities; these utilities take up more conventional memory than she'd like. The goal here is to free up as much conventional memory as possible while accommodating her favorite programs. Melissa also has an external floppy drive which requires a device driver. Listing 4-29 shows the problem configuration files.

System Description

- 80486SX
- 4 Megabytes of RAM
- Serial Mouse
- External Floppy Controller

Listing 4-29 Problem #2—Configuration Files

```
AUTOEXEC.BAT contents
---------------------
&ECHO OFF
CLS
PATH C:\DOS;C:\FILES;C:\321;
LOADHIGH C:\MOUSE\MOUSE
LOADHIGH C:\DOS\DOSKEY
LOADHIGH C:\SUPERPOP\POP


CONFIG.SYS contents
---------------------
FILES=20
BUFFERS=10
DEVICE=C:\DOS\HIMEM.SYS
DEVICE=C:\DOS\EMM386.EXE
DOS=HIGH,UMB
DEVICE=C:\DRIVERS\FDCTRL.SYS
```

Solving the Problem

Melissa's complaint is that she cannot run some programs because of low conventional memory. The expanded memory application is not performing well either. At first glance it may look like a fairly good configuration. EMM386.EXE is simulating expanded memory from extended. She is attempting to load the memory-resident utilities with LOADHIGH. However, are they actually loaded high?

The first place to go to work immediately is the EMM386.EXE line in CONFIG.SYS. Recall that the use of this driver and no switches simulates the default amount of expanded memory (256K) and it does not provide access to upper memory. Therefore, the following line (DOS=HIGH,UMB) loads DOS high, but UMB option does nothing. She must change the EMM386.EXE line by adding the RAM switch. This will now allow the LOADHIGH command to load the memory-resident programs in upper memory.

After a quick look at her program's documentation she finds that the program works best with at least 2 megabytes of expanded memory. So, her next step is to override the default of 256K and add 2048 to the EMM386.EXE line. This will simulate desired 2 megabytes of EMS.

The final thing that needs fixing is the last line in the CONFIG.SYS file. The external floppy controller driver is not loaded into high memory. She replaces DEVICE with DEVICEHIGH to accomplish this.

Now she has a system that has over a megabyte of free extended memory, 2 megabytes of expanded memory, and a large increase in conventional memory. This configuration is optimal for her situation.

There is another alternative she may want to consider: an upgrade to DOS 6 or a third-party memory manager. This would allow her to run programs requiring extended or expanded memory without worrying about specifying a specific amount (like the 2 megabytes in this example).

The solution files for Melissa's system are shown in Listing 4-30. The additions and modifications are shown in boldface. There are only three changes in these files, although they produced significant results. The RAM switch enables upper memory access and 2048 simulates the 2 megabytes of expanded memory. The DEVICEHIGH command loads the floppy driver into upper memory.

Watch Your Upper Memory

The amount of free upper memory varies from system to system based on configuration. You may or may not have enough room to load every driver and TSR into upper memory.

Listing 4-30 Solution #2—Configuration Files

```
AUTOEXEC.BAT contents
---------------------
&ECHO OFF
CLS
PATH C:\DOS;C:\FILES;C:\321;
LOADHIGH C:\MOUSE\MOUSE
LOADHIGH C:\DOS\DOSKEY
LOADHIGH C:\SUPERPOP\POP
```

continued on next page

continued from previous page

```
CONFIG.SYS contents
---------------------
FILES=20
BUFFERS=10
DEVICE=C:\DOS\HIMEM.SYS
DEVICE=C:\DOS\EMM386.EXE RAM 2048
DOS=HIGH,UMB
DEVICEHIGH=C:\DRIVERS\FDCTRL.SYS
```

Problem #3—Extended Memory Shortage

Our next user is Pat, who has two memory problems. First, he does not have the free extended memory he expects with his current configuration. Also, he is having trouble getting enough free upper memory to load his drivers and memory-resident programs. Pat also has a sound card installed which requires another device driver line in CONFIG.SYS. Listing 4-31 shows the problem configuration files.

System Description

- 80486DX
- 4 Megabytes of RAM
- Serial Mouse
- Sound Card

Listing 4-31 Problem #3—Configuration Files

```
AUTOEXEC.BAT contents
---------------------
&ECHO OFF
CLS
PATH C:\DOS;C:\GAMES;C:\UTILS;
LOADHIGH C:\MOUSE\MOUSE
LOADHIGH C:\DOS\DOSKEY
LOADHIGH C:\CAL\CALENDAR
LOADHIGH C:\UTIL\CALC


CONFIG.SYS contents
---------------------
FILES=20
BUFFERS=10
DEVICE=C:\DOS\HIMEM.SYS
DEVICE=C:\DOS\EMM386.EXE RAM
DOS=HIGH,UMB
DEVICEHIGH=C:\SOUND\SOUNDMAN.SYS
```

Solving the Problem

Once again this looks like a decent configuration on the surface. For example, he is attempting to load every driver and TSR in upper memory. He is also using the RAM switch which enables access to upper memory (combined with the DOS=UMB line).

Recall that Pat's complaints are low extended memory and available upper memory drivers. He can make one simple change to EMM386.EXE and solve both problems by replacing the RAM switch with the NOEMS switch. Besides enabling access to upper memory, the RAM switch simulates 256K expanded memory (which Pat doesn't need). This creates the drop in extended memory.

Also, recall that when you use expanded memory, EMM386.EXE reserves a 64K page frame in upper memory. This takes up memory that is best served for drivers and TSRs.

Pat isn't out of the woods yet, however. His system doesn't have enough free upper memory to store all his drivers and TSRs. Although he could opt to upgrade to DOS 6 or a third-party memory manager, he decides to create two configurations: GAME and WORK. He decides that he rarely uses the TSR programs when he uses the computer to play games. On the other hand, he never uses the sound card when he is using his computer for work. His solution is to create multiple configurations. One configuration loads the TSRs in upper memory and omits the sound driver, the other loads the sound driver in upper memory and omits the TSRs (except for the mouse driver).

Listing 4-32 shows the solution with two sets of configuration files. Pat can use CHANGE.BAT and STORE.BAT to manage these files. CHANGE.BAT and STORE.BAT are covered in Chapter 3, *Managing Configuration Files.*

Listing 4-32 Solution #3—Configuration Files

```
WORK CONFIGURATION (Store as WORK.BAT and WORK.SYS)
--------------------------------------------------

AUTOEXEC.BAT contents
--------------------

&ECHO OFF
CLS
PATH C:\DOS;C:\GAMES;C:\UTILS;
LOADHIGH C:\MOUSE\MOUSE
LOADHIGH C:\DOS\DOSKEY
LOADHIGH C:\CAL\CALENDAR
LOADHIGH C:\UTIL\CALC

CONFIG.SYS contents
--------------------

FILES=20
BUFFERS=10
```

continued on next page

continued from previous page

```
DEVICE=C:\DOS\HIMEM.SYS
DEVICE=C:\DOS\EMM386.EXE NOEMS
DOS=HIGH,UMB

GAME CONFIGURATION (Store as GAME.BAT and GAME.SYS)
----------------------------------------------------
AUTOEXEC.BAT contents
---------------------
&ECHO OFF
CLS
PATH C:\DOS;C:\GAMES;C:\UTILS;
LOADHIGH C:\MOUSE\MOUSE

CONFIG.SYS contents
---------------------
FILES=20
BUFFERS=10
DEVICE=C:\DOS\HIMEM.SYS
DEVICE=C:\DOS\EMM386.EXE NOEMS
DOS=HIGH,UMB
DEVICEHIGH=C:\SOUND\SOUNDMAN.SYS
```

Problem #4—A Challenge with Multimedia

Our last user, Jack, has gone all out and filled his machine with modern technology. He has a fast system with a sound card, SCSI adapter (which supports his CD-ROM), and a fancy new video card. Unfortunately, all of these devices require drivers. In fact, his CD-ROM requires two!

After getting the hardware to work properly, Jack found that he lacks the conventional memory necessary to run most multimedia applications (which is why he added the hardware in the first place). Listing 4-33 shows the problem configuration files.

System Description

- 80486DX
- 8 Megabytes of RAM
- Serial Mouse
- Sound Card
- CD-ROM
- Accelerator Video Card

Listing 4-33 Problem #4—Configuration Files

```
AUTOEXEC.BAT contents
---------------------
&ECHO OFF
CLS
PATH C:\DOS;C:\GAMES;C:\MEDIA;
C:\SCSI\MSCDEX
LOADHIGH C:\MOUSE\MOUSE
LOADHIGH C:\DOS\DOSKEY

CONFIG.SYS contents
---------------------
FILES=20
BUFFERS=10
DEVICE=C:\DOS\HIMEM.SYS
DEVICE=C:\DOS\EMM386.EXE NOEMS
DOS=HIGH,UMB
DEVICEHIGH=C:\SOUND\SOUNDMAN.SYS
DEVICEHIGH=C:\SCSI\ADAPTER.SYS
DEVICEHIGH=C:\VIDEO\VESA.SYS
```

Solving the Problem

Jack has no problem getting his drivers into upper memory—with the exception of the MSCDEX driver. This is the Microsoft CD Extension driver. If you own a CD-ROM, you are probably using this driver. After the drivers in CONFIG.SYS are loaded (for the sound, SCSI, and video card), he doesn't have enough room in upper memory.

Fortunately, the MSCDEX driver has an optional switch (/e) that loads the driver into extended memory (if it's available). This is no problem since Jack has plenty of extended RAM. After testing this configuration, he realizes that the DOSKEY program will not fit into upper memory. After weighing the small conventional memory gain versus how much he uses the utility, he decides to omit it from the configuration.

Listing 4-34 Solution #4—Configuration Files

```
AUTOEXEC.BAT contents
---------------------
&ECHO OFF
CLS
PATH C:\DOS;C:\GAMES;C:\MEDIA;
C:\SCSI\MSCDEX /e
LOADHIGH C:\MOUSE\MOUSE
```

continued on next page

continued from previous page

```
CONFIG.SYS contents
--------------------
FILES=20
BUFFERS=10
DEVICE=C:\DOS\HIMEM.SYS
DEVICE=C:\DOS\EMM386.EXE NOEMS
DOS=HIGH,UMB
DEVICEHIGH=C:\SOUND\SOUNDMAN.SYS
DEVICEHIGH=C:\SCSI\ADAPTER.SYS
DEVICEHIGH=C:\VIDEO\VESA.SYS
```

These examples should provide some insight to the thought process that is necessary when configuring your system. If you have a loaded system, you may find you must make compromises or use multiple configurations to meet your needs. Let's look at a summary of the topics for this chapter.

Summary

We've covered a number of topics in this chapter that pertain to DOS 5.0 memory management. Let's review these topics before moving to DOS 6 and/or Windows. If you are unsure of any area, you can always return to the specific section and review it in more depth.

- The DOS 5.0 MEM command lets you view the way your system's memory is configured. Using MEM without switches provides a summary of conventional, expanded (if any), and extended memory.
- The MEM /C, or /CLASSIFY, switch provides a listing of programs (including their size) installed in conventional and upper memory as well as the memory summary.
- The MEM /P, or /PROGRAM, switch provides more detailed information such as the starting address and size (in hexadecimal) of each loaded program.
- The MEM /D, or /DEBUG, switch provides additional information on system device drivers, their locations, and their sizes.
- The main goal of DOS 5.0 memory management is to free up as much conventional memory as possible.
- Loading the HIMEM.SYS driver in your CONFIG.SYS file provides access to extended memory. It also enables the high memory area, where you can ultimately place a large portion of DOS, freeing up

conventional memory. The HIMEM.SYS driver must be installed in conventional memory.

- Loading the EMM386.EXE driver in your CONFIG.SYS file can simulate expanded memory and/or enable access to the upper memory block. EMM386.EXE requires HIMEM.SYS to be loaded first.
- Using EMM386.EXE with no switches simulates expanded memory, but does not enable upper memory access. Using EMM386.EXE with the NOEMS switch enables access to upper memory, but does not simulate expanded memory. Using EMM386 with the RAM switch both simulates expanded memory and enables access to upper memory.
- Adding the DOS=HIGH command to your CONFIG.SYS file will relocate a large portion of MS-DOS, COMMAND, and HIMEM to high memory. You must load HIMEM.SYS before using DOS=HIGH.
- Adding the DOS=UMB command to your CONFIG.SYS file informs DOS that you will load programs and/or device drivers into upper memory blocks. This line must be after the HIMEM.SYS and EMM386.EXE lines.
- You can combine the DOS=HIGH and DOS=UMB on one line using DOS=HIGH, UMB.
- You can load memory-resident (TSR) programs in upper memory using the LOADHIGH command in your AUTOEXEC.BAT file. This requires that the HIMEM.SYS, EMM386.EXE, and DOS=UMB lines are in your CONFIG.SYS file.
- You can load device drivers in upper memory using the DEVICEHIGH command in your CONFIG.SYS file. This requires that the HIMEM.SYS, EMM386.EXE, and DOS=UMB lines are in your CONFIG.SYS file before any DEVICEHIGH line.
- You can create a temporary RAM disk drive using the RAMDRIVE.SYS device driver. The RAM disk either uses conventional memory (no switches), extended memory (/e switch), or expanded memory (/a switch). Always use extended memory if possible. The contents of a RAM disk are lost as soon as you turn off your computer; therefore, use a RAM disk only for temporary purposes.
- You can create a disk cache using the SMARTDRV.SYS device driver. SMARTDrive can speed up your system by storing data that is repeatedly requested from disk in memory. You can create your disk

cache in extended (no switches) or expanded memory (/a switch). You can set the maximum and minimum sizes of the disk cache when loading SMARTDRV.SYS.

Now you have seen the essentials for managing memory in DOS 5.0 The next chapter will cover memory management for DOS 6. If you are thinking about upgrading to version 6, read the next chapter to see if it's for you. We will go through the same exercises we went through in this chapter so you can easily compare the two DOS versions.

DOS 6 Memory Management

This chapter covers memory management techniques using DOS 6.0 (and the DOS 6.2 upgrade). If you are currently using DOS 6, you will find the necessary information to configure your computer memory. If you are currently using DOS 5.0, and are considering upgrading to DOS 6, you can use the information provided in this chapter to help you decide whether the new features of DOS 6 would benefit you.

> The use of the term DOS 6 in this chapter refers to DOS 6.0 and 6.2. References to a specific version are called out where necessary.

As with the last chapter, we'll start with modifications that you can make to your CONFIG.SYS file to increase the amount of free conventional memory. Our goal is to free as much conventional memory as possible. At the same time, we want to configure the computer memory for programs that require other types of memory (extended or expanded).

This chapter will also build a configuration, one step at a time. In each step we will describe exactly what is taking place along with what you will gain (or lose) by performing the step. You can modify your own configuration files along the way (using STORE.BAT to store them), or you can read the entire chapter and develop your configurations on paper before creating them.

We'll also use the MEMAKER utility supplied with DOS 6 to create and modify configuration files. You'll learn how to use MEMMAKER effectively and what to do if something goes wrong.

At the end of this chapter, we'll provide some real-world examples of memory management in DOS 6. These examples include multimedia and nonmultimedia systems.

In this chapter, we will concentrate on memory management as it relates to DOS applications. You will find information that specifically relates to DOS 6. If you are using DOS 6 and Windows you will want to read this chapter and Chapter 6, *Windows Memory Management.* It is important to understand the DOS commands and device drivers before proceeding to the Windows chapter.

Let's start with an overview of the topics we will discuss in this chapter.

DOS 6 TOPICS COVERED

Getting Detailed Memory Information Using the DOS 6 MEM Command

Managing Extended Memory Using HIMEM.SYS

Simulating Expanded Memory Using the EMM386.EXE Driver

Providing Access to Upper Memory Using the EMM386.EXE Driver

Loading DOS in High Memory Using the DOS= Command

Loading Programs in Upper Memory Using the LOADHIGH Command

Loading Device Drivers in Upper Memory Using the DEVICEHIGH Command

Loading Multimedia Drivers High

Using MEMMAKER

Creating a RAM Disk Using the RAMDRIVE.SYS Driver

Creating a Disk Cache Using the SMARTDRV.EXE Driver

Solving Memory Problems in DOS 6

Memory Management Using DOS 6

This section will explore memory management as it relates to DOS 6. We will start with a more in-depth look at the MEM command followed by a step-by-step procedure using memory configuration commands and drivers. In each step of the procedure, we will introduce a new feature to the configuration files. We

Switch	Example	Purpose
/C or /CLASSIFY	MEM /C or MEM /CLASSIFY	Provides a list of programs in first megabyte (conventional and upper).
/D or /DEBUG	MEM /D or MEM /DEBUG	Shows the status of programs, and system drivers loaded in memory.
/F or /FREE	MEM /F or MEM /FREE	Shows the status of free conventional and upper memory.
/M or /MODULE	MEM/ M *name* or MEM /MODULE *name*	Displays the status of one module (program).
/P or /PAGE	MEM /D /P or MEM /DEBUG /PAGE	Causes lengthy MEM listings to be displayed a page at a time.

Table 5-1 MEM command line switches

will show what the feature does and its various options, if any. As we progress, we will show the memory layout in graphical form so you can see what is taking place and what effects it has on your system. This will be followed by a description of MEMMAKER, DOS 6's new memory management assistant.

A 4-Megabyte System Example

We are using a system with 4 megabytes of memory for the examples in this chapter. You will see differences in the MEM output if your system has more or less memory than 4MB.

Viewing Your Memory Configuration Using MEM in DOS 6

In Chapter 2, *Memory and Your Computer,* you used the DOS MEM command to find out the general details of your current memory configuration. We will now demonstrate how you can use the MEM command to gain more detailed memory information. This is done by using a *switch* on the command line when you type **MEM**. A switch is nothing more than a few characters on the command line (in addition to MEM itself). Table 5-1 shows the possible MEM switches and what they accomplish. The DOS 6 version of MEM has different switches than the DOS 5.0 version we showed last chapter.

Up until now, we used the MEM command by itself, which produced a memory summary similar to the one shown in Listing 5-1.

Listing 5-1 Sample MEM Output (No Switches)

```
Memory Type        Total =  Used  +  Free
----------------  ------  ------  ------
Conventional        640K     21K    619K
Upper               155K     31K    124K
Adapter RAM/ROM     384K    384K      0K
Extended (XMS)     2917K   1241K   1676K
----------------  ------  ------  ------
Total memory       4096K   1676K   2420K

Total under 1 MB    795K     51K    744K

Largest executable program size     619K  (634096 bytes)
Largest free upper memory block     124K  (127296 bytes)
MS-DOS is resident in the high memory area.
```

Note that this version of MEM supplies much more information than the one supplied with DOS 5.0. For example, the DOS 6 version of MEM provides details about upper memory and adapter RAM and ROM.

Let's look at some sample output produced by each of the DOS 6 MEM switches. The examples use the same memory configuration that produced the previous output.

> **MEM Requires a PATH to Your DOS Directory**
>
> MEM was installed to your DOS directory when you installed DOS itself. In order to run MEM from any directory other than DOS, you must have a path to DOS in your AUTOEXEC.BAT file. This may be in combination with other paths. For example: PATH=C:\WINDOWS;C:\DOS; provides a path to both the WINDOWS directory and the DOS directory. The DOS 6 installation program automatically adds the PATH statement to your AUTOEXEC.BAT file. It should be there now unless you manually deleted it.

MEM /CLASSIFY—Program Classification

The /C, or /CLASSIFY, switch provides a list of the programs in memory by type. For example, each program in the first megabyte of memory is listed by conventional and upper memory usage. The remaining information is the same memory summary you see when using MEM without a switch. Listing 5-2 shows some example output from MEM /C. Any additions or changes to the material are in boldface.

Listing 5-2 MEM /C Output

```
Modules using memory below 1 MB:

  Name           Total        =   Conventional    +   Upper Memory
  --------  ----------------   ----------------   ----------------
  MSDOS       13885   (14K)      13885   (14K)          0    (0K)
  HIMEM        1168    (1K)       1168    (1K)          0    (0K)
  EMM386       3120    (3K)       3120    (3K)          0    (0K)
  COMMAND      2912    (3K)       2912    (3K)          0    (0K)
  SMARTDRV    27280   (27K)          0    (0K)      27280   (27K)
  DOSKEY       4144    (4K)          0    (0K)       4144    (4K)
  Free       761584  (744K)     634192  (619K)     127392  (124K)

Memory Summary:

  Type of Memory       Total       =       Used         +       Free
  ----------------  -----------------   -----------------   -----------------
  Conventional        655360   (640K)      21168    (21K)     634192   (619K)
  Upper               158816   (155K)      31424    (31K)     127392   (124K)
  Adapter RAM/ROM     393216   (384K)     393216   (384K)          0     (0K)
  Extended (XMS)     2986912  (2917K)    1270688  (1241K)    1716224  (1676K)
  ----------------  -----------------   -----------------   -----------------
  Total memory       4194304  (4096K)    1716496  (1676K)    2477808  (2420K)

  Total under 1 MB    814176   (795K)      52592    (51K)     761584   (744K)

  Largest executable program size         634096   (619K)
  Largest free upper memory block         127296   (124K)
  MS-DOS is resident in the high memory area.
```

MEM /DEBUG—Listing Programs and Device Drivers in Memory

By typing **MEM /DEBUG** or **MEM /D**, we can get a much more detailed memory listing. An example of this is shown in Listing 5-3. The listing provides specific information regarding system device drivers. This information is usually not necessary in memory management, so we'll use MEM /C in most of this chapter's examples. The differences between MEM and MEM /D are in boldface.

Listing 5-3 MEM /D Output

```
Conventional Memory Detail:

  Segment           Total         Name         Type
  -------     ----------------   -----------  --------
   00000          1039    (1K)                 Interrupt Vector
   00040           271    (0K)                 ROM Communication Area
   00050           527    (1K)                 DOS Communication Area
   00070          2752    (3K)   IO            System Data
```

continued on next page

continued from previous page

```
                                             CON         System Device Driver
                                             AUX         System Device Driver
                                             PRN         System Device Driver
                                             CLOCK$      System Device Driver
                                             A: - D:     System Device Driver
                                             COM1        System Device Driver
                                             LPT1        System Device Driver
                                             LPT2        System Device Driver
                                             LPT3        System Device Driver
                                             COM2        System Device Driver
                                             COM3        System Device Driver
                                             COM4        System Device Driver
  0011C                  5104      (5K)    MSDOS         System Data
  0025B                  8416      (8K)    IO            System Data
                         1152      (1K)      XMSXXXX0    Installed Device=HIMEM
                         3104      (3K)      EMMQXXX0    Installed Device=EMM386
                          960      (1K)                  FILES=21
                          256      (0K)                  FCBS=4
                          512      (1K)                  BUFFERS=15
                          448      (0K)                  LASTDRIVE=E
                         1856      (2K)                  STACKS=9,128
  00469                    80      (0K)    MSDOS         System Program
  0046E                  2640      (3K)    COMMAND       Program
  00513                    80      (0K)    MSDOS         -- Free --
  00518                   272      (0K)    COMMAND       Environment
  00529                    96      (0K)    MEM           Environment
  0052F                 88608     (87K)    MEM           Program
  01AD1                545504    (533K)    MSDOS         -- Free --

Upper Memory Detail:

  Segment  Region       Total          Name          Type
  -------  ------  ----------------  -----------   --------
   0C93A      1          96    (0K)  MSDOS         -- Free --
   0C940      1       27280   (27K)  SMARTDRV      Program
   0CFE9      1        4144    (4K)  DOSKEY        Program
   0D0EC      1      127296  (124K)  MSDOS         -- Free --

Memory Summary:

  Type of Memory       Total        =       Used          +       Free
  ----------------  -----------------   -----------------   -----------------
  Conventional        655360   (640K)     21168     (21K)     634192   (619K)
  Upper               158816   (155K)     31424     (31K)     127392   (124K)
  Adapter RAM/ROM     393216   (384K)    393216    (384K)          0     (0K)
  Extended (XMS)     2986912  (2917K)   1270688   (1241K)    1716224  (1676K)
  ----------------  -----------------   -----------------   -----------------
  Total memory       4194304  (4096K)   1716496   (1676K)    2477808  (2420K)

  Total under 1 MB    814176   (795K)     52592     (51K)     761584   (744K)

  Memory accessible using Int 15h             0      (0K)
  Largest executable program size        634096    (619K)
  Largest free upper memory block        127296    (124K)
```

```
MS-DOS is resident in the high memory area.

XMS version  3.00; driver version  3.09
```

Let's break the MEM output in Listing 5-3 into pieces. The first line starts at the bottom of conventional memory (00000h) and is 1,039 bytes. This is the area in which DOS stores *interrupt vectors.* Interrupt vectors are a collection of addresses that DOS uses internally. We do not have to worry about them in memory management. They'll always be there no matter how we manage our memory.

The same goes for the next few lines. For example, the ROM communication area is at segment 00040h (address 000400h). Again, these are addresses that DOS uses internally. This is followed by the DOS communication area at segment 00050h (address 000500h).

The next two sections, IO and MSDOS, are the hidden files that are required on a boot disk: IO.SYS and MSDOS.SYS. Up to this point we haven't had much control over the system memory; however, we haven't taken up much conventional memory (just 0023B0h bytes or 9,648 bytes). Note that the column on the left drops the offset number (last digit). For example, 0025B actually represents address 0025B0.

The block of lines that begins at address 0025B0h is at the point where we have some level of control. This is the *DOS environment block.* This is where DOS stores information such as FILES= and BUFFERS= from the CONFIG.SYS file. The more files and buffers we specify in the CONFIG.SYS file, the more space is allocated to this environment block.

The remainder of the Conventional Memory Detail section is the MS-DOS program, free memory, and the MEM program itself.

The Upper Memory Detail section shows the status of programs and free memory in upper memory. For example, in the listing you will see a DOS TSR program at address CFE90h. This is DOSKEY, a utility supplied with DOS that makes command line entries easier. Notice that it takes up 4,144 bytes (around 4K).

The Memory Summary section also contains two new entries. The first new entry lists the amount of memory accessible by interrupt 15h. This information is used by programmers and doesn't concern us while managing memory. The second new line, and also the last line of the MEM /D output, shows the extended memory specification version (3.0) and the version of the XMS driver (3.09).

We'll examine more about addresses and programs in memory as this chapter progresses. Now let's look at a free memory summary: MEM /F.

MEM /FREE—Free Memory Summary

Typing **MEM /F** and pressing ENTER provides a summary of free memory. Listing 5-4 shows some example output from MEM /F.

The first section in the free memory summary is conventional memory. In this example, there are four separate areas of free conventional memory. The listing shows the starting segment of each free block as well as the size of the block. The last line of the conventional memory section shows the total free conventional memory.

The other section of this summary shows the status of free upper memory. This is divided into the largest free contiguous block, the total free upper memory, and the total size of upper memory. In this case, the total upper memory is around 155K with 124K free and in one piece.

Listing 5-4 MEM /F—Free Memory Summary

```
Free Conventional Memory:

  Segment          Total
  -------     ----------------
   00513           80      (0K)
   00529           96      (0K)
   0052F        88608     (87K)
   01AD1       545504    (533K)

  Total Free: 634288    (619K)

Free Upper Memory:

  Region    Largest Free      Total Free       Total Size
  ------  --------------  --------------  --------------
       1   127296 (124K)   127392 (124K)   158816 (155K)
```

MEM /MODULE *name*—List a Specific Module's Memory Information

The /M switch, along with a program name, provides the location and size of the program in memory. Listing 5-5 shows the output if you typed **MEM /M HIMEM**. This requires HIMEM.SYS to be in memory. Note that you do not type the extension of a program (.COM, .EXE, or .SYS).

Listing 5-5 MEM /M—Individual Module Information

```
HIMEM is using the following memory:

  Segment  Region        Total          Type
  -------  ------  ----------------  --------
   0025B                1152    (1K)  Installed Device=HIMEM
                   ----------------
  Total Size:           1152    (1K)
```

In this example, HIMEM starts at segment 0025Bh and is 1,152 bytes in size. If you type a name of a program that is not in memory, the system displays a message indicating the situation. For example, if you type **MEM /M DOSKEY** and DOSKEY is not in memory, the system displays:

```
DOSKEY is not currently in memory.
```

MEM /PAGE—Display Output a Screen at a Time

The /PAGE or /P switch can be used in combination with any MEM switch. This is similar to typing **DIR /P** to get a directory a page at a time. This switch is more useful with the /CLASSIFY and /DEBUG switches, because they usually display more than one page of information. Here are a few examples of the MEM /P switch.

```
MEM /C/P
```

This would display the memory classify information one page at a time.

```
MEM /DEBUG /PAGE
```

This would display the memory debug information one page at a time.

We will use the MEM command throughout this chapter to see the effects on modifying the configuration files (CONFIG.SYS and AUTOEXEC.BAT). If you are trying some of these examples, remember that the /P switch breaks the MEM output into pages.

A Bare-Bones Configuration

In order to build a set of working configuration files, we will start with a simple, minimal configuration. This way you can see the effects of each step in the process. For each example, we will show the MEM output and a graphic indicating the effects of each change. For DOS 5.0 users, we also provide a short comparison of the DOS versions after each stage. Listing 5-6 shows the contents of the AUTOEXEC.BAT and CONFIG.SYS files for this minimal configuration.

Listing 5-6 Minimal AUTOEXEC.BAT and CONFIG.SYS

```
Contents of AUTOEXEC.BAT
------------------------
@ECHO OFF
CLS
PROMPT $p$g
PATH=C:\DOS;
```

continued on next page

continued from previous page

```
Contents of CONFIG.SYS
----------------------
FILES=21
BUFFERS=15
```

The AUTOEXEC.BAT file in this example has an ECHO OFF command followed by a CLS (clear screen). It also has the PROMPT command and a path to DOS. None of these commands take up any memory, with the exception of the PATH statement (which is part of the DOS environment block). However, DOS automatically reserves 256 bytes of environment space; so we might as well use it to store a path to the DOS directory.

> **Remove CLS and &ECHO OFF When Troubleshooting Memory**
>
> It's a good idea to remove the CLS and &ECHO OFF commands from your AUTOEXEC.BAT when troubleshooting memory problems. These commands prevent DOS from displaying important information during the boot process.

Now that we've seen the contents of the configuration files, let's look at the output from the MEM command for this minimal configuration. Listing 5-7 shows the MEM /C output.

Listing 5-7 MEM /C—Minimal Configuration

```
Modules using memory below 1 MB:

  Name           Total       =   Conventional    +   Upper Memory
  --------  ----------------   ----------------   ----------------
  MSDOS       58989    (58K)     58989    (58K)          0    (0K)
  COMMAND      4992     (5K)      4992     (5K)          0    (0K)
  Free       591280   (577K)    591280   (577K)          0    (0K)

Memory Summary:

  Type of Memory       Total       =       Used        +       Free
  ----------------  ----------------   ----------------   ----------------
  Conventional        655360   (640K)     64080    (63K)    591280   (577K)
  Upper                    0     (0K)         0     (0K)         0     (0K)
  Adapter RAM/ROM     393216   (384K)    393216   (384K)         0     (0K)
  Extended (XMS)     3145728  (3072K)   3145728  (3072K)         0     (0K)
  ----------------  ----------------   ----------------   ----------------
  Total memory       4194304  (4096K)   3603024  (3519K)    591280   (577K)

  Total under 1 MB    655360   (640K)     64080    (63K)    591280   (577K)

  Largest executable program size        591184   (577K)
  Largest free upper memory block             0     (0K)
```

Note that the output from MEM /C does not show any usage of upper memory. This is because we do not have the necessary drivers to access upper memory yet. We are also using more conventional memory because we are not loading DOS high yet. This accounts for low initial conventional memory (577K).

The first section of MEM/C output (see Listing 5-7) is *Modules using memory below 1MB.* There are three entries in this section and all are in conventional memory. The first line is MS-DOS itself and it takes up 58,989 bytes, or about 58K. The second line is COMMAND; this is the command interpreter of DOS. Its purpose is to interpret command line internal DOS commands (such as DIR, COPY, and so on). It is using 4,992 bytes, or around 5K.

The last entry in the first section is labeled Free. This indicates free conventional memory. Our goal is to keep this value as high as possible. With no other programs loaded in conventional memory, there are 591,280 bytes free (around 577K).

The next section, *Memory Summary,* provides the status of conventional, upper, adapter RAM/ROM, and extended memory. This is followed by a line indicating the largest executable program size. In this case it's 591,184 bytes (around 577K). The last line shows the largest free upper memory block. It's zero at this point because we have not installed the necessary drivers to access upper memory.

Comparing DOS 5.0 and DOS 6—Minimal Configuration

This is our first comparison between the two latest versions of DOS. The same configuration in DOS 5.0 resulted in a largest executable program size of 592,256 bytes. The DOS 6 configuration resulted in a largest executable program size of 591,184 bytes. Therefore, DOS 5.0 has 1,072 more bytes with which to run programs. This difference is due to the fact that the MSDOS and COMMAND modules are slightly larger in DOS 6.

Now let's look at a graphic that represents the memory for this minimal configuration. Figure 5-1 shows this graphic.

The left side of Figure 5-1 shows the entire range of the 4-megabyte example system. The right side shows an enlarged depiction of the first megabyte (conventional and upper memory) and the high memory area (HMA). Recall that the HMA is the first 64K of extended memory. Upper memory and the HMA do not come into play in this example.

Notice that the COMMAND program and MS-DOS are loaded in conventional memory. There are also small pieces of conventional memory (at its lowest point) used for system purposes. Also note that the relative sizes of COMMAND and MS-DOS are not to exact scale.

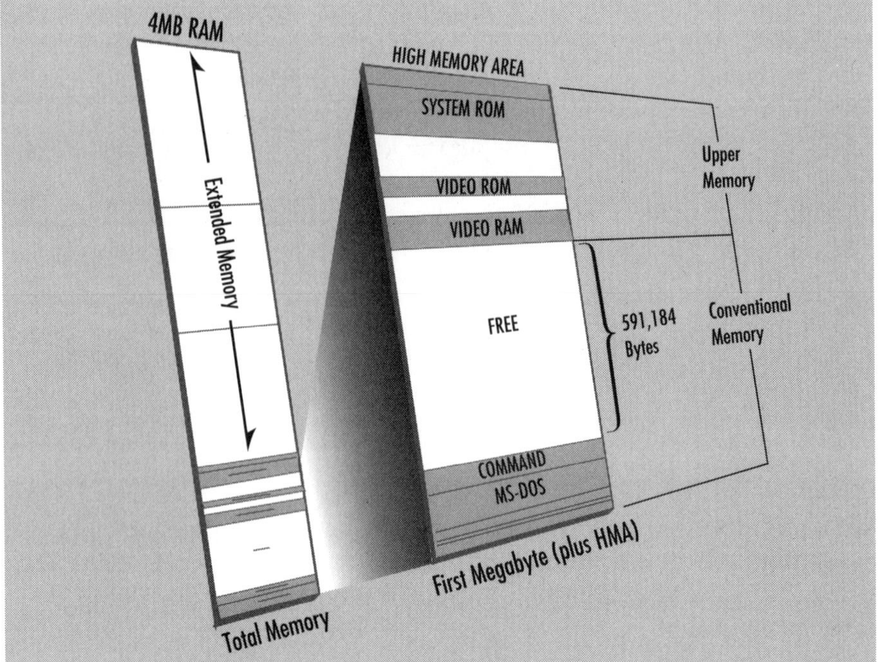

Figure 5-1 Memory configuration for the Minimal example

Remember that most DOS programs (especially multimedia programs) require as much conventional memory as you can supply. We'll continue with our example configurations one step at a time, with the ultimate goal being maximized conventional memory. Let's expand on this example by loading the DOS supplied extended memory driver, HIMEM.SYS.

Adding HIMEM.SYS—Extended Memory Driver

Our next set of configuration files adds the DOS extended memory driver, HIMEM.SYS. The version of HIMEM.SYS supplied with DOS 6 is compatible with the XMS specification version 3.0. Do not confuse this with the version of the driver itself. Recall that the XMS and XMS driver versions are listed at the bottom of an MEM /D output.

Always use the most recent version of HIMEM.SYS that you have available. If you buy a copy of Microsoft Windows (which also contains a copy of HIMEM.SYS), compare the versions by examining the time and date stamp on the file. The most recent date will be the newest version. As of the time of this writing, DOS 6's HIMEM.SYS is newer than Windows 3.1's version. Windows 3.1's HIMEM.SYS is newer than DOS 5.0's.

Now, let's look at our new configuration file. This time we only modified CONFIG.SYS, so it's the only file in the listing. Listing 5-8 shows the new CONFIG.SYS adding the HIMEM.SYS driver.

Listing 5-8 Modified CONFIG.SYS—Adding the HIMEM.SYS Driver

```
Contents of CONFIG.SYS
----------------------
FILES=21
BUFFERS=15
DEVICE=C:\DOS\HIMEM.SYS
```

Note that only one line in the CONFIG.SYS file is required to load the HIMEM.SYS. This line consists of the DEVICE= statement followed by the full pathname and filename of the driver. You must supply the pathname in this case. Because the system loads the CONFIG.SYS before the AUTOEXEC.BAT file, the PATH statement in AUTOEXEC.BAT has no effect yet.

One difference between DOS 6 and DOS 5.0 is that the messages from drivers, such as HIMEM.SYS, are not displayed during power up. You must add a /V, or /VERBOSE switch to the HIMEM.SYS driver to see the messages. Another alternative is to press and hold the ALT key during power up.

When the HIMEM.SYS driver is successfully loaded on power up (and you're holding down the ALT key or using the /VERBOSE switch), you will see a message similar to the following:

```
HIMEM: DOS XMS Driver, Version 3.09 - 02/23/93
Extended Memory Specification (XMS) Version 3.0
Copyright 1988-1993 Microsoft Corp.

Installed A20 handler number 1.
64K High Memory Area is available.
```

This message indicates the version of the driver on the first line (in this case, version 3.09, although your system may differ). The fourth line indicates that a handler for the A20 address line has been installed. Recall that we cannot address the high memory area without a 21st address line. Because the first twenty address lines are A0 through A19, A20 becomes the twenty-first.

Now let's see the effects on the MEM output when we add the new driver and reboot the computer. Remember you must always reboot after making a change to CONFIG.SYS. Listing 5-9 shows the new MEM output.

Listing 5-9 MEM /C—After Loading HIMEM.SYS

```
Modules using memory below 1 MB:

  Name           Total        =   Conventional     +   Upper Memory
  --------  ----------------   ----------------   ----------------
  MSDOS        59005   (58K)      59005   (58K)           0   (0K)
  HIMEM         3792    (4K)       3792    (4K)           0   (0K)
  COMMAND       4992    (5K)       4992    (5K)           0   (0K)
  Free        587488  (574K)     587488  (574K)           0   (0K)

Memory Summary:

  Type of Memory        Total        =       Used          +       Free
  ----------------  ----------------   ----------------   ----------------
  Conventional        655360   (640K)     67872    (66K)     587488   (574K)
  Upper                    0     (0K)         0     (0K)          0     (0K)
  Adapter RAM/ROM     393216   (384K)    393216   (384K)          0     (0K)
  Extended (XMS)     3145728  (3072K)     65536    (64K)    3080192  (3008K)
  ----------------  ----------------   ----------------   ----------------
  Total memory       4194304  (4096K)    526624   (514K)    3667680  (3582K)

  Total under 1 MB    655360   (640K)     67872    (66K)     587488   (574K)

  Largest executable program size        587392   (574K)
  Largest free upper memory block             0     (0K)
  The high memory area is available.
```

Notice that the HIMEM driver now appears in the first section of the MEM output. It is 3,792 bytes in size. This reduces the amount of conventional memory available by a similar amount. This in turn reduces our largest executable program size.

The last line of the MEM /C output indicates that the high memory area is available. This is a function of the HIMEM.SYS driver.

> **Comparing DOS 5.0 and DOS 6—HIMEM.SYS Configuration**
>
> The HIMEM.SYS configuration in DOS 5.0 resulted in a largest executable program size of 589,040 bytes. The DOS 6 configuration resulted in a largest executable program size of 587,392 bytes. Therefore, DOS 5.0 has 1,648 more bytes with which to run programs. This difference is due to the fact that the HIMEM.SYS driver is slightly larger in DOS 6.

It may seem like we're going in the wrong direction, but don't despair. There is a method to this madness, as you will see later in this chapter. The main thing the HIMEM.SYS driver buys us is access to the HMA. We just aren't taking advantage of it yet.

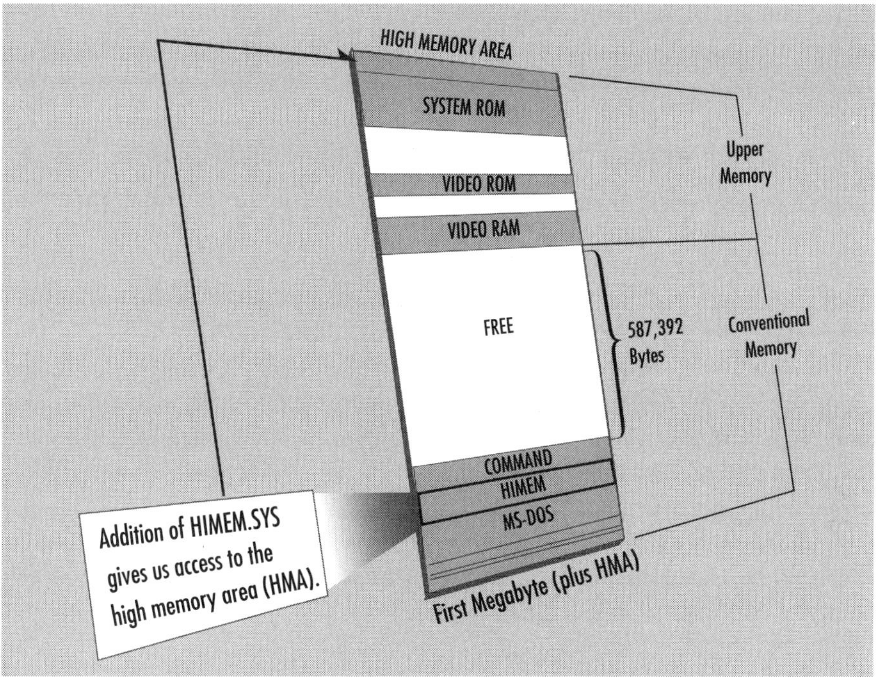

Figure 5-2 Memory configuration—added HIMEM.SYS

Let's look at a graphic to see the addition of the HIMEM.SYS driver. Figure 5-2 shows this addition. We've omitted the overview of the entire 4-megabyte range because nothing there has changed for this example.

Adding EMM386.EXE—Expanded Memory Driver

In addition to the HIMEM.SYS driver, DOS 6 also supplies an expanded memory driver, EMM386.EXE. This driver performs more than one purpose. EMM386.EXE can do the following:

- Simulate expanded memory using extended memory.
- Provide access to the upper memory blocks (UMB).
- Combine expanded memory simulation and UMB access.

Using EMM386.EXE in CONFIG.SYS

When you add a line for EMM386.EXE in your CONFIG.SYS file, you can specify a number of options in the form of switches. For example, you can specify the amount of expanded memory (in kilobytes) you want to simulate. Here is an example:

```
DEVICE=C:\DOS\EMM386.EXE 512
```

This allocates 512K of expanded memory. Of course, as a result, the amount of free extended memory decreases. However, DOS 6 can modify the amount of free extended and expanded memory on the fly. We'll see more about this in a moment. There are also switches to set the page frame, include or exclude particular addresses, and do other things. However, these switches are usually not required. Consult your DOS manual for more information on these switches.

Two switches are important in our discussion of memory management: RAM and NOEMS. We will look at three examples of EMM386.EXE usage. The first example is with no switches, the second is with the RAM switch, and the third is with the NOEMS switch. Table 5-2 shows the effects of these switches on expanded memory simulations and UMB access.

You can see in Table 5-2 that the switch you use affects whether you require simulated expanded memory, access to the UMBs, or both. Let's look at the three examples. We'll start out using no switches.

EMM386.EXE with No Switch

This example loads EMM386.EXE with no switch. According to our table, this should simulate expanded memory without access to the UMBs. Listing 5-10 shows the new CONFIG.SYS for this example. Once again, the AUTOEXEC.BAT file remains unchanged.

Listing 5-10 Modified CONFIG.SYS—Added EMM386.EXE (No Switches)

```
Contents of CONFIG.SYS
----------------------
FILES=21
BUFFERS=15
DEVICE=C:\DOS\HIMEM.SYS
DEVICE=C:\DOS\EMM386.EXE
```

Switch	Example	Expanded Memory?	UMB Access?
none	C:\DOS\EMM386.EXE	YES	NO
RAM	C:\DOS\EMM386.EXE RAM	YES	YES
NOEMS	C:\DOS\EMM386.EXE NOEMS	NO	YES

Table 5-2 EMM386.EXE with RAM, NOEMS, or no switches

Note that this example CONFIG.SYS file also loads the HIMEM.SYS driver, which is required by EMM386.EXE. You cannot load the expanded memory driver without first loading the extended memory driver.

Use the ALT Key or the VERBOSE Switch to See Power Up Messages

There are two ways to view messages from EMM386.EXE on power up. The first is to press and hold the ALT key during the boot process. The other is to add the VERBOSE switch to the EMM386.EXE line in the CONFIG.SYS file. Do not use a slash (/) in front of the VERBOSE switch as we did with HIMEM.SYS

During the boot process, the system will display the following message to indicate that the expanded memory driver is installed correctly. This is in addition to the message from HIMEM.SYS.

```
MICROSOFT Expanded Memory Manager 386  Version 4.45
(C) Copyright Microsoft Corporation 1986, 1993

EMM386 successfully installed.

  Available expanded memory . . . . . . . .  3008 KB

  LIM/EMS version . . . . . . . . . . . . .  4.0
  Total expanded memory pages . . . . . . .  212
  Available expanded memory pages . . . . .  188
  Total handles . . . . . . . . . . . . . .  64
  Active handles  . . . . . . . . . . . . .  1
  Page frame segment  . . . . . . . . . . .  E000 H

EMM386 Active.
```

This message provides quite a bit of information. The lines that are important for our purposes are in boldface. For example, the first line following the copyright message indicates that EMM386 has been successfully installed. The next line indicates that we have 3,008K of expanded memory available. This is much different compared to DOS 5.0 which used a default of 256K. The main difference is that DOS 6 can change the amount of extended/expanded memory on the fly, depending on program needs. For example, if you started Microsoft Windows, DOS 6 would provide extended memory. As a result, the amount of available expanded memory would decrease.

There are 212 pages of expanded memory and only 188 pages available. The difference is 24 pages. This difference is caused by the system using 24 expanded memory pages (24 x 16K = 384K) to backfill upper memory. However, we cannot use it in this configuration because we are not using the RAM or NOEMS switch.

The second to last line indicates the page frame segment. This is a 64K section of upper memory where programs that utilize expanded memory can keep up to four pages at a time. The default page frame segment for DOS 6 is E000h. In DOS 5.0, the default page frame segment is D000h.

Now let's look at the MEM /C output for this example. Listing 5-11 provides this information.

Listing 5-11 MEM /C—After Loading EMM386.EXE (No Switches)

```
Modules using memory below 1 MB:

  Name           Total       =   Conventional   +   Upper Memory
  --------  ----------------   ----------------   ----------------
  MSDOS       59021   (58K)      59021   (58K)          0    (0K)
  HIMEM        3792    (4K)       3792    (4K)          0    (0K)
  EMM386       8112    (8K)       8112    (8K)          0    (0K)
  COMMAND      4992    (5K)       4992    (5K)          0    (0K)
  Free       579376  (566K)     579376  (566K)          0    (0K)

Memory Summary:

  Type of Memory         Total    =      Used     +      Free
  ----------------  ----------------  ----------------  ----------------
  Conventional        655360  (640K)     75984   (74K)    579376  (566K)
  Upper                    0    (0K)         0    (0K)         0    (0K)
  Adapter RAM/ROM     393216  (384K)    393216  (384K)         0    (0K)
  Extended (XMS)*    3145728 (3072K)    491520  (480K)   2654208 (2592K)
  ----------------  ----------------  ----------------  ----------------
  Total memory       4194304 (4096K)    960720  (938K)   3233584 (3158K)

  Total under 1 MB    655360  (640K)     75984   (74K)    579376  (566K)

  Total Expanded (EMS)                 3473408 (3392K)
  Free Expanded (EMS)*                 2899968 (2832K)

  * EMM386 is using XMS memory to simulate EMS memory as needed.
    Free EMS memory may change as free XMS memory changes.

  Largest executable program size       579280  (566K)
  Largest free upper memory block            0    (0K)
  The high memory area is available.
```

Note in the first section of the listing that the EMM386 driver now resides in conventional memory. As a result, our free conventional memory is shrinking even more. But we'll correct that soon.

Also note that there are four new lines near the end of the summary. The first new line indicates 3,392K (3,473,408 bytes) total EMS memory. The next line indicates 2,832K (2,899,968 bytes) of free EMS memory. Remember that 384K of the expanded memory is upper memory backfill.

The next two lines form an important message marked with an asterisk. This indicates that EMM386 is using extended memory to simulate expanded memory. However, the free expanded memory will change with the demands of extended memory. Notice that both the free expanded and free extended entries are marked with an asterisk.

Comparing DOS 5.0 and DOS 6—EMM386.EXE Configuration

The EMM386.EXE (with no switch) configuration in DOS 5.0 resulted in a largest executable program size of 580,624 bytes. The DOS 6 configuration resulted in a largest executable program size of 579,280 bytes. Therefore, DOS 5.0 has 1,344 more bytes with which to run programs. This difference is due to the fact that the EMM386.EXE driver is slightly smaller in DOS 6.

Even though this configuration takes slightly more conventional memory in DOS 6, the newer version gives your system the capability to flexibly adapt to program memory needs in terms of expanded and extended memory. This benefit outweighs the 1,344-byte difference.

To help solidify what happened here, let's look at another graphic. Figure 5-3 shows the memory configuration with EMM386 installed.

As you can see by the illustration, the EMM386 driver takes up space in conventional memory. Once again this reduces the amount of conventional memory. At this point we have MS-DOS, HIMEM, EMM386, and the COMMAND interpreter loaded in conventional memory. This is in addition to the conventional memory that the system always requires.

Because we did not specify a switch on the EMM386.EXE line, we end up creating expanded memory with no access to upper memory. This results in a 64K page frame being located in upper memory. By default, the address of the EMS page frame is E0000h (the default address is D0000h in DOS 5.0). The 64K page frame is divided into four pages, each being 16K. The contents of the page frames can be any available page from the expanded memory. The left side of Figure 5-3 shows a section of extended memory converted to expanded memory. This amount can grow and shrink based on program memory demands.

Programs must be specifically written to use expanded memory. If none of the programs you run use expanded memory, there is no point in configuring to allow for it.

There is a drawback to using EMM386.EXE without any switches. True, this configuration provides expanded memory; however, it does not provide access to the upper memory blocks, or UMBs. Let's look at an example that starts to open up access to the UMBs.

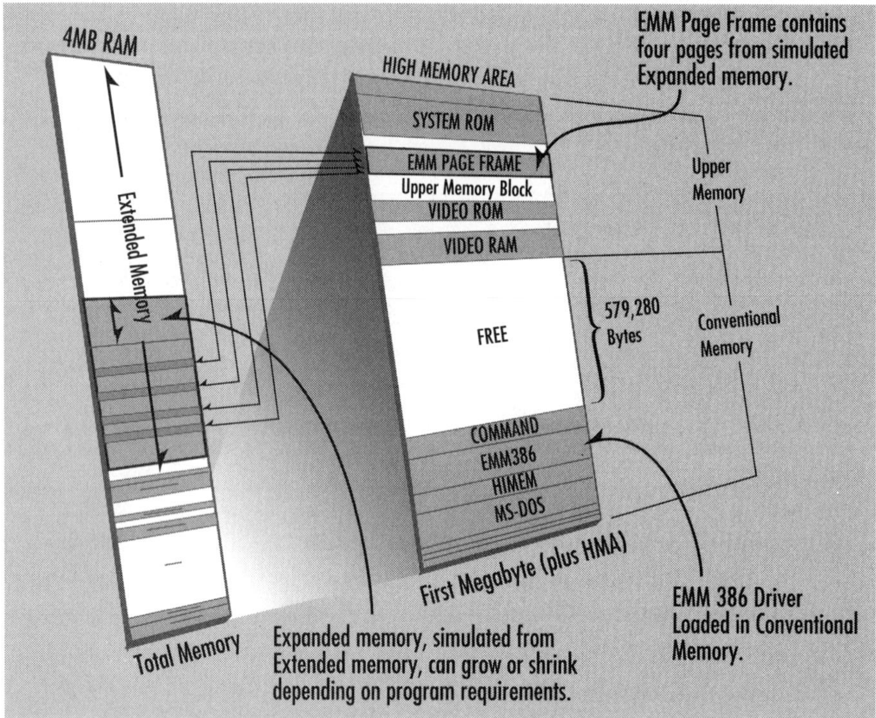

Figure 5-3 Memory configuration—EMM386.EXE loaded with no switches

EMM386.EXE with the RAM Switch

Our next example modifies the CONFIG.SYS line that loads EMM386.EXE by adding the RAM switch. The configuration files are identical except for this line. Using the RAM switch simulates expanded memory and also provides access to the UMBs. Here is the new line:

```
DEVICE=C:\DOS\EMM386.EXE RAM
```

Note the addition of the RAM switch. This switch, unlike the switches used with the MEM command, does not require the forward slash character (/). The first indication of this change appears during the boot process. Listing 5-12 shows the messages that EMM386.EXE displays.

Listing 5-12 EMM386.EXE Startup Messages

```
MICROSOFT Expanded Memory Manager 386  Version 4.45
(C) Copyright Microsoft Corporation 1986, 1993

EMM386 successfully installed.
```

```
  Available expanded memory . . . . . . . .  3008 KB

  LIM/EMS version . . . . . . . . . . . . .  4.0
  Total expanded memory pages . . . . . . .  212
  Available expanded memory pages . . . . .  188
  Total handles . . . . . . . . . . . . . .  64
  Active handles  . . . . . . . . . . . . .  1
  Page frame segment  . . . . . . . . . . .  E000 H

  Total upper memory available  . . . . . .    91 KB
  Largest Upper Memory Block available  . .    91 KB
  Upper memory starting address . . . . . .  C800 H

EMM386 Active.
```

Notice that in addition to the expanded memory information, EMM386.EXE also displays information regarding upper memory. In this example, 91K of upper memory is available. We can use this memory to load some device drivers and memory-resident programs. However, this will require additional steps, as we'll see in a moment. Simply loading EMM386.EXE with the RAM switch doesn't move programs to upper memory. It simply makes upper memory *available.*

The last new line in the EMM386.EXE output shows the address (it's actually the segment address) of the start of *available* upper memory. Recall that upper memory actually starts at A0000h, but this area is normally reserved for video RAM.

Let's see the effects of EMM386.EXE RAM on the MEM /C output. This is shown in Listing 5-13.

Listing 5-13 MEM /C—After Loading EMM386.EXE with the RAM Switch

```
Modules using memory below 1 MB:

  Name          Total       =   Conventional    +   Upper Memory
  --------  ----------------   ----------------    ----------------
  MSDOS        59021   (58K)      59021   (58K)           0     (0K)
  HIMEM         3792    (4K)       3792    (4K)           0     (0K)
  EMM386        3120    (3K)       3120    (3K)           0     (0K)
  COMMAND       4992    (5K)       4992    (5K)           0     (0K)
  Free        584368  (571K)     584368  (571K)           0     (0K)

Memory Summary:

  Type of Memory         Total       =        Used        +        Free
  ----------------  -----------------   -----------------   -----------------
  Conventional        655360   (640K)       70992    (69K)     584368   (571K)
  Upper                    0     (0K)           0     (0K)          0     (0K)
```

continued on next page

continued from previous page

```
Adapter RAM/ROM      393216    (384K)     393216    (384K)          0      (0K)
Extended (XMS)*     3145728   (3072K)     589824    (576K)    2555904   (2496K)
---------------- -----------------  -----------------  -----------------
Total memory        4194304   (4096K)    1054032   (1029K)    3140272   (3067K)

Total under 1 MB     655360    (640K)      70992     (69K)     584368    (571K)

Total Expanded (EMS)                     3473408   (3392K)
Free Expanded (EMS)*                     2801664   (2736K)

* EMM386 is using XMS memory to simulate EMS memory as needed.
  Free EMS memory may change as free XMS memory changes.

Largest executable program size           584272    (571K)
Largest free upper memory block                0      (0K)
The high memory area is available.
```

Note that the only major change is a slight increase in extended memory. This is because EMM386.EXE takes up less memory with the RAM switch (8,112 bytes without the RAM switch, 3,120 bytes with the RAM switch).

Another noticeable difference between this and the corresponding DOS 5.0 configuration is that MEM /C in DOS 6 does not show that the upper memory block is available. It will not show that upper memory is available until we use the DOS=UMB command. We'll use this command later in this chapter.

Comparing DOS 5.0 and DOS 6—EMM386.EXE RAM Configuration

The EMM386.EXE RAM configuration in DOS 5.0 resulted in a largest executable program size of 580,624 bytes. The DOS 6 configuration resulted in a largest executable program size of 584,272 bytes. Therefore, DOS 6 has 3,648 more bytes with which to run programs. This difference is due to the fact that the EMM386.EXE driver is slightly smaller in DOS 6.

Another difference between the DOS 6 and DOS 5.0 configurations is the amount of upper memory. The amount in DOS 5.0 is 31K and the amount in DOS 6 is 91K. This is because DOS 6 provides a more aggressive approach to upper memory. The amount of free upper memory will vary from system to system depending on the hardware you have installed. For example, a network adapter card may use addresses in upper memory for its ROM. This would decrease the amount of upper memory available.

Figure 5-4 shows an illustration for the EMM386.EXE RAM configuration. Note that the upper memory block is now available. The starting address is C8000h. This is just above the video ROM addresses in the first megabyte of memory. This value may vary from computer to computer.

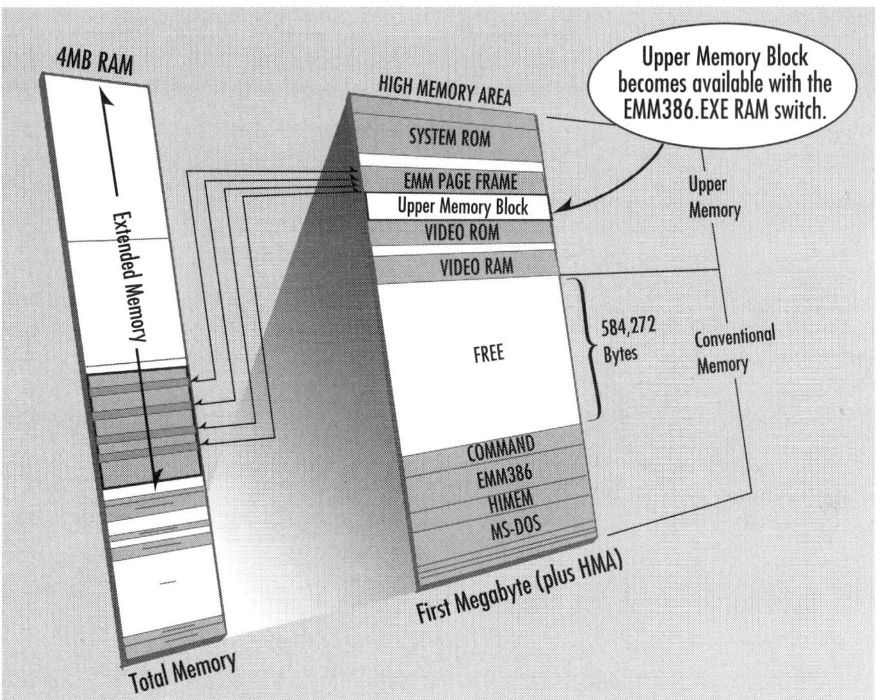

Figure 5-4 Memory configuration—EMM386.EXE loaded with the RAM switch

The RAM switch is good for situations where you want both expanded memory and access to the upper memory area. If you do not need expanded memory, or you need more upper memory, the next situation is for you.

EMM386.EXE with the NOEMS Switch

Next, we modify the CONFIG.SYS file so the EMM386.EXE driver is loaded using the NOEMS switch. As you might have guessed, this switch means no expanded memory services. However, it does provide access to the upper memory blocks. It also provides a greater amount of upper memory for you to load device drivers or memory-resident programs. Here is the modified EMM386.EXE line:

```
DEVICE=C:\DOS\EMM386.EXE NOEMS
```

Note the addition of the NOEMS switch. As with the RAM switch the first noticeable change appears during the boot process. Listing 5-14 shows the new message that EMM386.EXE displays.

Listing 5-14 EMM386.EXE Startup Message (NOEMS)

```
MICROSOFT Expanded Memory Manager 386  Version 4.45
(C) Copyright Microsoft Corporation 1986, 1993

EMM386 successfully installed.

Expanded memory services unavailable.

  Total upper memory available  . . . . . .    155 KB
  Largest Upper Memory Block available  . .    155 KB
  Upper memory starting address . . . . . .  C800 H

EMM386 Active.
```

The message from EMM386.EXE is considerably smaller when using the NOEMS switch. This is primarily due to the fact that there is no expanded memory information. This information has been replaced by a line indicating that EMS is unavailable. Also notice that the amount of upper memory has increased to 155K. We'll see why this occurred in a moment. First let's look at the MEM output which is shown in Listing 5-15.

Listing 5-15 MEM /C—After Loading EMM386.EXE with the NOEMS Switch

```
Modules using memory below 1 MB:

  Name           Total       =   Conventional    +   Upper Memory
  --------  ----------------   ----------------   ----------------
  MSDOS       59021    (58K)     59021    (58K)          0    (0K)
  HIMEM        3792     (4K)      3792     (4K)          0    (0K)
  EMM386       3120     (3K)      3120     (3K)          0    (0K)
  COMMAND      4992     (5K)      4992     (5K)          0    (0K)
  Free       584368   (571K)    584368   (571K)          0    (0K)

Memory Summary:

  Type of Memory        Total       =       Used          +        Free
  ----------------  -----------------   -----------------   -----------------
  Conventional        655360   (640K)      70992    (69K)     584368   (571K)
  Upper                    0     (0K)          0     (0K)          0     (0K)
  Adapter RAM/ROM     393216   (384K)     393216   (384K)          0     (0K)
  Extended (XMS)     3145728  (3072K)     380928   (372K)    2764800  (2700K)
  ----------------  -----------------   -----------------   -----------------
  Total memory       4194304  (4096K)     845136   (825K)    3349168  (3271K)

  Total under 1 MB    655360   (640K)      70992    (69K)     584368   (571K)

  Largest executable program size         584272   (571K)
  Largest free upper memory block              0     (0K)
  The high memory area is available.
```

The new MEM /C output has two distinct changes. First, the expanded memory lines are gone because we are no longer simulating expanded memory. Second, the available extended memory increased.

Comparing DOS 5.0 and DOS 6—EMM386.EXE RAM Configuration

The EMM386.EXE NOEMS configuration in DOS 5.0 resulted in a largest executable program size of 580,624 bytes. The DOS 6 configuration resulted in a largest executable program size of 584,272 bytes. Therefore, DOS 6 has 3,648 more bytes with which to run programs. This difference is due to the fact that the EMM386.EXE driver is slightly smaller in DOS 6.

Another difference between the DOS 6 and DOS 5.0 configurations is the amount of upper memory. The amount in DOS 5.0 is 95K and the amount in DOS 6 is 155K. Again, this is because DOS 6 provides a more aggressive approach to upper memory. The amount of free upper memory will vary from system to system depending on the hardware you have installed. For example, a network adapter card may use addresses in upper memory for its ROM, decreasing the amount of upper memory available.

Let's look at a graphic that illustrates the increase in upper memory. Figure 5-5 shows the memory configuration for the EMM386.EXE NOEMS switch.

You can see from the figure that the increase in available upper memory is a result of the absence of the EMM page frame. Recall that the EMM page frame is always 64K. Our first two examples (with the page frame) had 91K of upper memory available. Now that the page frame is gone, we have 155K (64K + 91K) of upper memory available.

We still have only 584,272 free bytes of conventional memory because we are not loading any programs or drivers in upper memory yet. Before we do that, however, let's burden the system with an additional device driver and a memory-resident program.

Loading a Device Driver and a TSR in Lower Memory

Let's tax the system a little more to demonstrate how device drivers and terminate-and-stay-resident programs consume more of our precious conventional memory. In a multimedia system, you usually have to load drivers for things such as sound cards, CD-ROMs, and even some video cards. In this example, we'll use the DOS program DOSKEY and the ANSI.SYS driver. Listing 5-16 shows the new configuration files.

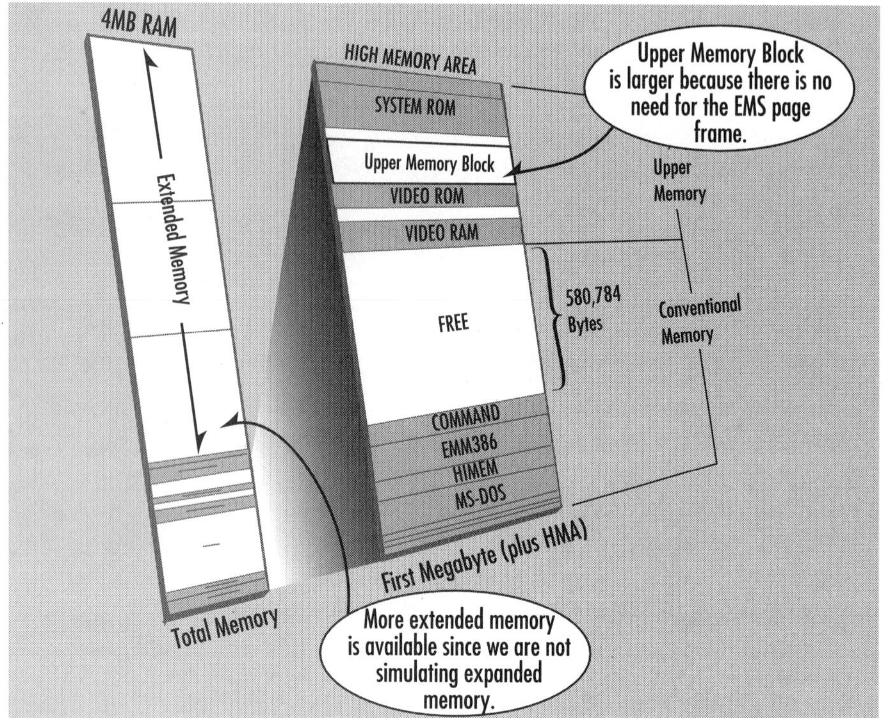

Figure 5-5 Memory configuration—EMM386.EXE loaded with the NOEMS switch

Listing 5-16 AUTOEXEC.BAT and CONFIG.SYS—Loading Drivers and TSRs

```
Contents of AUTOEXEC.BAT
------------------------
@ECHO OFF
CLS
PROMPT $p$g
PATH=A:\DOS;
C:\DOS\DOSKEY

Contents of CONFIG.SYS
------------------------
FILES=21
BUFFERS=15
DEVICE=C:\DOS\HIMEM.SYS
DEVICE=C:\DOS\EMM386.EXE NOEMS
DEVICE=C:\DOS\ANSI.SYS
```

Note that the ANSI driver (ANSI.SYS) and the memory-resident program (DOSKEY) are loaded by the CONFIG.SYS and AUTOEXEC.BAT file respectively. For our purposes, it's not important what these drivers do. We are using them in this case to demonstrate that drivers and memory-resident programs consume memory. You can find information about DOSKEY and ANSI.SYS in your DOS documentation.

To prove that the driver and program are consuming additional conventional memory, let's use the MEM program once again. Listing 5-17 shows the MEM output after these items are loaded.

Listing 5-17 MEM /C—After Loading a Device Driver and TSR

```
Modules using memory below 1 MB:

  Name           Total        =   Conventional    +   Upper Memory
  --------  ----------------   ----------------   ----------------
  MSDOS       59037    (58K)     59037    (58K)          0     (0K)
  HIMEM        3792     (4K)      3792     (4K)          0     (0K)
  EMM386       3120     (3K)      3120     (3K)          0     (0K)
  ANSI         4208     (4K)      4208     (4K)          0     (0K)
  COMMAND      4992     (5K)      4992     (5K)          0     (0K)
  DOSKEY       4144     (4K)      4144     (4K)          0     (0K)
  Free       576016   (563K)    576016   (563K)          0     (0K)

Memory Summary:

  Type of Memory         Total        =       Used         +        Free
  ----------------  -----------------   -----------------   -----------------
  Conventional        655360   (640K)      79344    (77K)     576016   (563K)
  Upper                    0     (0K)          0     (0K)          0     (0K)
  Adapter RAM/ROM     393216   (384K)     393216   (384K)          0     (0K)
  Extended (XMS)     3145728  (3072K)     380928   (372K)    2764800  (2700K)
  ----------------  -----------------   -----------------   -----------------
  Total memory       4194304  (4096K)     853488   (833K)    3340816  (3263K)

  Total under 1 MB    655360   (640K)      79344    (77K)     576016   (563K)

  Largest executable program size         575920   (562K)
  Largest free upper memory block              0     (0K)
  The high memory area is available.
```

Note that our conventional memory list is growing longer as our free conventional memory is shrinking. We are down to 575,920 bytes of conventional memory. Not having enough conventional memory is a common problem for multimedia PC users and PC users in general. Figure 5-6 shows the memory layout with DOSKEY and ANSI in conventional memory.

No DOS 5.0/6 Comparison

We can't accurately compare this configuration to the DOS 5.0 equivalent. We loaded SMARTDRV.SYS and DOSKEY in DOS 5.0. In the DOS 6 example, we loaded ANSI.SYS and DOSKEY. In DOS 6, SMARTDRV.EXE is loaded by a command in the AUTOEXEC.BAT file.

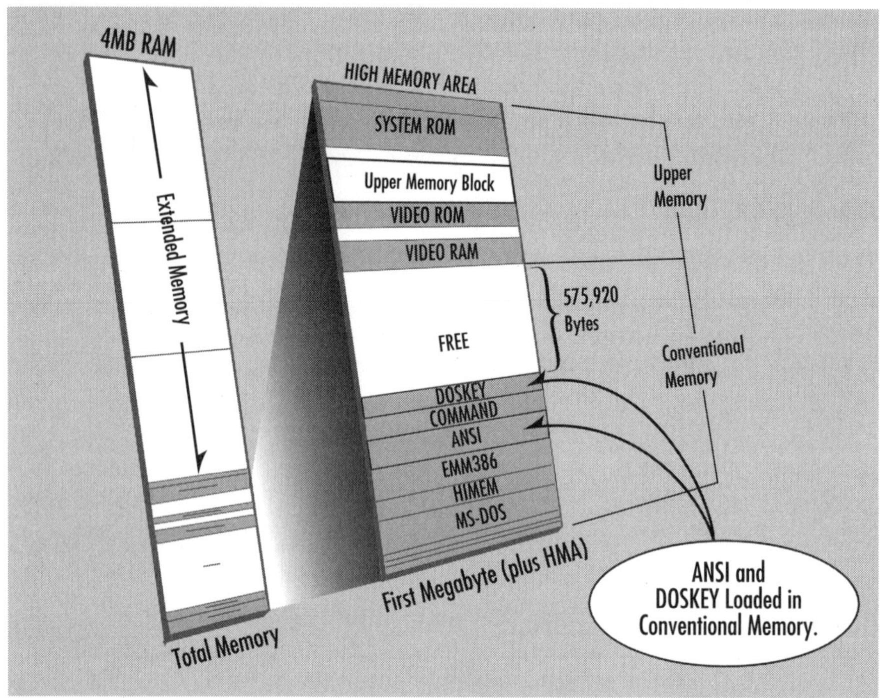

Figure 5-6 Memory configuration—DOSKEY and SMARTDRV.SYS in conventional memory

This figure shows that conventional memory is shrinking as we load more and more programs and drivers. The time has finally come to reverse this trend! Let's start by relocating part of DOS to high memory.

Adding the DOS Command to CONFIG.SYS

DOS 5.0 was the first DOS version to provide a command that relocates a significant amount of the DOS code into the high memory area. The command is also named DOS. Simply adding this command to your CONFIG.SYS file frees up a significant amount of conventional memory. Listing 5-18 shows the CONFIG.SYS file with the DOS command set to HIGH. You can also use DOS=LOW, but because that is the default, it is never necessary.

Listing 5-18 CONFIG.SYS—Adding DOS=HIGH

```
Contents of CONFIG.SYS
-----------------------
FILES=21
BUFFERS=15
```

```
DEVICE=C:\DOS\HIMEM.SYS
DOS=HIGH
DEVICE=C:\DOS\EMM386.EXE NOEMS
DEVICE=C:\DOS\ANSI.SYS
```

Notice that the DOS=HIGH line is placed after the HIMEM.SYS driver in CONFIG.SYS. This is necessary because the HIMEM.SYS driver gives us access to the HMA. It does not, however, have to be the line immediately following HIMEM.SYS. Any location following the extended memory driver is fine.

Now for the moment of truth. Let's check the memory status using MEM. Listing 5-19 shows the MEM output after using the DOS=HIGH command.

Listing 5-19 MEM/C—After DOS=HIGH

```
Modules using memory below 1 MB:

  Name           Total       =   Conventional   +   Upper Memory
  --------  ----------------   ----------------   ----------------
  MSDOS        13901   (14K)      13901   (14K)          0    (0K)
  HIMEM         1168    (1K)       1168    (1K)          0    (0K)
  EMM386        3120    (3K)       3120    (3K)          0    (0K)
  ANSI          4208    (4K)       4208    (4K)          0    (0K)
  COMMAND       2912    (3K)       2912    (3K)          0    (0K)
  DOSKEY        4144    (4K)       4144    (4K)          0    (0K)
  Free        625856  (611K)     625856  (611K)          0    (0K)

Memory Summary:

  Type of Memory         Total       =       Used        +       Free
  ----------------  -----------------   -----------------   -----------------
  Conventional        655360   (640K)      29504    (29K)     625856   (611K)
  Upper                    0     (0K)          0     (0K)          0     (0K)
  Adapter RAM/ROM     393216   (384K)     393216   (384K)          0     (0K)
  Extended (XMS)     3145728  (3072K)     380928   (372K)    2764800  (2700K)
  ----------------  -----------------   -----------------   -----------------
  Total memory       4194304  (4096K)     803648   (785K)    3390656  (3311K)

  Total under 1 MB    655360   (640K)      29504    (29K)     625856   (611K)

  Largest executable program size         625760   (611K)
  Largest free upper memory block              0     (0K)
  MS-DOS is resident in the high memory area.
```

This MEM output shows a great gain in conventional memory, all due to one line in the CONFIG.SYS file. Notice that three programs have been reduced in size significantly. They are MSDOS, HIMEM, and COMMAND. This resulted in approximately 48K of DOS being moved into the HMA. Also note that the summary at the bottom of the MEM output indicates that DOS has been moved to the HMA. Figure 5-7 shows the results.

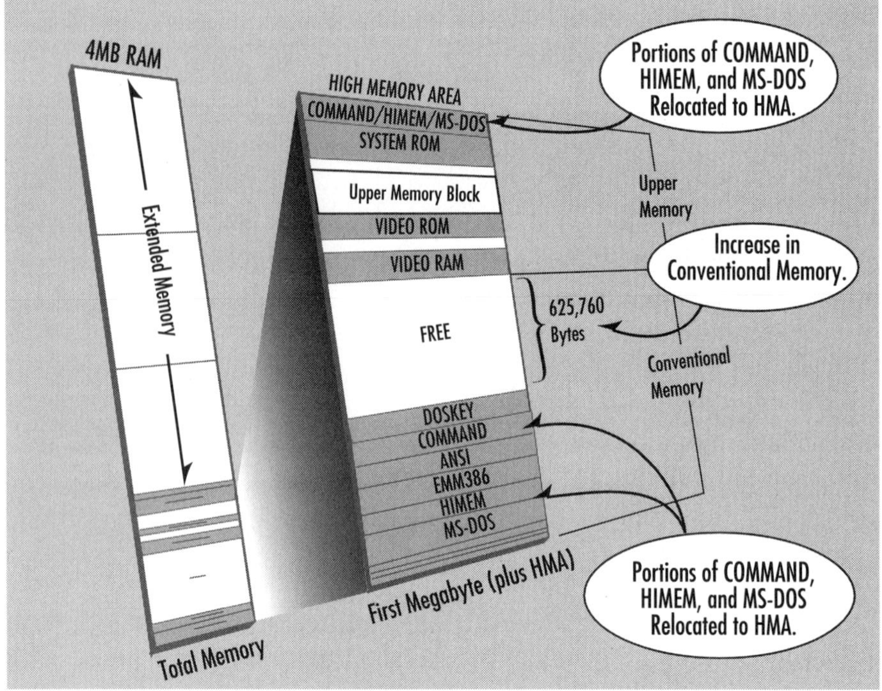

Figure 5-7 Memory configuration—DOS loaded in the HMA

Notice that the MS-DOS, HIMEM, and COMMAND programs were reduced in size in conventional memory. They now reside in the HMA providing us with more conventional memory for our memory hungry programs. Now let's get greedy and squeeze out even more conventional memory.

Loading Programs and Device Drivers in Upper Memory

Recall that we loaded HIMEM.SYS to provide an extended memory manager and also to gain access to the HMA. Then we loaded EMM386 (using the RAM or NOEMS switch) to gain access to the upper memory block. We also loaded a device driver (ANSI.SYS) and a memory-resident program (DOSKEY) into conventional memory. Now let's move the driver and program into upper memory.

In order to gain complete access to upper memory, we must add a line to the CONFIG.SYS file. This line is DOS=UMB. After this line is executed, we can load device drivers into upper memory using DEVICEHIGH= instead of DEVICE=. We can also load memory-resident programs into high memory using LOADHIGH in the AUTOEXEC.BAT file. Let's look at the CONFIG.SYS and AUTOEXEC.BAT files which perform this action. Listing 5-20 shows these configuration files.

Listing 5-20 Loading Device Drivers and Memory-Resident Programs High

```
Contents of CONFIG.SYS
------------------------
FILES=21
BUFFERS=15
DEVICE=C:\DOS\HIMEM.SYS
DEVICE=C:\DOS\EMM386.EXE NOEMS
DOS=HIGH, UMB
DEVICEHIGH=C:\DOS\ANSI.SYS

Contents of AUTOEXEC.BAT
------------------------
@ECHO OFF
CLS
PROMPT $p$g
PATH=C:\DOS;
LOADHIGH C:\DOS\DOSKEY
```

The first step in loading drivers and programs high is in the CONFIG.SYS file. This is done by using the line: DOS=HIGH, UMB. In this case, we are combining DOS=HIGH and DOS=UMB into one line. This is perfectly legal. However, if you use UMB, you must place it after the line that loads the EMM386.EXE driver. This is because the expanded memory driver is required to access the upper memory blocks.

To load the device driver high, we use DEVICEHIGH (in CONFIG.SYS), instead of the usual DEVICE command. To load the memory-resident program high, we place LOADHIGH (in AUTOEXEC.BAT) on the line preceding the program name, in this case it's DOSKEY.

A Shortcut for LOADHIGH

You can use LH in place of LOADHIGH in your AUTOEXEC.BAT file. You cannot, however, abbreviate DEVICEHIGH in CONFIG.SYS.

Let's look at the MEM /D output to check two things. First, we'll see another gain in conventional memory. Second, we can check to see if the driver and program are actually loaded high. Listing 5-21 shows the MEM /D output.

Listing 5-21 MEM /D—Loading SMARTDRV.SYS and DOSKEY High

```
Conventional Memory Detail:

  Segment          Total          Name         Type
  -------     ----------------  -----------  --------
   00000           1039    (1K)                Interrupt Vector
```

continued on next page

continued from previous page

```
  00040             271     (0K)                 ROM Communication Area
  00050             527     (1K)                 DOS Communication Area
  00070            2752     (3K)   IO            System Data
                                      CON        System Device Driver
                                      AUX        System Device Driver
                                      PRN        System Device Driver
                                      CLOCK$     System Device Driver
                                      A: - D:    System Device Driver
                                      COM1       System Device Driver
                                      LPT1       System Device Driver
                                      LPT2       System Device Driver
                                      LPT3       System Device Driver
                                      COM2       System Device Driver
                                      COM3       System Device Driver
                                      COM4       System Device Driver
  0011C            5104     (5K)   MSDOS         System Data
  0025B            8416     (8K)   IO            System Data
                   1152     (1K)      XMSXXXX0   Installed Device=HIMEM
                   3104     (3K)      EMMQXXX0   Installed Device=EMM386
                    960     (1K)                 FILES=21
                    256     (0K)                 FCBS=4
                    512     (1K)                 BUFFERS=15
                    448     (0K)                 LASTDRIVE=E
                   1856     (2K)                 STACKS=9,128
  00469              80     (0K)   MSDOS         System Program
  0046E            2640     (3K)   COMMAND       Program
  00513              80     (0K)   MSDOS         -- Free --
  00518             272     (0K)   COMMAND       Environment
  00529              96     (0K)   MEM           Environment
  0052F           88608    (87K)   MEM           Program
  01AD1          545504   (533K)   MSDOS         -- Free --

Upper Memory Detail:

  Segment  Region       Total          Name         Type
  -------  ------  ----------------  -----------  --------
  0C93A       1       4224     (4K)  IO           System Data
                      4192     (4K)    CON        Installed Device=ANSI
  0CA42       1         96     (0K)  MSDOS        -- Free --
  0CA48       1       4144     (4K)  DOSKEY       Program
  0CB4B       1     150352   (147K)  MSDOS        -- Free --

Memory Summary:

  Type of Memory       Total        =      Used        +      Free
  ----------------  ----------------   ----------------   ----------------
  Conventional      655360   (640K)     21168    (21K)    634192   (619K)
  Upper             158832   (155K)      8384     (8K)    150448   (147K)
  Adapter RAM/ROM   393216   (384K)    393216   (384K)         0     (0K)
  Extended (XMS)   2986896  (2917K)    222096   (217K)   2764800  (2700K)
  ----------------  ----------------   ----------------   ----------------
  Total memory     4194304  (4096K)    644864   (630K)   3549440  (3466K)
```

```
Total under 1 MB    814192   (795K)      29552    (29K)     784640   (766K)

Memory accessible using Int 15h              0     (0K)
Largest executable program size         634096   (619K)
Largest free upper memory block         150352   (147K)
MS-DOS is resident in the high memory area.

XMS version  3.00; driver version  3.09
```

As you can see in the MEM output, we now have even more conventional memory available. We've increased this amount by 8,336 bytes (around 8K) by loading ANSI.SYS and DOSKEY in upper memory.

The MEM /D output also provides verification that the program and driver were actually loaded into upper memory. We can determine this by checking the starting address. For example, ANSI's starting address is 0C93A0h. Recall that the starting address for upper memory in this example is C8000. Any value below this address is in conventional memory. Any value above this address is in upper memory.

Let's look at an illustration that shows the results of this example. Figure 5-8 shows the results of the usage of LOADHIGH and DEVICEHIGH. Table 5-3 shows a summary of the DEVICEHIGH and LOADHIGH commands.

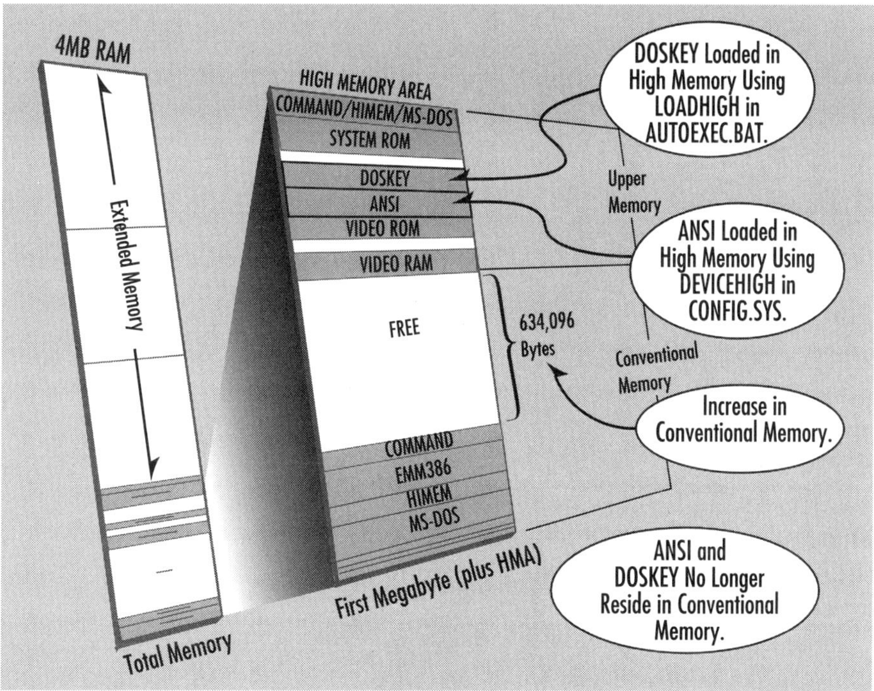

Figure 5-8 Memory configuration—after LOADHIGH and DEVICEHIGH

Command	Used In	Used to Load	Example Usage
DEVICEHIGH	CONFIG.SYS	Device drivers	DEVICEHIGH=C:\CDROM\DRIVER.SYS
LOADHIGH	AUTOEXEC.BAT	TSR programs	LOADHIGH C:\MOUSE\MOUSE

Table 5-3 DEVICEHIGH and LOADHIGH summary

You can see in Figure 5-8 that relocating DOSKEY (with LOADHIGH) and SMARTDRV (with DEVICEHIGH) to upper memory has removed them from conventional memory. This resulted in an increase of more than 17K of free conventional memory.

Loading Multimedia Drivers HIGH

You can use LOADHIGH and DEVICEHIGH to relocate the multimedia drivers (sound, CD-ROM, video, and so on) on your system as well. However, you may run into some drivers that do not behave properly when loaded high. If this occurs, try rearranging the order of lines in your CONFIG.SYS and AUTOEXEC.BAT files to find a solution that works. As a last resort, you can always load the offending driver in low (conventional memory). As always, make a backup of your configuration files before trying something new.

Using MemMaker

DOS 6 provides a new utility to help you tailor your configuration files automatically. MemMaker analyzes your AUTOEXEC.BAT and CONFIG.SYS files and makes adjustments if necessary. MemMaker gets some information from you at the start of the program. Figure 5-9 shows an overview of the process that MemMaker follows.

Welcome Screen and Setup Option

To start the utility, type **MemMaker** and press ENTER. The first screen MemMaker displays is a welcome screen. This screen provides information such as how to make selections (SPACEBAR), abort the program (F3), get help (F1), or continue (ENTER).

Upon pressing ENTER at the welcome screen, MemMaker asks you if you want express or custom setup. The default is the express setup, so let's follow that path first.

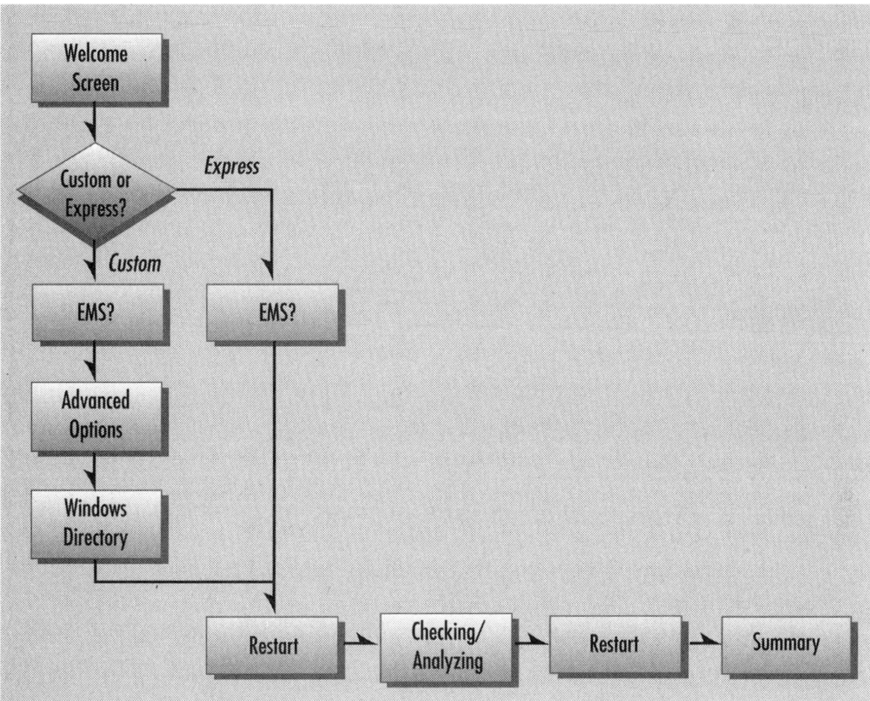

Figure 5-9 MemMaker process

MemMaker Express Setup

Let's take a look at the screens you will encounter upon selecting express setup. After following this scenario to its conclusion, we'll examine the custom setup.

Do You Want EMS?

MemMaker asks you if you will be using programs that require expanded memory. If you know you have programs that require expanded memory, answer YES. If you know you will not require expanded memory, or if you are making a custom configuration to store for later use, select NO. Pressing ENTER takes us to the next screen.

First Restart Notification

MemMaker notifies you that it will restart your system. Press ENTER to restart your computer. If your computer does not restart automatically, try your reset button. If you do not have a reset button, or your button fails, turn your computer off, wait ten seconds and turn it on again. At this point, you may need to bypass the faulty configuration files by pressing F5 during the boot process.

First Restart

MemMaker uses the first restart of your computer to check and analyze the possible combinations of CONFIG.SYS and AUTOEXEC.BAT entries. After a few moments, you are prompted to restart your computer again. Press ENTER to restart your computer a second time.

Second Restart

MemMaker uses the second restart to see if the changes to AUTOEXEC.BAT and CONFIG.SYS are successful. If your computer does not restart, manually reset or turn your computer off for ten seconds and try again.

What If MemMaker Locks Me Up?

If MemMaker locks your system up during a restart, it will prompt you (on the next restart) if you want to try more conservative settings. If you answer YES, MemMaker will attempt to configure your system again, just not as aggressively. You can also (using the SPACEBAR) to cycle between two options) return to the last configuration or try the current configuration again.

If you continue to lock up, try pressing F5 as you power up. Pressing the F5 key will tell DOS to bypass the AUTOEXEC.BAT and CONFIG.SYS files. This will allow you to manually edit the files and correct the problem or go back to your backup files. One method is to remove one line at a time and restart to see if it has a positive effect.

Is Your System Working Properly?

If the computer restarts properly, MemMaker will ask if the system is working properly. If the system were not working properly, you probably wouldn't be able to see the question!

MemMaker Summary

After MemMaker completes its job, it displays a summary that includes before and after memory amounts for conventional, upper, and expanded memory. Upper memory is further divided into: memory used by programs, memory reserved for Windows, memory reserved for EMS, and free upper memory. This screen allows you to see the effects of MemMaker's changes to your system. You can press ESC at this screen to undo the changes and return to the previous configuration.

MemMaker also notifies you that it saved your previous configuration files with UMB extensions. This includes CONFIG.UMB, AUTOEXEC.UMB, and SYSTEM.UMB (if MemMaker modified your Windows file SYSTEM.INI). We'll discuss changes to SYSTEM.INI in the next chapter. Pressing (ENTER) returns us to the DOS prompt.

This completes the express setup using MemMaker. Let's examine the differences in the custom setup.

MemMaker Custom Setup

You can use the custom setup option of MemMaker to further tailor your memory configuration. Custom setup in MemMaker also starts with the expanded memory question. If you are using programs that require expanded memory, answer YES. If you are not going to require expanded memory, or you are creating a custom configuration to store, answer NO. After pressing (ENTER), the advanced options screen appears.

Advanced Options

This is the heart of a custom MemMaker setup. The Advanced Options screen has six YES/NO questions. Answer YES or NO based on your system and your needs. Let's look at them one at a time.

- Specify which drivers and TSRs to include in the optimization?

  Answer NO if no drivers or TSRs caused problems in earlier configurations. Answer YES if a driver or TSR caused a problem (such as a lockup) in an earlier configuration. If you answer YES, you will be prompted later for which driver(s) and/or TSR(s) to include in the optimization.

- Scan the upper memory area aggressively?

  Answer YES if you have not had a problem with this option in earlier configurations. Answer NO if you experienced a problem with this option in a previous configuration. This option causes MemMaker to scan the F000h through F7FFh segments of upper memory, which causes problems on some computers.

- Optimize upper memory for use with Windows?

  Answer YES if you run MS-DOS programs from Windows. Answer NO if you do not have Windows, or if you run only Windows applications from Windows. Answering NO creates more conventional memory when you are not using Windows.

- Use monochrome region (B000h-BFFFh) for running programs?

  Answer YES if you have an EGA or VGA adapter. Answer NO if you have a Super VGA or a monochrome adapter. The B000h to BFFFh addresses are not used with EGA or VGA video adapters; therefore, you can use this address range for upper memory addresses.

- Keep current EMM386 memory exclusions and inclusions?

  Answer YES if you are using the /I= or /X= switches with EMM386.EXE, and you want to save them. Answer NO if you are not using the switches, or if you do not want to save the exclusions/inclusions.

- Move Extended BIOS Data Area from conventional to upper memory?

  Answer YES if you have not had a problem with this option in earlier configurations. Answer NO if you experienced a problem with this option in a previous configuration. This option causes MemMaker to move extended BIOS data into upper memory, which causes problems on some systems.

After answering the advanced option questions, press ENTER to move on to the next screen.

Providing a Path to Windows

The next screen attempts to locate Microsoft Windows on your hard disk. If it finds a copy, it asks you to verify the path. This is useful if you have installed Windows to two locations on your hard disk. If the path is incorrect, type in the correct path.

After entering the correct path to Windows, press ENTER to proceed. You will not see this screen if you do not have Microsoft Windows installed.

Including/Excluding TSRs or Drivers

If you answered YES to the first advanced option, you are prompted at this point to decide which drivers and TSRs should be included in the memory optimization. Use the SPACEBAR to choose YES or NO for each driver and TSR. The device drivers and TSRs displayed are read from your current CONFIG.SYS and AUTOEXEC.BAT.

Two Restarts and Back In Business!

At this point, we go through the same two restarts that we did in the express setup. The first restart examines the combinations (if any) of configuration files.

The second restart tests your configuration. If your system does not restart properly, try the reset switch, or power off your system for ten seconds and try again. Remember, pressing F5 during the boot process will bypass CONFIG.SYS and AUTOEXEC.BAT.

If your custom setup is successful, you will see a summary that indicates the before and after memory amounts for conventional, upper, and expanded memory.

A MemMaker Example

Let's take a configuration—where DOSKEY and ANSI.SYS were loaded in conventional memory—and run the MemMaker express setup. Listing 5-22 shows the AUTOEXEC.BAT and CONFIG.SYS files before running MemMaker.

Listing 5-22 AUTOEXEC.BAT and CONFIG.SYS—Before MemMaker

```
Contents of AUTOEXEC.BAT
------------------------
&ECHO OFF
CLS
PROMPT $p$g
PATH C:\DOS
C:\DOS\DOSKEY

Contents of CONFIG.SYS
----------------------
FILES=21
BUFFERS=15
DEVICE=C:\DOS\HIMEM.SYS
DEVICE=C:\DOS\EMM386.EXE NOEMS
DEVICE=C:\DOS\ANSI.SYS
```

Now let's run MemMaker (express setup) and see the results. Listing 5-23 shows the same configuration files *after* MemMaker is finished.

Listing 5-23 AUTOEXEC.BAT and CONFIG.SYS—After MemMaker

```
Contents of AUTOEXEC.BAT
------------------------
@ECHO OFF
CLS
PROMPT $p$g
PATH C:\DOS
LH /L:1,6400 C:\DOS\DOSKEY
```

continued on next page

continued from previous page

```
Contents of CONFIG.SYS
----------------------
DEVICE=C:\DOS\HIMEM.SYS
DEVICE=C:\DOS\EMM386.EXE NOEMS
BUFFERS=15,0
FILES=21
DOS=UMB
LASTDRIVE=D
FCBS=4,0
DEVICEHIGH /L:1,9072 =C:\DOS\ANSI.SYS
```

Note that MemMaker has added and modified entries to the configuration files. It is using the advanced /L: switch on LOADHIGH (LH) and DEVICEHIGH. This attempts to locate the driver in a particular location in upper memory. MemMaker has more knowledge about the structure of upper memory than we do.

MemMaker also added an option to BUFFERS (no secondary cache), although this is the same as the default. It also added lines for upper memory block access (DOS=UMB), the LASTDRIVE command (one past the last logical drive), and file control blocks (FCBS). Four is the default number of file control blocks even if you do not specify it in CONFIG.SYS.

You can see that MemMaker can do most of the work for you when it comes to managing memory in DOS 6. However, it still helps to know the details about memory, especially if MemMaker has a problem.

Now that we have covered the DOS 6 memory configuration topics, let's look at a few more features that can improve the performance of your system.

Creating a RAM Disk with the RAMDRIVE.SYS Driver

You can create a simulated disk drive in RAM by using the RAMDRIVE.SYS device driver. This driver is supplied with DOS 6. A RAM disk is useful for storing temporary data that you will use only during the current time your computer is turned on. As soon as you turn your computer off, the RAM disk is gone.

Many programs use temporary files. If your programs allow you to specify where the temporary files are stored, you can direct them to the RAM disk. A RAM disk is much faster than a hard disk. Typical RAM access times are normally measured in microseconds, or millionths of a second. Typical hard disk access times are normally measured in milliseconds, or thousandths of a second.

There is a downside when creating a RAM disk, however. It takes up memory. You can install an MS-DOS RAM disk in conventional, extended, or expanded memory. Because our goal in memory management is to free up as much conventional memory as possible, we don't want to put our RAM disk there. Let's look at an example of creating a RAM disk in extended memory.

Creating an Extended Memory RAM Disk

In order to create a RAM disk, we must install the RAMDRIVE.SYS device driver in the CONFIG.SYS file. This requires the DEVICE or DEVICEHIGH command, the path to the driver, the driver name, and some options. Listing 5-24 shows an example CONFIG.SYS file loading the RAMDRIVE.SYS into upper memory, and the RAM disk itself into extended memory.

Listing 5-24 CONFIG.SYS—Creating a RAM Disk in Extended Memory

```
FILES=21
BUFFERS=15
DEVICE=C:\DOS\HIMEM.SYS
DEVICE=C:\DOS\EMM386.EXE NOEMS
DOS=HIGH, UMB
DEVICEHIGH=C:\DOS\RAMDRIVE.SYS 512 /e
```

Notice that we're loading the RAMDRIVE.SYS driver into upper memory using DEVICEHIGH. This requires that both HIMEM.SYS and EMM386.EXE (with either the RAM or NOEMS switch) are loaded. In order to place the RAMDISK in extended memory, we need at least the HIMEM.SYS driver. These lines must be before the RAMDRIVE line.

Now let's look at the RAMDRIVE line in Listing 5-24. We must specify the entire path because the AUTOEXEC.BAT file has not executed yet. Following the driver name is the size we want for a RAM disk, in kilobytes. In this case, we are using 512 so we will create a 512K RAM disk. The last portion of the line, /e, tells DOS to place the RAM disk in extended memory.

The drive letter will be one letter past the existing drives. For example, if your last disk drive is C:, the RAM disk will be D:. Here is a typical output during the boot process:

```
Microsoft RAMDrive version 3.07 virtual disk D:
    Disk size: 512K
    Sector size: 512 bytes
    Allocation unit: 1 sectors
    Directory entries: 64
```

Notice that the RAM drive is labeled drive D:. The second line indicates that the disk size is indeed 512K. The remaining lines indicate the sector size, allocation unit, and directory entries. You usually don't have to worry about these values. You can modify them with additional options in the CONFIG.SYS file, but this is almost never necessary. Consult your DOS manual about additional options for RAMDRIVE.SYS.

Now let's look at the MEM output for this CONFIG.SYS file. In this example, we don't load any programs in the AUTOEXEC.BAT file. Listing 5-25 shows the MEM /C output after installing the RAM disk.

Listing 5-25 MEM /C—512K RAM Drive Installed (Extended)

```
Modules using memory below 1 MB:

  Name           Total        =    Conventional     +    Upper Memory
  --------  ----------------     ----------------     ----------------
  MSDOS        13885   (14K)       13885   (14K)            0     (0K)
  HIMEM         1168    (1K)        1168    (1K)            0     (0K)
  EMM386        3120    (3K)        3120    (3K)            0     (0K)
  COMMAND       2912    (3K)        2912    (3K)            0     (0K)
  RAMDRIVE      1232    (1K)           0    (0K)         1232     (1K)
  Free        791792  (773K)      634192  (619K)       157600   (154K)

Memory Summary:

  Type of Memory         Total        =        Used          +        Free
  ----------------  -----------------    -----------------    -----------------
  Conventional        655360   (640K)       21168    (21K)      634192   (619K)
  Upper               158832   (155K)        1232     (1K)      157600   (154K)
  Adapter RAM/ROM     393216   (384K)      393216   (384K)           0     (0K)
  Extended (XMS)     2986896  (2917K)      746384   (729K)     2240512  (2188K)
  ----------------  -----------------    -----------------    -----------------
  Total memory       4194304  (4096K)     1162000  (1135K)     3032304  (2961K)

  Total under 1 MB    814192   (795K)       22400    (22K)      791792   (773K)

  Largest executable program size          634096   (619K)
  Largest free upper memory block          157600   (154K)
  MS-DOS is resident in the high memory area.
```

Notice that we have not affected conventional memory in any way. The RAMDRIVE.SYS device driver is located in upper memory. We can see the effect of the RAM disk on extended memory by looking at the bytes available for XMS memory. This has dropped to accommodate the RAM disk.

Now we have a RAM disk, named drive D:. We can direct our programs that store temporary data to this drive. Just remember, if you turn off your computer, drive D: vanishes. Only use a RAM disk for temporary data.

That example created the RAM disk in extended memory. Let's create the same drive in expanded memory.

Creating an Expanded Memory RAM Disk

Creating a RAM disk in expanded memory is nearly the same as creating the extended memory version. However, we first must ensure that the correct amount of expanded memory is available. We take care of that when we load

EMM386.EXE in the CONFIG.SYS file. Listing 5-26 shows the CONFIG.SYS file for this example.

Listing 5-26 CONFIG.SYS—Creating a RAM Disk in Expanded Memory

```
FILES=21
BUFFERS=15
DEVICE=C:\DOS\HIMEM.SYS
DEVICE=C:\DOS\EMM386.EXE 512 RAM
DOS=HIGH, UMB
DEVICEHIGH=C:\DOS\RAMDRIVE.SYS 512 /a
```

Notice the differences between this and the expanded memory driver. First, we add the number 512 to the EMM386.EXE line. This creates 512K of expanded memory, which we'll need to place the RAM disk. We're also using the RAM switch; this simulates expanded memory and provides access to the upper memory blocks, where we'll store RAMDRIVE.SYS.

The other change is replacing the /e switch with /a on the RAMDRIVE.SYS line. The /a switch tells DOS to create the RAM disk in expanded memory. When we reboot to install the RAM disk, DOS displays the following message:

```
Microsoft RAMDrive version 3.07 virtual disk D:
    Disk size: 512K
    Sector size: 512 bytes
    Allocation unit: 1 sectors
    Directory entries: 64
```

This is no different from the extended memory RAM disk example. The new drive is still labeled D: and the size is 512K. There is no indication from RAMDRIVE of where the RAM disk is located in memory.

Now let's look at the MEM output for this CONFIG.SYS file. Once again, we are not loading any programs in the AUTOEXEC.BAT file. Listing 5-27 shows the MEM /C output after installing the RAM disk in expanded memory.

Listing 5-27 MEM /C—512K RAM Drive Installed (Expanded)

```
Modules using memory below 1 MB:

  Name           Total       =   Conventional    +   Upper Memory
  --------  ----------------   ----------------    ----------------
  MSDOS       13885    (14K)      13885    (14K)          0     (0K)
  HIMEM        1168     (1K)       1168     (1K)          0     (0K)
  EMM386       3120     (3K)       3120     (3K)          0     (0K)
  COMMAND      2912     (3K)       2912     (3K)          0     (0K)
  RAMDRIVE     1280     (1K)          0     (0K)       1280     (1K)
  Free       726208   (709K)     634192   (619K)      92016    (90K)
```

continued on next page

continued from previous page

```
Memory Summary:

  Type of Memory         Total       =       Used        +       Free
  ----------------  -----------------  -----------------  -----------------
  Conventional        655360   (640K)     21168    (21K)    634192   (619K)
  Upper                93296    (91K)      1280     (1K)     92016    (90K)
  Adapter RAM/ROM     393216   (384K)    393216   (384K)         0     (0K)
  Extended (XMS)*    3052432  (2981K)    762768   (745K)   2289664  (2236K)
  ----------------  -----------------  -----------------  -----------------
  Total memory       4194304  (4096K)   1178432  (1151K)   3015872  (2945K)

  Total under 1 MB    748656   (731K)     22448    (22K)    726208   (709K)

  Total Expanded (EMS)                   917504   (896K)
  Free Expanded (EMS)*                        0     (0K)

  * EMM386 is using XMS memory to simulate EMS memory as needed.
    Free EMS memory may change as free XMS memory changes.

  Largest executable program size        634096   (619K)
  Largest free upper memory block         92016    (90K)
  MS-DOS is resident in the high memory area.
```

Once again, notice that we have not affected conventional memory in any way. The RAMDRIVE.SYS device driver is located in upper memory. We can see the effect of the RAM disk on extended memory in two places. First, there are 917,504 bytes of total EMS (expanded) memory. This is 896K of expanded memory; 512K that we requested and 384K to backfill upper memory. This drops immediately to 0 because we are using upper memory and the 512K for the RAM disk. Also, the XMS (extended) memory has dropped to accommodate the EMS memory, and ultimately the RAM disk.

You may be wondering: Why go through all the trouble of creating expanded memory for the RAM disk when you can simply place it in extended memory? The answer is: Always place your RAM disk in extended memory if you have it. If you have an expanded memory board (and no extended memory available), however, you must use the /a switch to place your RAM disk there.

Disk Caching with the SMARTDRV.EXE Driver

The SMARTDRV.EXE driver (also supplied with DOS 6 and Windows 3.1) creates a disk *cache* (pronounced cash). A disk cache is useful for programs that repeatedly request the same information from disk. The majority of programs do this to some degree.

The SMARTDrive disk cache keeps track of when the disk is read and what data is being read into memory. The cache keeps data in memory if it is being requested frequently. This way, the next time a program tries to read the data off disk, the disk cache intercepts the read and provides the data directly from memory. As we mentioned in the discussion of RAMDRIVE.SYS, memory access is much faster than disk access.

The overall performance increase depends on the size of the disk cache and how often similar data is requested. In other words, if your programs never request the same data twice (or more times), a disk cache is of no use.

A Note to Windows 3.1 Users

If you are running DOS 6 and Windows 3.1, you will want to use the SMARTDRV.EXE driver supplied with DOS 6. Always check the versions of HIMEM.SYS, EMM386.EXE, RAMDRIVE.SYS, and SMARTDRV.SYS/.EXE to see if you are loading the newest driver in your configuration files. To do this, check the date of the drivers in your \DOS and \WINDOWS directories.

SMARTDRV.SYS is loaded in your CONFIG.SYS file and SMARTDRV.EXE is loaded in your AUTOEXEC.BAT file. Refer to Chapter 4, *DOS 5.0 Memory Management,* for the DOS 5.0 version of SMARTDRV.SYS. Refer to Chapter 6, *Windows Memory Management,* for the Windows 3.1 version of SMARTDRV.EXE.

As with a RAM disk, you can create a SMARTDrive disk cache in either extended or expanded memory. Unlike the RAM disk, you cannot create a disk cache in conventional memory (you wouldn't want to anyway). Let's look at creating a disk cache using SMARTDRV.EXE.

Creating a SMARTDrive Disk Cache

In order to create a disk cache using SMARTDRV.EXE, we must load its driver in the AUTOEXEC.BAT file. This consists of the path and filename of the driver. Listing 5-28 shows the CONFIG.SYS file for our example extended memory disk cache.

Listing 5-28 AUTOEXEC.BAT—SMARTDrive Disk Cache

```
LOADHIGH C:\DOS\SMARTDRV.EXE
PROMPT $p$g
PATH C:\DOS
```

In this example, we use the LOADHIGH command. This loads the SMARTDRV.EXE device driver into upper memory. We also install HIMEM.SYS

Extended Memory	Initial Cache Size	Windows Cache Size
To 1MB	All extended memory	0
To 2MB	1MB	256K
To 4MB	1MB	512K
To 6MB	2MB	1MB
Over 6MB	2MB	2MB

Table 5-4 SMARTDrive initial cache and Windows cache defaults

and EMM386.EXE (with the NOEMS switch) in our CONFIG.SYS file to gain access to upper memory.

We use two command line parameters with SMARTDRV.SYS in DOS 5.0. The first sets the maximum size of the cache; the second parameter sets the minimum size of the cache. Using SMARTDRV.EXE we can still use these parameters. However, the first parameter is labeled *initial cache size;* the second parameter is known as the *Windows cache size.* This is the value to which SMARTDRV will shrink if you run Microsoft Windows.

If you omit the parameters (as we did in Listing 5-25), you will get the default initial and Windows cache sizes. These values depend on the amount of extended memory installed in your system. Table 5-4 shows the default SMARTDrive cache sizes for different amounts of extended memory.

When you use this table, keep in mind that the memory amounts are for extended memory only. For example, if you have a 2-megabyte system, you have 1 megabyte of extended memory; therefore, you would fall into the first category.

Unlike SMARTDRV.SYS, SMARTDRV.EXE is always loaded into extended memory. There is no support for loading SMARTDRV.EXE into expanded memory.

After adding this line to our CONFIG.SYS file, let's reboot and look at the results of loading SMARTDrive. We are not loading any other programs in the AUTOEXEC.BAT file for this example. SMARTDrive does not display any power up messages as SMARTDRV.SYS did in DOS 5.0.

After rebooting, you can type SMARTDRV and press ENTER to see the current status of your disk cache. For example, our 4-megabyte machine gives the output shown in Listing 5-29.

Listing 5-29 SMARTDrive Startup Message

```
Microsoft SMARTDrive Disk Cache version 4.1
Copyright 1991,1993 Microsoft Corp.

Cache size:  1,048,576 bytes
Cache size when running Windows:   524,288

            Disk Caching Status:
drive   read cache   write cache   buffering
--------------------------------------------
  A:       yes           no            no
  B:       yes           no            no
  C:       yes           yes           no
```

After the copyright message, SMARTDrive displays two lines. The first line is the initial cache size. The second line is the Windows cache size. Because we are using a 4-megabyte system, we have 3 megabytes of extended memory. Referring back to Table 5-4, this would fall into the "to 4MB" category. This results in a 1MB initial cache size and a 512K Windows cache size.

Caution When Using Write Cache

SMARTDrive enables write caching on any hard drives installed in your system. This means that at any given time, data that is supposed to be written to disk is still in memory. If you press CTRL-ALT-DEL to reboot your computer, you will receive the message "Waiting for system shutdown" in the upper left corner of the display. SMARTDrive intercepts the CTRL-ALT-DEL combination to give your system time to write any unwritten data to disk.

If you shut off your PC using the power switch, you run the risk of losing data or damaging files. If your system is idle at the DOS prompt, and no disk activity is present, it is safe to turn off your PC.

After the cache sizes, SMARTDrive displays the disk caching status for all drives in your system. Hard disks are usually read and write cached. This means that SMARTDrive can hold both read and write data for this drive. Floppy drives (such as A: and B: in our example) are normally only read cached. If you write data to a floppy disk, it will occur immediately.

The buffering entry is only for disk drives that are not compatible with SMARTDRV.EXE. Consult your MS-DOS documentation to see if your drive is affected. Most drives do not need to use buffering.

To see the full effect of SMARTDrive on our 4-megabyte test system, let's use the MEM command to view the status of memory. Listing 5-30 shows the MEM /C output for our extended memory disk cache.

Listing 5-30 MEM /C—SMARTDrive Disk Cache

```
Modules using memory below 1 MB:

  Name           Total       =   Conventional    +   Upper Memory
  --------  ----------------   ----------------   ----------------
  MSDOS      13885    (14K)      13885    (14K)          0    (0K)
  HIMEM       1168     (1K)       1168     (1K)          0    (0K)
  EMM386      3120     (3K)       3120     (3K)          0    (0K)
  COMMAND     2912     (3K)       2912     (3K)          0    (0K)
  SMARTDRV   27280    (27K)          0     (0K)      27280   (27K)
  Free      765728   (748K)     634192   (619K)     131536  (128K)

Memory Summary:

  Type of Memory       Total       =       Used          +       Free
  ----------------  ----------------   ----------------   ----------------
  Conventional        655360   (640K)      21168    (21K)     634192   (619K)
  Upper               158816   (155K)      27280    (27K)     131536   (128K)
  Adapter RAM/ROM     393216   (384K)     393216   (384K)          0     (0K)
  Extended (XMS)     2986912  (2917K)    1270688  (1241K)    1716224  (1676K)
  ----------------  ----------------   ----------------   ----------------
  Total memory       4194304  (4096K)    1712352  (1672K)    2481952  (2424K)

  Total under 1 MB    814176   (795K)      48448    (47K)     765728   (748K)

  Largest executable program size         634096   (619K)
  Largest free upper memory block         131440   (128K)
  MS-DOS is resident in the high memory area.
```

We're using the LOADHIGH command to create our disk cache and not affect conventional memory in any way.

The largest change in the MEM output is the effect the SMARTDrive disk cache has on extended memory. In this case, it has dropped to 1,716,224 bytes (1676K). Of course, this amount could increase back up to 2,188K (512K + 1,676K) when running Microsoft Windows because we specified a Windows cache size of 512K.

In general, it's a good idea to use SMARTDrive. As a last resort, when you need the extended memory for other programs, you can remove its line in AUTOEXEC.BAT. We'll look at the SMARTDrive program again in the next chapter when we discuss memory management in Windows.

Solving Memory Problems in DOS 6

The introduction of DOS 6 eased some users' memory configuration problems; however, there are still situations that present configuration difficulty. For example, even though DOS 6 usually finds more available upper memory, you still have to configure your system properly to use it. Also, upper memory still has its limit; you can easily run out of memory if you use TSRs and several device drivers.

There are two major factors that ultimately determine how difficult it will be to configure your system. The first factor is hardware. Basically, the more extra hardware (SCSI adapters, sound cards, etc.) you have installed in your system, the more troublesome configuring your system becomes. Hardware conflicts are covered in Chapter 9, *IRQs, DMA, and Other Mysteries.* However, some hardware devices require drivers which take up memory.

The other major factor affecting your configurations is the type and complexity of your software collection. For example, if you run nothing but Windows programs, configuring the system is easy. However, if you have DOS applications, Windows applications, and DOS applications that require expanded memory, you'll have a bit of work to do to find the optimum configuration.

Let's look at four situations of multimedia and nonmultimedia systems. Each of these systems has a problem with memory configuration. We'll use the drivers (HIMEM.SYS, EMM386.EXE, etc.) supplied with DOS 6 to provide solutions to these problems. Each situation starts with an overview of the problem system, its configuration files, and the objective of the user. This is followed by a solution and a new set of configuration files. Let's start with a nonmultimedia system.

Problem #1—The Memory Hungry Game Predicament

Our first user, Steve, has a system that has seemed adequate in recent years. However, he recently purchased a new hot game that introduced a problem he has not seen before. After going through the obligatory installation ritual, he types in the filename that starts the program. Instead of seeing what he hoped to be a colorful graphic opening screen he receives an ugly message: NOT ENOUGH MEMORY. Of course, most programs are friendlier than this.

Steve consults the game's documentation which indicates that the program requires 595K of free conventional memory. He types the **MEM** command and finds he only has 561K free. It appears that Steve is about 34K short of what is required to run this game. Before we start to consider a solution, let's take a closer look at Steve's system. Listing 5-31 shows the configuration files.

System Description

- 80386DX
- 2 Megabytes of RAM
- Serial Mouse

Listing 5-31 Problem #1—Configuration Files

```
AUTOEXEC.BAT contents
---------------------
&ECHO OFF
CLS
PATH C:\DOS;C:\MYFILES;
C:\MOUSE\MOUSE

CONFIG.SYS contents
---------------------
FILES=20
BUFFERS=10
DEVICE=C:\DOS\HIMEM.SYS
```

Solving the Problem

The first thing that should jump out at you is that Steve is loading HIMEM.SYS. Although this provides extended memory support, he is not taking advantage of something else HIMEM.SYS offers: access to high memory. The first thing he needs to do is add a DOS=HIGH after the HIMEM.SYS line.

The previous change alone would free up enough memory to run the game; however, he could go further and provide access to upper memory (with EMM386.EXE). This would allow him to relocate the mouse driver in high memory (using LOADHIGH). Even though we have to load the EMM386.EXE driver into conventional memory, the relocation of the mouse driver more than makes up for it.

The solution files for Steve's system are shown in Listing 5-32. The additions and modifications are shown in boldface. He is using the NOEMS switch with EMM386.EXE because he does not use programs that require expanded memory. Not only can Steve load his game now, in the future he will be able to load other resident programs and device drivers in upper memory. This should keep his conventional memory at a high enough level.

Listing 5-32 Solution #1—Configuration Files

```
AUTOEXEC.BAT contents
---------------------
&ECHO OFF
```

```
CLS
PATH C:\DOS;C:\MYFILES;
LOADHIGH C:\MOUSE\MOUSE

CONFIG.SYS contents
--------------------
FILES=20
BUFFERS=10
DEVICE=C:\DOS\HIMEM.SYS
DEVICE=C:\DOS\EMM386.EXE NOEMS
DOS=HIGH,UMB
```

Problem #2—The EMS Versus XMS Dilemma

Our next candidate for a memory checkup is Melissa. Melissa has been fortunate enough to receive a computer "hand-me-down." It's not an outdated system by any means; however, she wants to run certain kinds of programs and is having no luck. Her two favorite applications are quite different in their memory needs. One program requires extended memory and the other requires expanded memory.

Melissa also likes memory-resident utilities; these utilities take up more conventional memory than she'd like. The goal here is to free up as much conventional memory as possible while accommodating her favorite programs. Melissa also has an external floppy drive which requires a device driver. Listing 5-33 shows the problem configuration files.

If you read Chapter 4, *DOS Memory Management*, this problem will seem familiar. The problem is the same; however, with DOS 6 the solution is slightly different.

System Description

- 80486SX
- 4 Megabytes of RAM
- Serial Mouse
- External Floppy Controller

Listing 5-33 Problem #2—Configuration Files

```
AUTOEXEC.BAT contents
--------------------
&ECHO OFF
CLS
PATH C:\DOS;C:\FILES;C:\321;
LOADHIGH C:\MOUSE\MOUSE
LOADHIGH C:\DOS\DOSKEY
LOADHIGH C:\SUPERPOP\POP
```

continued on next page

continued from previous page

```
CONFIG.SYS contents
--------------------
FILES=20
BUFFERS=10
DEVICE=C:\DOS\HIMEM.SYS
DEVICE=C:\DOS\EMM386.EXE
DOS=HIGH,UMB
DEVICE=C:\DRIVERS\FDCTRL.SYS
```

Solving the Problem

Melissa's complaint is that she cannot run some programs because of low conventional memory. The expanded memory application is not performing well either. At first glance it may look like a fairly good configuration. EMM386.EXE is simulating expanded memory from extended. She is attempting to load the memory-resident utilities with LOADHIGH. However, are they actually loaded high?

The first place to go to work is the EMM386.EXE line in CONFIG.SYS. Recall that using this driver with no switches does not provide access to upper memory. Therefore, the following line (DOS=HIGH,UMB) loads DOS high, but the UMB option does nothing. She must change the EMM386.EXE line by adding the RAM switch. This will now allow the LOADHIGH command to load the memory-resident programs in upper memory.

One advantage Melissa gains with DOS 6 is that the entire range of extended memory can be used for extended or simulated expanded memory. EMM386.EXE makes the necessary adjustments based on program demands. There is no need to specify the amount of simulated expanded memory on the EMM386.EXE line (as we did in DOS 5.0).

The last thing that needs fixing is the last line in the CONFIG.SYS file. The external floppy controller driver is not loaded into high memory. She replaces DEVICE with DEVICEHIGH to accomplish this.

Now she has a system that has nearly 3 megabytes of free extended (or expanded) memory and a large increase in conventional memory. This configuration is optimal for her situation.

The solution files for Melissa's system are shown in Listing 5-34. The additions and modifications are shown in boldface. There are only two changes to these files, although they produced significant results. The EMM386.EXE RAM switch enables upper memory access. The DEVICEHIGH command loads the floppy driver into upper memory.

Watch Your Upper Memory

The amount of free upper memory varies from system to system based on configuration. You may or may not have enough room to load every driver and TSR into upper memory.

Listing 5-34 Solution #2—Configuration Files

```
AUTOEXEC.BAT contents
---------------------
&ECHO OFF
CLS
PATH C:\DOS;C:\FILES;C:\321;
LOADHIGH C:\MOUSE\MOUSE
LOADHIGH C:\DOS\DOSKEY
LOADHIGH C:\SUPERPOP\POP


CONFIG.SYS contents
---------------------
FILES=20
BUFFERS=10
DEVICE=C:\DOS\HIMEM.SYS
DEVICE=C:\DOS\EMM386.EXE RAM
DOS=HIGH,UMB
DEVICEHIGH=C:\DRIVERS\FDCTRL.SYS
```

Problem #3—DoubleSpace and MemMaker's Limitations

Our next user is Pat who has three memory problems. First, he does not see the free extended memory he expects with his current configuration. Second, he is having trouble getting enough free upper memory to load his drivers and memory-resident programs. Third, he is using MemMaker which requires a fairly large device driver. Pat also has a sound card installed which requires another device driver line in CONFIG.SYS. Listing 5-35 shows the problem configuration files.

System Description

- 80486DX
- 4 Megabytes of RAM
- Serial Mouse
- Sound Card
- Hard Drive Using DoubleSpace

Listing 5-35 Problem #3—Configuration Files

```
AUTOEXEC.BAT contents
---------------------
&ECHO OFF
CLS
PATH C:\DOS;C:\GAMES;C:\UTILS;
LOADHIGH C:\MOUSE\MOUSE
LOADHIGH C:\DOS\DOSKEY
LOADHIGH C:\CAL\CALENDAR
LOADHIGH C:\UTIL\CALC


CONFIG.SYS contents
---------------------
DEVICE=FILES=20
BUFFERS=10
DEVICE=C:\DOS\HIMEM.SYS
DEVICE=C:\DOS\EMM386.EXE RAM
DOS=HIGH,UMB
DEVICEHIGH=C:\SOUND\SOUNDMAN.SYS
DEVICEHIGH=C:\DOS\DOUBLESPACE /MOVE
```

Solving the Problem

Once again this looks like a decent configuration on the surface. For example, he is attempting to load every driver and TSR in upper memory. He is also using the RAM switch which enables access to upper memory (combined with the DOS=UMB line).

Pat attempts to use MemMaker to straighten out his problems. This case illustrates an important point. Although MemMaker is a nice utility, it cannot solve all of your memory problems. You have to analyze the results after running MemMaker to determine if the outcome is acceptable to you.

After running MemMaker, Pat ended up with the configuration files shown in Listing 5-36. Pat told the MemMaker program that he is not using expanded memory. Therefore, MemMaker did the right thing and changed the EMM386.EXE RAM switch to NOEMS. This frees up more upper memory and doesn't simulate any expanded memory.

Listing 5-36 Problem #3—After MemMaker

```
AUTOEXEC.BAT contents
---------------------
&ECHO OFF
CLS
PATH C:\DOS;C:\GAMES;C:\UTILS;
LOADHIGH C:\MOUSE\MOUSE
LOADHIGH C:\DOS\DOSKEY
```

```
LOADHIGH C:\CAL\CALENDAR
LOADHIGH C:\UTIL\CALC

CONFIG.SYS contents
---------------------
FILES=20
BUFFERS=10
DEVICE=C:\DOS\HIMEM.SYS
DEVICE=C:\DOS\EMM386.EXE NOEMS
DOS=HIGH,UMB
DEVICEHIGH=C:\SOUND\SOUNDMAN.SYS
DEVICEHIGH=C:\DOS\DOUBLESPACE /MOVE
```

Also, recall that when you use expanded memory, EMM386.EXE reserves a 64K page frame in upper memory. This takes memory that is best served for drivers and TSRs.

Pat isn't out of the woods yet, however. Because of the large DoubleSpace driver, his system still doesn't have enough free upper memory to store all drivers and TSRs. Although he could opt to upgrade to a third-party memory manager, he decides to create two configurations: GAME and WORK. He decides that he rarely uses the TSR programs when he uses the computer to play games. On the other hand, he never uses the sound card when he is using his computer for work. His solution is to create multiple configurations. One configuration loads the TSRs in upper memory and omits the sound driver, the other loads the sound driver in upper memory and omits the TSRs (except for the mouse driver). Both configurations must load the DoubleSpace driver because Pat won't be able to use his hard drive without it.

Listing 5-37 shows the solution with two sets of configuration files. Pat can use CHANGE.BAT and STORE.BAT to manage these files. CHANGE.BAT and STORE.BAT are covered in Chapter 3, *Managing Configuration Files.*

Listing 5-37 Solution #3—Configuration Files

```
WORK CONFIGURATION (Store as WORK.BAT and WORK.SYS)
----------------------------------------------------
AUTOEXEC.BAT contents
---------------------
&ECHO OFF
CLS
PATH C:\DOS;C:\GAMES;C:\UTILS;
LOADHIGH C:\MOUSE\MOUSE
LOADHIGH C:\DOS\DOSKEY
LOADHIGH C:\CAL\CALENDAR
LOADHIGH C:\UTIL\CALC
```

continued on next page

continued from previous page

```
CONFIG.SYS contents
--------------------
FILES=20
BUFFERS=10
DEVICE=C:\DOS\HIMEM.SYS
DEVICE=C:\DOS\EMM386.EXE NOEMS
DOS=HIGH,UMB
DEVICEHIGH=C:\DOS\DOUBLESPACE /MOVE

GAME CONFIGURATION (Store as GAME.BAT and GAME.SYS)
---------------------------------------------------
AUTOEXEC.BAT contents
--------------------
&ECHO OFF
CLS
PATH C:\DOS;C:\GAMES;C:\UTILS;
LOADHIGH C:\MOUSE\MOUSE

CONFIG.SYS contents
--------------------
FILES=20
BUFFERS=10
DEVICE=C:\DOS\HIMEM.SYS
DEVICE=C:\DOS\EMM386.EXE NOEMS
DOS=HIGH,UMB
DEVICEHIGH=C:\SOUND\SOUNDMAN.SYS
DEVICEHIGH=C:\DOS\DOUBLESPACE /MOVE
```

Problem #4—A Challenge with Multimedia

Our last user, Jack, has gone all out and filled his machine with modern technology. He has a fast system with a sound card, SCSI adapter (which supports his CD-ROM), and a fancy new video card. Unfortunately all of these devices require drivers. In fact, his CD-ROM requires two!

After getting the hardware to work properly, Jack has found that he lacks the conventional memory necessary to run most multimedia applications (which is why he added the hardware in the first place). Listing 5-38 shows the problem configuration files.

System Description

- 80486DX
- 8 Megabytes of RAM
- Serial Mouse
- Sound Card
- CD-ROM
- Accelerator Video Card

Listing 5-38 Problem #4—Configuration Files

```
AUTOEXEC.BAT contents
---------------------
&ECHO OFF
CLS
PATH C:\DOS;C:\GAMES;C:\MEDIA;
C:\SCSI\MSCDEX
LOADHIGH C:\MOUSE\MOUSE
LOADHIGH C:\DOS\DOSKEY

CONFIG.SYS contents
---------------------
FILES=20
BUFFERS=10
DEVICE=C:\DOS\HIMEM.SYS
DEVICE=C:\DOS\EMM386.EXE NOEMS
DOS=HIGH,UMB
DEVICEHIGH=C:\SOUND\SOUNDMAN.SYS
DEVICEHIGH=C:\SCSI\ADAPTER.SYS
DEVICEHIGH=C:\VIDEO\VESA.SYS
```

Solving the Problem

Jack has no problem getting his drivers into upper memory. This is with the exception of the MSCDEX driver, which is the Microsoft CD Extension driver. If you own a CD-ROM, you will probably use this driver. After the drivers in CONFIG.SYS are loaded (for the sound, SCSI, and video card), he doesn't have enough room in upper memory.

Fortunately, the MSCDEX driver has an optional switch (/e) that will load the driver into extended memory (if it's available). This is not a problem because Jack has plenty of extended RAM. After testing this configuration, he realizes that the DOSKEY program will not fit into upper memory. After weighing the small conventional memory gain versus how much he uses the utility, he decides to omit it from the configuration. Listing 5-39 shows Jack's new configuration files.

Listing 5-39 Solution #4—Configuration Files

```
AUTOEXEC.BAT contents
---------------------
&ECHO OFF
CLS
PATH C:\DOS;C:\GAMES;C:\MEDIA;
C:\SCSI\MSCDEX /e
LOADHIGH C:\MOUSE\MOUSE

CONFIG.SYS contents
---------------------
FILES=20
BUFFERS=10
```

continued on next page

continued from previous page

```
DEVICE=C:\DOS\HIMEM.SYS
DEVICE=C:\DOS\EMM386.EXE NOEMS
DOS=HIGH,UMB
DEVICEHIGH=C:\SOUND\SOUNDMAN.SYS
DEVICEHIGH=C:\SCSI\ADAPTER.SYS
DEVICEHIGH=C:\VIDEO\VESA.SYS
```

These examples should provide some insight to the thought process that is necessary when configuring your system. If you have a loaded system, you may find you must make compromises or multiple configurations to meet your needs. Let's look at a summary of the topics covered in this chapter.

Summary

We've covered a number of topics in this chapter that pertain to DOS 6 memory management. Let's review these topics before moving to Windows memory management. If you are unsure of any area, you can always return to the specific section and review it in more depth.

- The DOS 6 MEM command lets you view the way your system's memory is configured. Using MEM without switches provides a summary of conventional, expanded (if any), and extended memory. The MEM command in DOS 6 provides more information than DOS 5.0's MEM command.
- The MEM /C, or /CLASSIFY, switch provides a listing of programs in the first megabyte (including their size), as well as a summary of conventional, upper, extended, and possibly expanded memory.
- The MEM /D, or /DEBUG, switch provides additional information on system device drivers, their locations, and their sizes.
- The MEM /F, or /FREE, switch provides the status of free conventional and upper memory.
- The MEM /M, or /MODULE, switch provides the status of one module (program). You must supply the module name immediately after the switch.
- As with DOS 5.0, the main goal of DOS 6 memory management is to free up as much conventional memory as possible.

- Loading the HIMEM.SYS driver in your CONFIG.SYS file provides access to extended memory. It also enables the high memory area, where you can ultimately place a large portion of DOS, freeing up conventional memory. The HIMEM.SYS driver must be installed in conventional memory.
- Loading the EMM386.EXE driver in your CONFIG.SYS file can simulate expanded memory and/or enable access to the upper memory block. EMM386.EXE requires HIMEM.SYS to be loaded first.
- Using EMM386.EXE with no switches simulates expanded memory, but does not enable upper memory access. Using EMM386.EXE with the NOEMS switch enables access to upper memory, but does not simulate expanded memory. Using EMM386 with the RAM switch both simulates expanded memory and enables access to upper memory.
- DOS 6's EMM386.EXE can switch amounts of extended and expanded memory on the fly. We could not do this in DOS 5.0.
- Adding the DOS=HIGH command to your CONFIG.SYS file will relocate a large portion of MS-DOS, COMMAND, and HIMEM. You must load HIMEM.SYS before using DOS=HIGH.
- Adding the DOS=UMB command to your CONFIG.SYS file informs DOS that you will load programs and/or device drivers into upper memory blocks. This line must be after the HIMEM.SYS and EMM386.EXE lines.
- You can combine the DOS=HIGH and DOS=UMB on one line using DOS=HIGH, UMB.
- You can load memory-resident (TSR) programs in upper memory using the LOADHIGH command in your AUTOEXEC.BAT file. This requires the HIMEM.SYS, EMM386.EXE, and DOS=UMB lines to be in your CONFIG.SYS file. You can abbreviate LOADHIGH with LH.
- You can load device drivers in upper memory using the DEVICEHIGH command in your CONFIG.SYS file. This requires the HIMEM.SYS, EMM386.EXE, and DOS=UMB lines to be in your CONFIG.SYS file *before* any DEVICEHIGH line.
- DOS 6 supplies a new utility, MemMaker, to help you configure and optimize your system's memory.

- You can create a temporary RAM disk drive using the RAMDRIVE.SYS device driver. The RAM disk either uses conventional memory (no switches), extended memory (/e switch), or expanded memory (/a switch). Always use extended memory if possible. The contents of a RAM disk are lost as soon as you turn off your computer; therefore, only use a RAM disk for temporary purposes.
- You can create a disk cache using the SMARTDRV.EXE device driver. SMARTDrive can speed up your system by storing data in memory that is repeatedly requested from disk. The SMARTDrive cache has an initial size and a Windows size.

Now you have seen the essentials for managing memory in DOS 6. The next chapter will cover memory management for Windows 3.1. You will see how to create configurations so your DOS and Windows applications can peacefully coexist.

Windows Memory Management

In this chapter, we will discuss memory management techniques for Microsoft Windows. Because Windows runs on the MS-DOS operating system, we must be aware of our DOS configuration files: CONFIG.SYS and AUTOEXEC.BAT. These files not only configure your system for DOS programs; they also provide a starting point for managing memory in Windows.

We'll begin this chapter by looking at a few sets of DOS configuration files. Some configurations are better for Windows, than others. What configuration you use depends on the types of applications you run. For example, if you run Windows applications exclusively, you can create a single DOS configuration that will meet your needs. However, if you want to run both DOS and Windows programs, or if you want to run DOS programs from within Windows, you will have to adjust your configuration files accordingly.

We'll also see how expanded and extended memory fit into the Windows memory management scheme. You'll find examples for when you want to configure expanded memory, or when you will want a configuration that is exclusively extended memory.

We'll also look at *virtual* memory in Windows. Virtual memory is actually disk space that represents memory while Windows is running. You can actually expand your Windows memory without purchasing additional physical memory. Virtual memory does have some drawbacks; we'll discuss those as well.

If you are a DOS 5.0 user, you will see that the Windows version of the SMARTDrive disk cache has changed. If you are a DOS 6 user, the disk caching software is very similar.

Let's look at an overview of the topics for this chapter.

TOPICS COVERED

Checking Memory In Microsoft Windows

Comparison of Windows Memory and DOS Memory

Standard Windows Mode and Requirements

Enhanced Windows Mode and Requirements

Windows and Extended Memory

Windows and Expanded Memory

Virtual Memory and Swap Files

Setting Up a Temporary or Permanent Swap File

SMARTDrive Disk Caching with Windows

Checking Memory in Windows

Before we get into managing memory in Microsoft Windows, we must first examine our current memory situation. This memory information can be found in a number of applications supplied by Windows, for example:

- Program Manager
- File Manager
- Control Panel
- Notepad

To check your memory configuration from any of the programs listed above, perform the following steps:

1. Select the Help menu by clicking on it (or press ALT+H).
2. Select the About menu option by clicking on it (or press A).
3. The program displays the About dialog box (shown in Figure 6-1).

4. Examine the results at the bottom of the About dialog box. This includes the Windows mode in which you are currently operating, the amount of free memory, and the percentage of free system resources available.

5. When you are done using the About box, click OK (or press ENTER).

We'll discuss Windows modes and system resources later in this chapter. Before we do that, however, let's look at what affects the free memory reported in the About box in Figure 6-1.

Windows Memory—From a DOS Point of View

Before we look at managing memory in Windows, we will first show how your configuration files are affected by the Windows installation. At the same time, we'll show how these configuration files affect Windows.

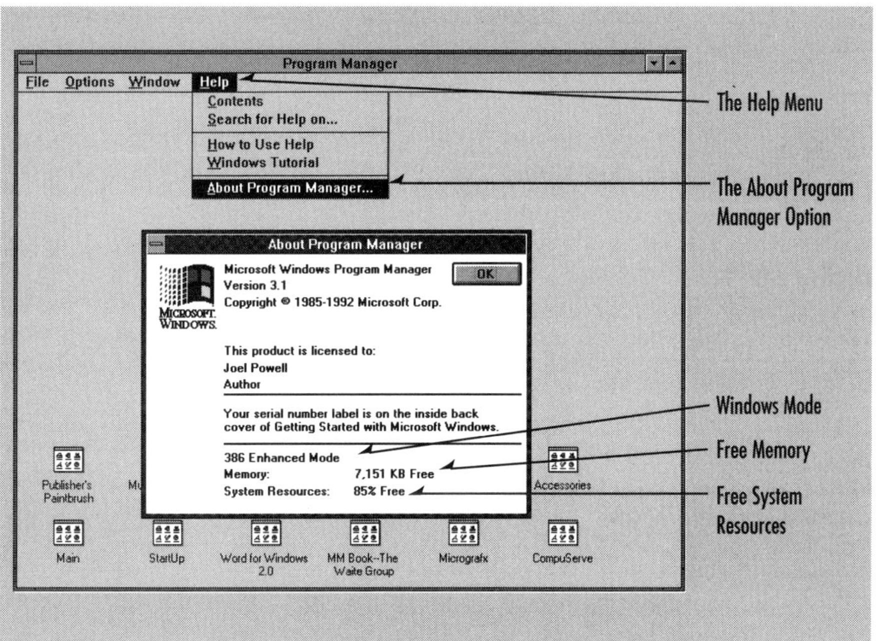

Figure 6-1 The Program Manager about box—Windows mode, free memory, and free space resources

When you install Windows, the Setup program modifies your AUTOEXEC.BAT and CONFIG.SYS files. This usually involves adding SMARTDRV.EXE and the SHARE program to your AUTOEXEC.BAT, and also modifying the PATH to include the path to the Windows directory. It also adds HIMEM.SYS to your CONFIG.SYS file (if it's not already there).

In addition, you can modify your CONFIG.SYS with EMM386.EXE and the DOS=HIGH,UMB command to access upper memory blocks and/or simulate expanded memory as discussed in the previous chapter. Listings 6-1 and 6-2 show two possibilities for Windows configuration files. Note that we are not loading any multimedia drivers in these examples. They simply supply a basic configuration on which we can build a final configuration. Lines that are added by the Windows setup program are in boldface.

Listing 6-1 Basic Windows Configuration—No Expanded Memory

```
Contents of AUTOEXEC.BAT
------------------------
C:\WINDOWS\SMARTDRV.SYS
@ECHO OFF
CLS
PROMPT $p$g
PATH C:\WINDOWS;C:\DOS;
C:\DOS\SHARE.EXE/f:4096

Contents of CONFIG.SYS
------------------------
FILES=21
BUFFERS=15
DEVICE=C:\DOS\HIMEM.SYS
DEVICE=C:\DOS\EMM386.EXE NOEMS
DOS=HIGH, UMB
```

Listing 6-2 Basic Windows Configuration—With Expanded Memory

```
Contents of AUTOEXEC.BAT
------------------------
C:\WINDOWS\SMARTDRV.SYS
@ECHO OFF
CLS
PROMPT $p$g
PATH C:\WINDOWS;C:\DOS;
C:\DOS\SHARE.EXE/f:4096

Contents of CONFIG.SYS
------------------------
FILES=21
BUFFERS=15
```

```
DEVICE=C:\DOS\HIMEM.SYS
DEVICE=C:\DOS\EMM386.EXE RAM
DOS=HIGH, UMB
```

Let's examine the Windows additions to the AUTOEXEC.BAT files in the two listings. The first line is SMARTDRV.EXE; this is the disk caching program we discussed for DOS 5.0 and 6 in the two previous chapters. However, the Windows install program automatically uses the SMARTDRV.EXE in the WINDOWS directory.

Always Use the Latest Version of SMARTDrive

It's a good idea to use the most recent driver for SMARTDrive (and all other DOS/Windows drivers for that matter). If you are using DOS 5.0 and Windows 3.1, you should use the SMARTDRV.EXE supplied with Windows. If you are using DOS 6 and Windows 3.1, you should use the SMARTDRV.EXE supplied with DOS 6.

Another modification by the Windows installation routine is the addition of C:\WINDOWS to the PATH statement. This way, you can type **WIN** at the DOS prompt and press ENTER to start Windows, regardless of which directory you are in at the time.

The last addition to AUTOEXEC.BAT is the SHARE program. The SHARE program keeps two programs from accessing the same file at the same time. You will see a sharing violation message in Windows if this occurs. Different Windows applications handle sharing violations in different ways. Figure 6-2 shows how Microsoft Word for Windows handles a sharing violation. In this case, it allows you to optionally make a copy of the document.

The /F switch allocates the amount of memory to store open filenames. In the listings, we are using 4,096 bytes (4K) to store filenames, although you can specify a different amount. The default value (if you do not use the /F switch) is 2,048 bytes. The Windows setup program added the /F switch to SHARE in this case.

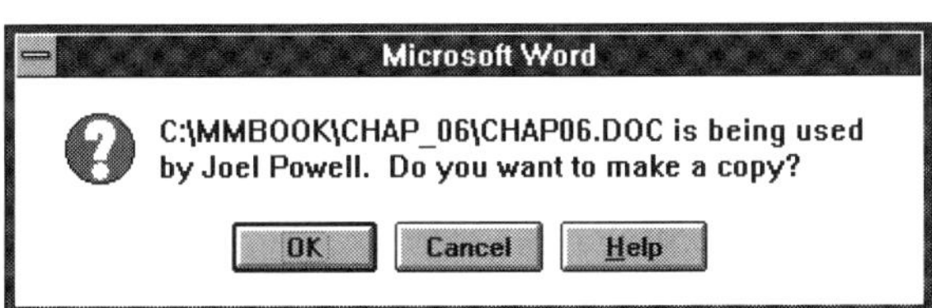

Figure 6-2 Microsoft Word handling a sharing violation

The Windows install program also places a line in CONFIG.SYS to load the HIMEM.SYS driver. This driver is required in Windows 3.1 as it requires extended memory.

The other CONFIG.SYS lines in Listings 6-1 and 6-2 load EMM386.EXE. The first listing uses the NOEMS switch, which provides access to upper memory, but doesn't simulate expanded memory. The second listing uses the RAM switch, which provides access to upper memory and simulates expanded memory. Windows itself does not require expanded memory. We'll see why you may need expanded memory in Windows later in this chapter.

Loading Programs High

The Windows installation may add the SMARTDRV.EXE and SHARE programs, but it does not automatically load them into high memory. Because both Listings 6-1 and 6-2 provide access to the upper memory area, we could modify AUTOEXEC.BAT to load these programs into high memory. Listing 6-3 shows the modified AUTOEXEC.BAT.

Listing 6-3 Loading SMARTDRV and SHARE into High Memory

```
Contents of AUTOEXEC.BAT
------------------------
LOADHIGH C:\WINDOWS\SMARTDRV.SYS
@ECHO OFF
CLS
PROMPT $p$g
PATH C:\WINDOWS;C:\DOS;
LOADHIGH C:\DOS\SHARE.EXE/f:4096
```

As long as you have the upper memory available, adding these commands will increase free conventional memory. Remember that adapter cards (network cards, hard drive cards, and so on) can reserve memory addresses in upper memory. As a result, this decreases the amount of free upper memory. Also, if you are simulating expanded memory, a 64K portion of upper memory is used for the EMM page frame.

Now that we've looked at the DOS configuration files for Windows, let's see how Windows uses memory.

Managing Memory in Windows

How Windows uses your system's memory depends on the amount of memory and in which *mode* Windows is running. Basically, the more extended memory you have, the better for running Windows programs. The amount of extended memory is also a factor in determining the mode in which Windows will run.

Windows Modes—Standard and Enhanced

The About Program Manager dialog box showed us the amount of free memory available to Windows programs. It also showed that Windows was operating in the *386 enhanced mode.* Let's look at the requirements for the standard and 386 enhanced modes of Windows.

Standard Mode Requirements

The requirements to run the standard mode are less stringent than for the 386 enhanced mode; however, the standard mode has limits. For example, you cannot simulate expanded memory and use it to run non-Windows applications. You must have a separate expanded memory board instead.

Here are the minimum requirements to run the Windows standard mode:

- An 80286 Processor or Higher
- 256K of Free Conventional Memory
- 192K of Free Extended Memory
- An Extended Memory Driver (for example, HIMEM.SYS)

Windows automatically detects your hardware configuration when it starts up. It automatically selects the appropriate mode for the hardware. If you want to force Windows into the standard mode, you can type **WIN /S** instead of **WIN** when starting Windows.

386 Enhanced Mode Requirements

This mode takes greater advantage of the 80386 or higher processor which makes Windows performance better in general. You also can use simulated expanded memory (using EMM386.EXE) to run non-Windows applications that require expanded memory. You do not need a separate expanded memory board.

Here are the minimum requirements to run the Windows 386 enhanced mode:

- An 80386 Processor or Higher
- 256K of Free Conventional Memory
- 1,024K of Free Extended Memory
- An Extended Memory Driver (for example, HIMEM.SYS)

Note the two differences between the standard and 386 mode requirements. 386 enhanced mode requires an 80386 processor because it uses the processor's advanced features. Because earlier processors do not contain these features, they would fail under the 386 enhanced mode.

The other difference is the extended memory requirement. The enhanced mode requires at least 1,024K (1 megabyte) of free extended memory. If you use a 2-megabyte system and simulate expanded memory, you will not have the free memory required to run Windows enhanced mode. If you are running DOS 6, remember that EMM386 can adjust the amount of free extended and expanded memory on the fly. We'll also see the effects of SMARTDrive on extended memory later in this chapter.

Windows and Conventional/Extended Memory

As we've already mentioned, Windows has a fondness for extended memory. Windows can swap both Windows and DOS applications into extended memory. However, Windows applications break the 640K conventional memory barrier that most DOS programs run up against. DOS programs still function in a 640K virtual memory space. A DOS application "sees" 640K of memory.

As shown in Figure 6-3, Windows treats conventional and extended memory as a single block of memory. Because we can run more than one application at a time, Windows is responsible for switching programs around in memory.

The figure also shows that this configuration can run Windows programs, which require extended and/or conventional memory. Windows can also run DOS programs which require extended and/or conventional memory. We cannot, however, run a DOS program which requires expanded memory. Let's look at the differences of Windows and its use of expanded memory.

Windows and Expanded Memory

Windows applications and the Windows system itself do not use expanded memory. The only reason you would want to simulate expanded memory is for DOS programs that require it. Otherwise it's best to configure your system so you have as much free conventional and extended memory as possible.

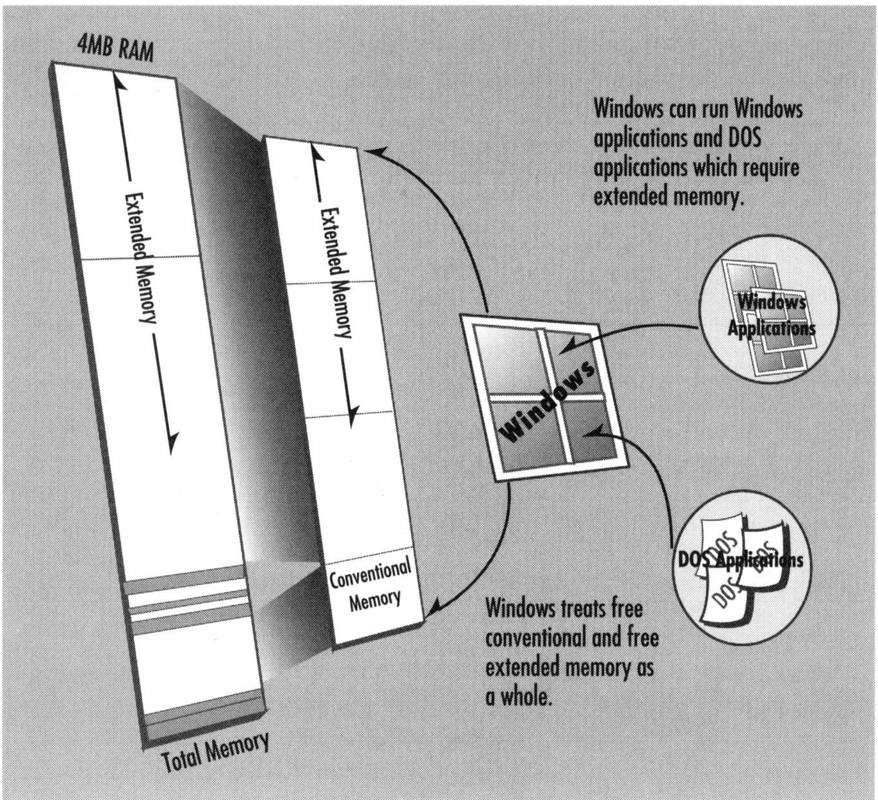

Figure 6-3 Windows using conventional and extended memory

Figure 6-4 shows that simulating expanded memory (using EMM386.EXE) reduces the amount of free extended memory. DOS 6 users should remember that amounts of free extended and expanded memory will change as requirements change. However, DOS 5.0 users must configure the amount of expanded memory they want, and as a result, lose the extended memory that was converted.

The main effect of simulating expanded memory is that it reduces the amount of free extended memory. This results in less memory for the Windows system, Windows applications, and DOS applications requiring extended memory.

The bottom line is: If you are not using a DOS application that requires expanded memory, do not simulate it. Use the EMM386.EXE switch with the NOEMS option. This will result in more memory for Windows and, as a result, it will perform better. Remember, you cannot simulate expanded memory if you are running Windows in standard mode. You must use an expanded memory card in this instance.

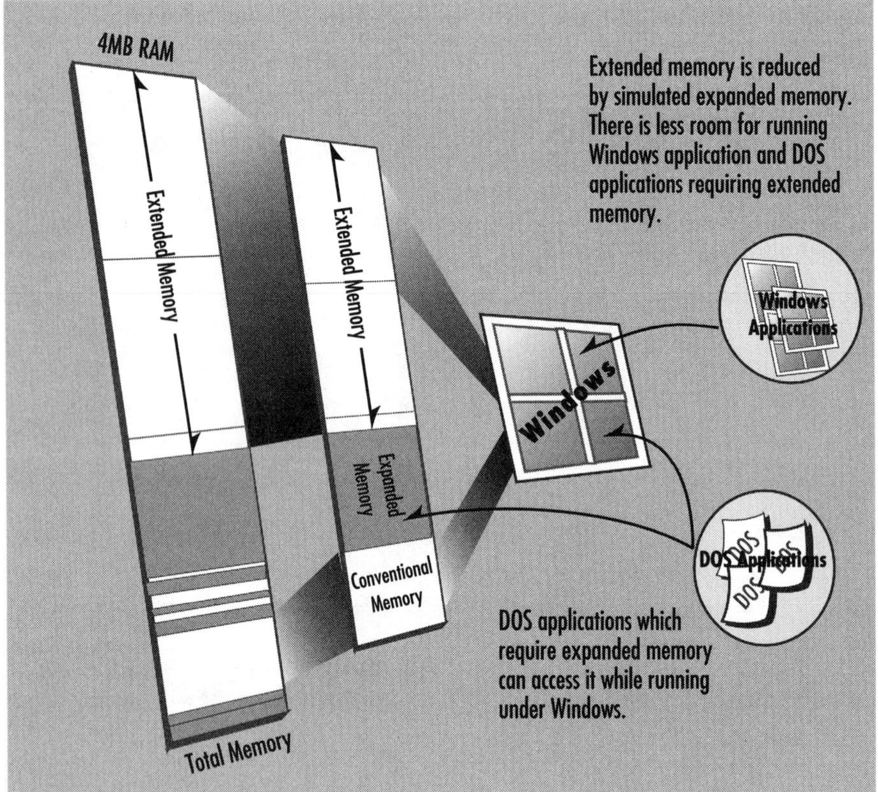

Figure 6-4 Effects of expanded memory on Windows, Windows applications, and DOS applications

Windows System Resources

We checked the amount of free memory earlier in this chapter using the About option on the Program Manager's Help menu. This About dialog box also displayed the percentage of free *system resources.* What are Windows system resources?

If you've used several Windows applications, by now you've noticed that they all have the same general appearance. For example, the windows in one application are similar to windows in other applications. The menu system is usually the same from one Windows application to another.

Windows does a lot of work for the program developer. Each Windows program a developer writes can access Windows system resources. For virtually every object (window, icon, menu, etc.) you encounter, it involves and consumes system resources.

We do not have direct control over the free resources. However, you should keep an eye on them especially if you run many applications simultaneously. Each Windows program consumes resources while it's running. If you close an application, the application will free the system resources it used.

If the amount of free system resources gets low, you may get out of memory messages from applications, even though you have a lot of free memory remaining. The only way to bring the free resource level back up is to close other applications, then recheck the value in the Program Manager About dialog box.

Now let's look at a way we can simulate additional memory (without going to the store and buying some!) in systems that use the 386 enhanced mode.

Virtual Memory—The Swap File

There is one way to increase your amount of Windows memory without spending a dime. You can create *virtual* memory if you use the 386 enhanced mode of Windows. Virtual memory is actually disk space that Windows maintains as free memory. This is known as a *swap file.* Figure 6-5 shows how the virtual memory and the swap file work.

Now that a swap file exists, Windows' total free memory consists of free conventional, free extended memory, and the swap file space. However, you will not see total free memory increase by the exact size of the swap file. Some of this space is used to manage the virtual memory.

How Virtual Memory Works

Virtual memory is controlled by a virtual memory manager within the Windows system. The virtual memory manager determines which of the running programs will get stored in actual memory or in virtual memory. It makes that decision by examining which programs have been active most recently. As a result of this examination, the memory manager can determine which applications should be in actual physical memory. When a program is idle (and other programs are active) its code and data are swapped to virtual memory.

Drawbacks of Virtual Memory and the Swap File

Using virtual memory is usually a good idea; it enhances the operation of Windows, especially when you are running several applications at once. However, it takes up hard disk space. If you are low on hard disk space you should use a

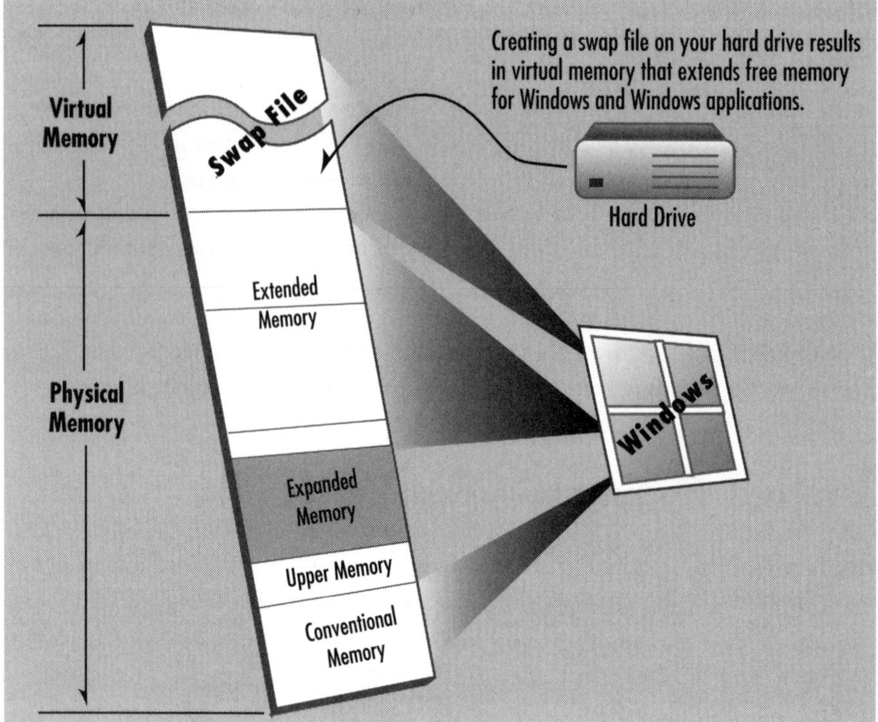

Figure 6-5 Virtual Memory—using a swap file to extend memory

temporary swap file, or none at all. Virtual memory is also slower than physical RAM because you are relying on disk access speed as opposed to memory access speed. Let's see how to create a swap file and virtual memory.

Setting up a Swap File On Your System

Let's look at the steps for creating a temporary or permanent swap file on your system. We started this example using a set of configuration files which did not simulate expanded memory. Figure 6-6 shows the Program Manager About box before creating virtual memory. Notice that 1,772K of Windows memory is free at this time.

Perform the following steps to set up your virtual memory:

1. Open the Main group in the Program Manager.
2. Start the Control Panel application; the control panel appears.

Windows Setup Defaults to a Temporary Swap File

The Windows Setup program automatically defaults to a temporary swap file. The size of this file varies depending on the amount of free disk space on your system. If you have a large amount of free disk space, or if your swap file has been damaged, use the following procedure to create a new (permanent or temporary) swap file.

3. Start the 386 Enhanced application; the 386 Enhanced window appears. Note: The 386 Enhanced icon will not appear if you are running in Windows standard mode. You cannot set up virtual memory in standard mode.
4. Select the Virtual Memory... option. Figure 6-7 shows an example of the initial Virtual Memory dialog box. Note that this dialog box does not show a drive because there is no swap file yet.
5. Select the Change>> option. The Virtual Memory dialog box grows as shown in Figure 6-8. Windows now makes a suggestion for a swap file for your system. In this example, Windows is suggesting a permanent swap file on drive C:. The suggested size is 7,786K. This is based on

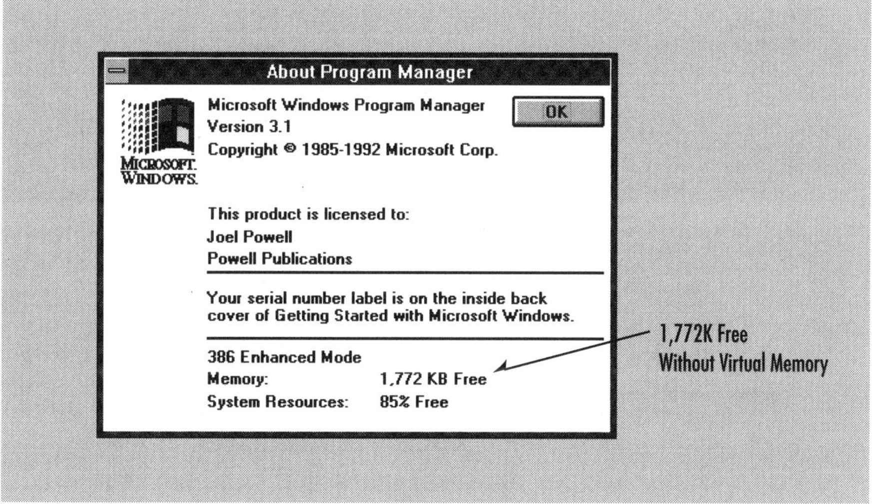

Figure 6-6 The Program Manager About box—before Virtual Memory

Virtual Memory
Current Settings
Drive:
Size: 0 KB
Type: None
OK
Cancel
Change>>
Help

Figure 6-7 Initial Virtual Memory dialog box

the amount of free space on the drive and the maximum size for a swap file.

You can override any of the suggestions at this point. For example, you could set the Type to Temporary or change the Drive selection to another hard disk (if you have one). See the tips that follow these steps for more information.

6. When you are satisfied with the selections, select OK. In our example, we are accepting the Windows suggestions for our swap file.

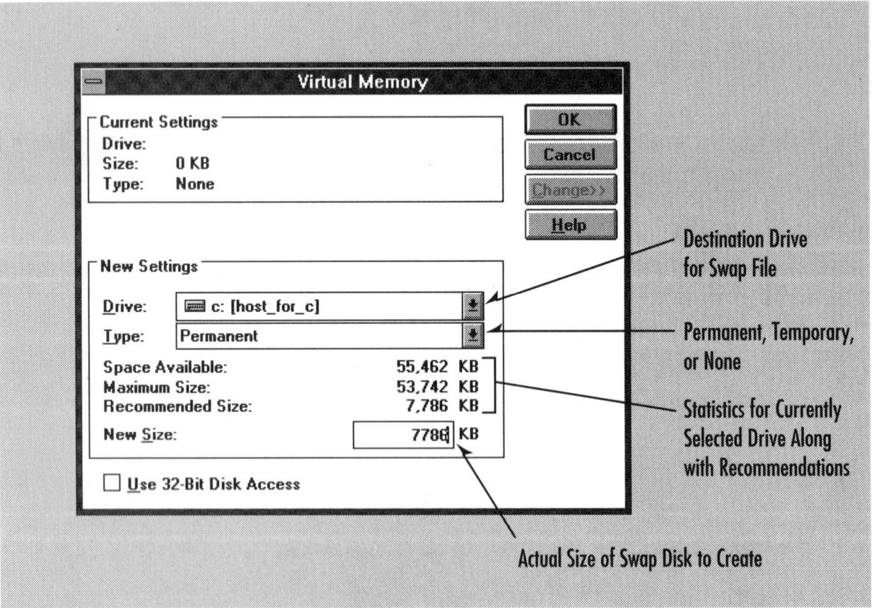

Figure 6-8 Windows suggests a swap file in the Virtual Memory dialog box

Warning to DoubleSpace Users

If you are a DOS 6 user and you are using DoubleSpace to increase the capacity of your drive, make sure you set up your swap file to an uncompressed drive (by default this is drive H:). To change the size of your uncompressed drive, consult your DoubleSpace documentation (supplied with MS-DOS).

7. Windows asks if you are sure you want to make the changes. If you are sure, select OK. If you select cancel, no swap file is created.
8. If this is a permanent swap file, Windows displays a message indicating that the swap file has been created. Select OK.
9. Windows asks you if you want to Continue or Reboot. If you select Continue, you will return to Windows and the swap file will be in effect the next time you start Windows. If you select Reboot, Windows will automatically restart, and the swap file is in effect.

Let's see the effects of the swap file in our example. Figure 6-9 shows the Program Manager About box after the new swap file is in place. Notice that the free memory has now risen to 7,029K. This is on a 4-megabyte system. Windows actually thinks it has more memory than is physically installed in our example system.

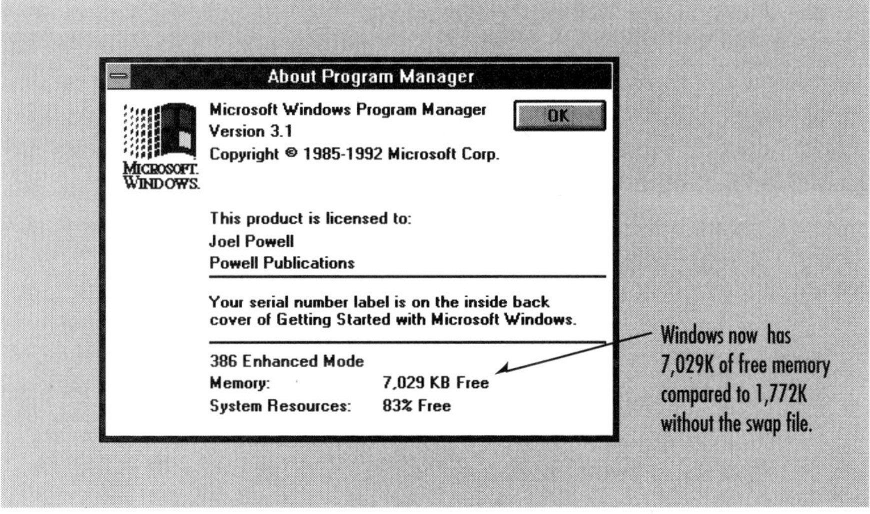

Figure 6-9 The Program Manager About box—with Virtual Memory

Tips For Creating a Swap File

Keep the following things in mind when setting up virtual memory on your system:

- If you are low on disk space, create a temporary swap file. Windows may automatically suggest this type if your disk space is low.
- If you have sufficient disk space, always create a permanent swap file. Permanent swap files are more efficient because they are always in the same place on disk. Temporary swap files are created and moved by the Windows system during each session. This reduces the effectiveness of the swap file.
- Never increase a permanent swap file size above what Windows suggests. This will take up more hard disk space and Windows will not use the additional space anyway.

Now let's take a look at disk caching in Windows.

SMARTDrive and Windows

If you are a DOS 5.0 user (and you skipped Chapter 5), this version of SMARTDRV is new to you, and because it is a newer version, you should use it instead of SMARTDRV.SYS. If you are a DOS 6 user, you should use the version of SMARTDRV supplied with DOS.

As with previous versions of SMARTDrive, this disk caching program keeps track of when the disk is read and what data is being read into memory. The cache keeps data in memory if it is frequently requested. This way, the next time a program tries to read the data off disk, the disk cache intercepts the read and provides the data directly from memory. As we mentioned in the discussion of RAMDRIVE.SYS, memory access is much faster than disk access.

The overall performance increase depends on the size of the disk cache and how often similar data is requested. In other words, if your programs never request the same data twice (or more times), a disk cache is of no use.

As with a the DOS 6 version of SMARTDrive, the Windows version only uses extended memory. Let's look at creating a disk cache using SMARTDRV.EXE.

In order to create a disk cache using SMARTDRV.EXE, we must load its driver in the AUTOEXEC.BAT file. This consists of the path and filename of the driver. Listing 6-4 shows the AUTOEXEC.BAT file for our example extended memory disk cache.

Listing 6-4 AUTOEXEC.BAT—SMARTDrive Disk Cache

```
LOADHIGH C:\DOS\SMARTDRV.EXE
PROMPT $p$g
PATH C:\WINDOWS;C:\DOS
```

In this example, we use the LOADHIGH command. This loads the SMARTDRV.EXE device driver into upper memory. We also install HIMEM.SYS and EMM386.EXE (with the NOEMS switch) in our CONFIG.SYS file to gain access to upper memory.

We use two command line parameters with SMARTDRV.SYS in DOS 5.0. The first sets the maximum size of the cache; the second parameter sets the minimum size of the cache. Using SMARTDRV.EXE we can still use these parameters. However, the first parameter is labeled *initial cache size*; the second parameter is known as the *Windows cache size*. This is the value to which SMARTDRV will shrink if you run Microsoft Windows. Recall that Windows can adjust the size of the SMARTDrive disk cache.

If you omit the parameters (as we did in Listing 6-4) you will get the default initial and Windows cache sizes. These values depend on the amount of extended memory installed in your system. Table 6-1 shows the default SMARTDrive cache sizes for different amounts of extended memory.

When using this table, keep in mind that the memory amounts are for extended memory only. For example, if you have a 2-megabyte system, you have 1 megabyte of extended memory; therefore, you would fall into the first category in this case. Notice that the system with only 1 megabyte of free extended memory has a Windows cache size of 0. This is because Windows needs 1 megabyte of free extended memory to run in enhanced mode.

Extended Memory	Initial Cache Size	Windows Cache Size
To 1MB	All extended memory	0
To 2MB	1MB	256K
To 4MB	1MB	512K
To 6MB	2MB	1MB
Over 6MB	2MB	2MB

Table 6-1 SMARTDrive initial cache and Windows cache defaults

After adding this line to our CONFIG.SYS file, let's reboot and look at the results of loading SMARTDrive. We are not loading any other programs in the AUTOEXEC.BAT file for this example. The Windows version of SMARTDrive does not display and power up messages as SMARTDRV.SYS did in DOS 5.0.

After rebooting, you can type **SMARTDRV** and press ENTER to see the current status of your disk cache. For example, our 4-megabyte machine gives the output.

```
Microsoft SMARTDrive Disk Cache version 4.0
Copyright 1991,1993 Microsoft Corp.

Cache size:  1,048,576 bytes
Cache size when running Windows:   524,288

            Disk Caching Status:
drive   read cache   write cache   buffering
--------------------------------------------
  A:        yes          no            no
  B:        yes          no            no
  C:        yes          yes           no
```

After the copyright message, SMARTDrive displays two lines. The first line is the initial cache size. The second line is the Windows cache size. Because we are using a 4-megabyte system, we have 3 megabytes of extended memory. Referring back to Table 5-3, this would fall into the "to 4MB" category. This results in a 1MB initial cache size and a 512K Windows cache size.

Caution When Using Write Cache

SMARTDrive enables write caching on any hard drives installed in your system. This means that at any given time, data that is supposed to be written to disk is still in memory. If you press CTRL-ALT-DEL to reboot your computer, you will receive the message "Waiting for system shutdown" in the upper left corner of the display. SMARTDrive intercepts the CTRL-ALT-DEL combination to give your system time to write any unwritten data to disk.

If you shut off your PC using the power switch, you run the risk of losing data or damaging files. If your system is idle at the DOS prompt, and no disk activity is present, it is safe to turn off your PC.

After the cache sizes, SMARTDrive displays the disk caching status for all drives in your system. Hard disks are usually read and write cached. This means that SMARTDrive can hold both read and write data for this drive. Floppy drives (such as A: and B: in our example) are normally only read cached. If you write data to a floppy disk, it will occur immediately.

The buffering entry is only for disk drives that are not compatible with SMARTDRV.EXE. Consult your MS-DOS documentation to see if your drive is affected. Most drives do not need to use buffering. DOS 6.2 also supports caching of CD-ROM drives.

To see the full effect of SMARTDrive on our 4-megabyte test system, let's use the MEM command to view the status of memory. We'll run the MEM command before loading Windows to see the total free extended memory. Listing 6-5 shows the MEM /C output for our extended memory disk cache.

Listing 6-5 MEM /C—SMARTDrive Disk Cache

```
Modules using memory below 1 MB:

  Name           Total       =   Conventional   +   Upper Memory
  --------  ----------------   ----------------   ----------------
  MSDOS        13885    (14K)     13885    (14K)         0     (0K)
  HIMEM         1168     (1K)      1168     (1K)         0     (0K)
  EMM386        3120     (3K)      3120     (3K)         0     (0K)
  COMMAND       2912     (3K)      2912     (3K)         0     (0K)
  SMARTDRV     27280    (27K)         0     (0K)     27280    (27K)
  Free        765728   (748K)    634192   (619K)    131536   (128K)

Memory Summary:

  Type of Memory        Total       =       Used       +       Free
  ----------------  ----------------   ----------------   ----------------
  Conventional        655360   (640K)      21168    (21K)     634192   (619K)
  Upper               158816   (155K)      27280    (27K)     131536   (128K)
  Adapter RAM/ROM     393216   (384K)     393216   (384K)          0     (0K)
  Extended (XMS)     2986912  (2917K)    1270688  (1241K)    1716224  (1676K)
  ----------------  ----------------   ----------------   ----------------
  Total memory       4194304  (4096K)    1712352  (1672K)    2481952  (2424K)

  Total under 1 MB    814176   (795K)      48448    (47K)     765728   (748K)

  Largest executable program size        634096   (619K)
  Largest free upper memory block        131440   (128K)
  MS-DOS is resident in the high memory area.
```

We're using the LOADHIGH command to create our disk cache and not affect conventional memory in any way.

The largest change in the MEM output is the effect the SMARTDrive disk cache has on extended memory. In this case it has dropped to 1,716,224 bytes (1676K). Of course, this amount could increase back up to 2,188K (512K +

1,676K) when running Microsoft Windows because we specified a Windows cache size of 512K.

In general, it's a good idea to use SMARTDrive. If it is a last resort, and you need the extended memory for other programs, you can remove its line in AUTOEXEC.BAT.

Multimedia Configurations in Windows 3.1

This section provides two example configurations for users running Windows 3.1 on a system equipped with multimedia devices. The first example is for DOS 5.0 users and the second is for DOS 6 users.

Windows gets the most out of extended memory; therefore, these configurations do not simulate expanded memory. Not only does Windows benefit from this configuration, you also benefit because you have more room in upper memory to load device drivers and TSRs (because no 64K upper memory page frame is required).

Listing 6-6 shows the Windows on DOS 5.0 configuration, and Listing 6-7 shows the configuration for Windows on DOS 6. Notice that the DOS 5.0 configuration uses the newer, Windows versions of EMM386.EXE and SMARTDRV.EXE. The DOS 6.0 configuration uses the newer, DOS 6 versions of EMM386.EXE and SMARTDRV.EXE.

Both configurations maximize extended memory by using the NOEMS switch with EMM386.EXE. Both configurations also load all device drivers and TSRs high using DEVICEHIGH and LOADHIGH. Keep in mind that the amount of free upper memory varies depending on the amount and types of hardware you have installed in your system. You may not be able to load every driver and memory-resident program on your system. In which case, it's better to find two configurations that suit your needs.

Notice that we are using the /e switch with the MSCDEX driver. This loads this driver into extended memory; therefore, it does not take up any upper memory.

Listing 6-6 Windows 3.1—DOS 5.0 Multimedia Configuration

```
AUTOEXEC.BAT contents
---------------------
&ECHO OFF
CLS
PATH C:\DOS;C:\GAMES;C:\MEDIA;
C:\WINDOWS\SMARTDRV.EXE
```

```
C:\SCSI\MSCDEX /e
LOADHIGH C:\MOUSE\MOUSE
LOADHIGH C:\DOS\DOSKEY

CONFIG.SYS contents
---------------------
FILES=20
BUFFERS=10
DEVICE=C:\WINDOWS\HIMEM.SYS
DEVICE=C:\WINDOWS\EMM386.EXE NOEMS
DOS=HIGH,UMB
DEVICEHIGH=C:\SOUND\SOUNDMAN.SYS
DEVICEHIGH=C:\SCSI\ADAPTER.SYS
DEVICEHIGH=C:\VIDEO\VESA.SYS
```

Listing 6-7 Windows 3.1—DOS 6 Multimedia Configuration

```
AUTOEXEC.BAT contents
---------------------
&ECHO OFF
CLS
PATH C:\DOS;C:\GAMES;C:\MEDIA;
C:\DOS\SMARTDRV.EXE
C:\SCSI\MSCDEX /e
LOADHIGH C:\MOUSE\MOUSE
LOADHIGH C:\DOS\DOSKEY

CONFIG.SYS contents
---------------------
FILES=20
BUFFERS=10
DEVICE=C:\DOS\HIMEM.SYS
DEVICE=C:\DOS\EMM386.EXE NOEMS
DOS=HIGH,UMB
DEVICEHIGH=C:\SOUND\SOUNDMAN.SYS
```

Other Drivers in Windows

Many multimedia devices such as Windows accelerators (video cards) and sound cards require more than the drivers in your configuration files. They also require a driver for Windows. Each device is usually accompanied by a disk that contains the driver. You can install drivers by using the Drivers option in the Control Panel. The Control Panel is located in the Main group in the Windows Program Manager. Figure 6-10 shows the Drivers screen.

At this screen you can select Add to add your new device driver. The screens that appear after this point vary depending on the type and manufacturer of the device. You can remove unwanted drivers at this point as well. The Setup option (shown grayed) is enabled for drivers with advanced setup.

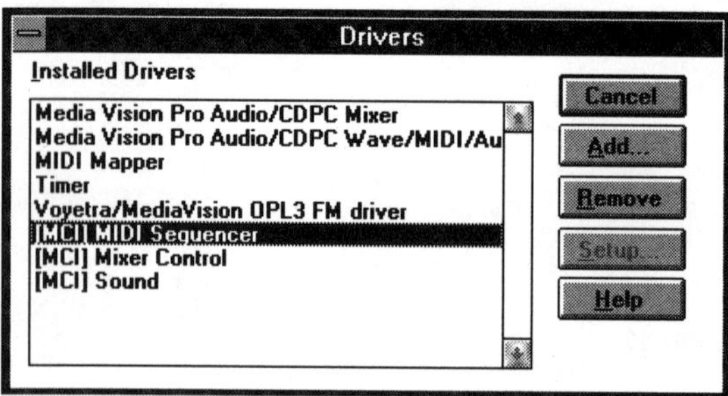

Figure 6-10 Drivers installation in Windows 3.1

This concludes our management of Windows memory. Let's review the topics covered in this chapter.

Summary

You can see that managing memory in Windows is relatively easy. Because Windows' system relies on DOS, Windows memory management starts with the DOS configuration files: AUTOEXEC.BAT and CONFIG.SYS. Here is a review of the topics covered in this chapter.

- You can get the status of free memory and system resources using the Program Manager About dialog box. Many other Windows applications also provide this information (File Manager, Notepad, etc.).
- The Windows installation program usually modifies your configuration files, adding SMARTDRV and SHARE to your AUTOEXEC.BAT file. It also modifies the PATH in AUTOEXEC.BAT and adds HIMEM.SYS to your CONFIG.SYS file (if it doesn't already exist).
- If you configure your system to use upper memory blocks (using EMM386.EXE and DOS=UMB), you can load SMARTDrive and SHARE programs into high memory (for example, LOADHIGH C:\WINDOWS\SMARTDRV.EXE).
- Windows has two basic operating modes: standard and 386 enhanced. Windows' standard mode requires at least an 80286 processor, 256K of free conventional memory, 192K of free extended memory, and an extended memory driver (for example, HIMEM.SYS). You cannot use

expanded memory that is simulated (using EMM386.EXE) in standard mode.

- The Windows 386 enhanced mode takes advantage of the design of the 80386 processor. As a result, this mode has broader requirements. The 386 enhanced mode requires at least an 80386 processor, 256K of free conventional memory, 1,024K (1MB) of free extended memory, and an extended memory driver. You can use EMM386.EXE to simulate expanded memory in 386 enhanced mode.
- Windows uses free conventional and extended memory to run Windows applications. Expanded memory is only used if a non-Windows application requires it. Windows programs never require expanded memory.
- If you are running 386 enhanced mode, you can extend your free physical memory with virtual memory. Virtual memory is a disk file, called a swap file, that appears as memory to Windows. Windows places the least recently used portions of programs in the swap file, while recently active programs are in physical memory.
- A permanent swap file is the most efficient. The major drawback of permanent swap files is that they take up disk space (even when not running Windows).
- Temporary swap files are less efficient than the permanent version, however. They only require disk space when Windows is running. The swap file is deleted when you exit Windows.

The key to managing memory in Windows is to free up as much conventional and extended memory as possible. The more extended memory you install, the better Windows will perform. The next chapter shows the main features and capabilities of two popular third-party memory managers.

Third-Party Memory Management

If you're willing to spend some extra money to help you with memory configuration, a third-party memory manager may be for you. Many of these memory managers take better advantage of upper memory addresses than DOS 5.0 or DOS 6.0's EMM386.EXE. This allows you to load even more drivers and memory-resident programs into upper memory, freeing up more conventional memory. They also allow switching between extended and expanded memory on the fly depending on the demands of your programs.

Another advantage of third-party memory managers is they usually come with utilities that help you configure your computer's memory. For example, some utilities analyze your current configuration and display it on your screen in graphical form. This helps you visualize how your system utilizes its memory.

In this chapter, we will examine the features, utilities, and basic functionality of two of the more popular memory managers: QEMM Version 7 by Quarterdeck and 386MAX Version 7 by Qualitas. These are the most recent versions at this time. Both products have been on the market for several years and have proven to be stable.

You can use this chapter as a guide to see if your system would benefit from one of these memory managers. We'll use typical DOS 6.0 configuration files as a point of comparison. You'll be able to see how much additional upper and conventional memory you would gain by using one of these products. Let's start with an overview of the topics for this chapter.

TOPICS COVERED

Why Use a Third-Party Memory Manager?

Quarterdeck QEMM Requirements

QEMM Features and Utilities

Comparison Between QEMM and DOS 6.0

Qualitas 386MAX Requirements

386MAX Features and Utilities

Comparison Between 386MAX and DOS 6.0

Why Use a Third-Party Memory Manager?

If your computer has lots of hardware that requires device drivers, you may need some additional assistance from a third-party memory manager. Both the DOS 5.0 and DOS 6.0 versions of EMM386.EXE have limitations. These limitations are in the utilization of upper memory. If you have several device drivers, you may run out of upper memory space to store them. When you run out, the rest of the drivers are loaded into conventional memory. If you are using DOS 6.0's DoubleSpace, you may run into trouble sooner because its driver is very large.

On the other hand, if your system does not require many device drivers, you may not need a third-party memory manager. It is important to note that these products are not limited to simply increasing free conventional memory. They each come with a host of utilities related to memory. Let's look at the requirements, features, utilities, and installation of Quarterdeck's QEMM.

QEMM—Quarterdeck Expanded Memory Manager

Quarterdeck's QEMM is one of the leading third-party memory managers. It does the job that EMM386.EXE did for us in DOS 5.0 and DOS 6.0. However, it is more aggressive in opening up additional upper memory addresses. You can move more drivers and TSRs into upper memory, as a result, increasing free conventional memory.

QEMM System Requirements

The following is a list of the minimum requirements to run 386QEMM:

- 80386SX Processor or Higher
- 1.5 Megabytes of RAM
- MS-DOS (Version 3.0 through 6.0) or DR DOS 6.0. If you are using DOS 6.0, you must have QEMM version 7.

Features of QEMM

Quarterdeck has introduced several new features with version 7.0 including DOS-Up and Stealth DoubleSpace. Here is a brief look at the features of QEMM along with the purpose and function of each feature.

DOS-Up

The DOS-Up feature frees up conventional memory by relocating a large portion of DOS into high memory. This is similar to the DOS=HIGH command used with DOS 5.0 and DOS 6.0 although DOS-Up is more effective than DOS=HIGH alone.

DOS-Up consists of two device drivers: DOSDATA.SYS and DOS-UP.SYS. These drivers are loaded and configured by the OPTIMIZE program on install. Your CONFIG.SYS file is modified automatically to add lines for the drivers.

QEMM386.SYS—QEMM's Device Driver

This driver is the heart of QEMM. QEMM386.SYS is essentially the replacement for EMM386.EXE. It is responsible for memory management when you're using QEMM. The installation program automatically adds the QEMM386.SYS line to your CONFIG.SYS file.

QDPMI.SYS—DOS Protected Mode Interface

The QDPMI.SYS driver is the Quarterdeck DOS Protected Mode Interface host. It is useful for programs that require DPMI support. This driver has no effect when you're running Microsoft Windows; Windows supplies its own DPMI driver for its applications. This driver is also automatically added to your CONFIG.SYS file on install.

LOADHI.SYS

This driver loads device drivers and memory-resident programs into high memory. It is the equivalent of the DEVICEHIGH, LOADHIGH, or LH command in DOS. You must use the entire filename (LOADHI.SYS) to load device drivers high in CONFIG.SYS. Only the main portion of the filename, LOADHI, is required to load memory-resident programs in AUTOEXEC.BAT. This calls up LOADHI.COM. OPTIMIZE automatically adds the LOADHI.SYS and LOADHI lines to your configuration files. References to LOADHIGH, LH, and DEVICEHIGH are removed by OPTIMIZE.

VIDRAM

VIDRAM is a memory-resident program that seizes unused video RAM address space. This program only works with systems with EGA or VGA adapters. Some EGA and VGA adapters do not require the 64K of memory above conventional memory. This increases the contiguous conventional memory by 64K. VIDRAM may also be able to extend conventional memory another 32K on some systems.

Stealth DoubleSpace

If you're using DOS 6.0 and DoubleSpace, you can use the Stealth DoubleSpace feature. The driver for DoubleSpace is around 43K which takes up a large amount of conventional or upper memory. Stealth DoubleSpace moves the DoubleSpace driver into an EMS page frame on demand. This frees conventional or upper memory, depending on where the driver was originally installed.

Stealth ROM

The Stealth ROM feature of QEMM creates up to 115K of upper memory address space. It essentially remaps the system ROMs freeing the memory addresses it originally occupied. Stealth ROM may or may not be enabled on installation depending on the configuration of your system.

OPTIMIZE

The OPTIMIZE program is run automatically by the installation program and is similar to MemMaker in DOS 6. It analyzes your system and makes adjustments to your configuration files. OPTIMIZE reboots your computer during this process. OPTIMIZE examines all possible configurations for your system and determines the one which is optimal for your system.

OPTIMIZE also uses a program to determine the size of TSRs and device drivers. With this information, it can load the drivers in an order that will best utilize upper memory space.

Let's see how OPTIMIZE fits into the installation scheme for QEMM.

Installing QEMM

Installing QEMM is fairly straightforward. Figure 7-1 shows an overview of the QEMM installation process. You start out with a decision: Express or Advanced Setup. If you choose Express Setup, the installation program will make all the decisions for you. For example, the installation program will remove any reference to HIMEM.SYS and replace it with the QEMM equivalent, DOS-Up. If you choose the Advanced install, you will have a chance later to confirm or deny the suggested changes.

In either case, the installation program copies the QEMM files to your hard disk. If you selected the Advanced Setup, the installation program will prompt you for each change.

The next step is the OPTIMIZE program. Similar to the Setup program, OPTIMIZE has two modes: Express and Custom. The Express mode uses default settings and makes all decisions for you. The Custom mode lets you override the default settings of OPTIMIZE.

After OPTMIZE knows the settings, it reboots your computer. When the system is restarting, OPTIMIZE takes over and determines the sizes of all drivers and memory-resident programs. It uses this information to get the most out of upper memory space.

OPTIMIZE reports the number of combinations for your system, selects the optimum configuration, and reboots again.

OPTIMIZE reports the gain in conventional memory on the final startup. At this point you are at the DOS prompt, ready to go. You now have a new CONFIG.SYS and AUTOEXEC.BAT. The old configuration files (just in case) are written to CONFIG.QDK and AUTOEXEC.QDK.

Getting Around QEMM On Startup

If something goes awry when rebooting (such as a lockup or system crash), you can bypass QEMM by holding down the ALT key on startup. It will prompt you to press ESC to bypass DOS-Up. After pressing ESC, immediately press and hold the ALT key again. QEMM will prompt you to press ESC to unload QEMM. Press ESC and you've bypassed QEMM.

Manifest—Many QEMM Utilities in One

QEMM does more than increase conventional memory and modify your configuration files. You also get Manifest, a utility program that provides just about every bit of information about your computer and memory. It provides details about both the hardware and software installed in your system.

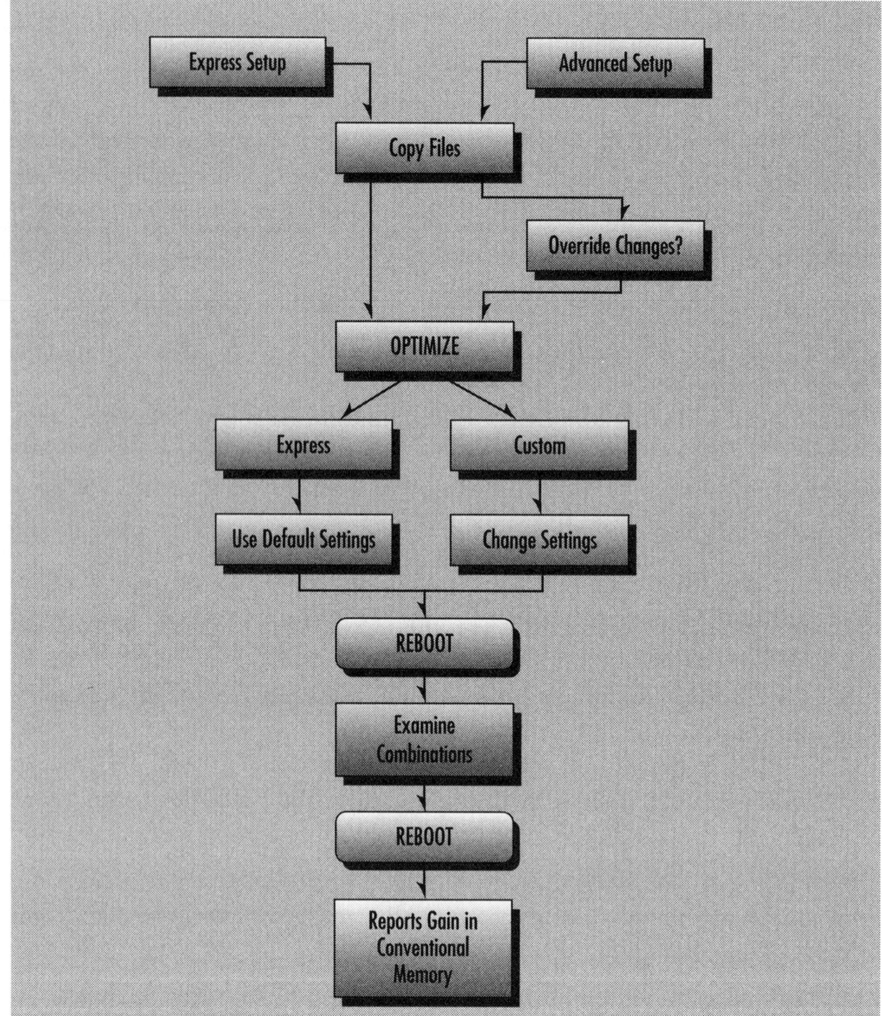

Figure 7-1 An overview of QEMM installation

Manifest has a built-in editor so you can easily modify your configuration files. Manifest also prints reports. You can print information about a specific topic, or you can print a comprehensive report on your system. Figure 7-2 shows one of the screens from QEMM Manifest.

QEMM's Manifest is similar to the Microsoft Diagnostics (MSD) program. However, the MSD program cannot edit configurations files. Manifest has a built-in text editor. This editor is shown in Figure 7-3.

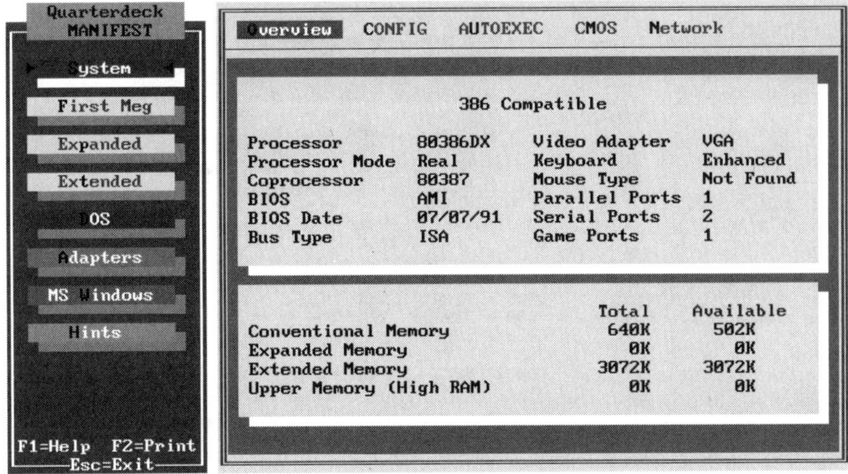

Figure 7-2 QEMM Manifest system overview screen

Figure 7-4 shows a screen from Manifest that provides a report on the first megabyte of memory. There are similar screens for expanded and extended memory.

Comparing QEMM to DOS 6.0

The only way to know exactly how much a third-party memory manager will help you is to buy it and try it. However, we have conducted a simple test to com-

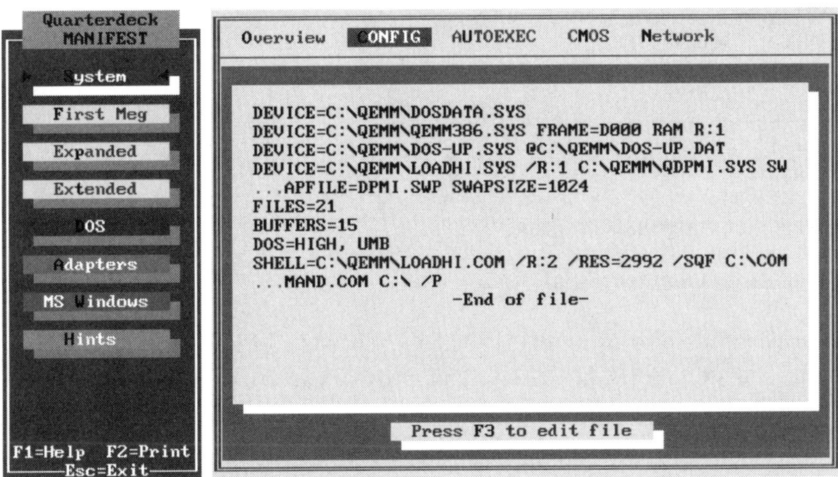

Figure 7-3 Manifest text editor

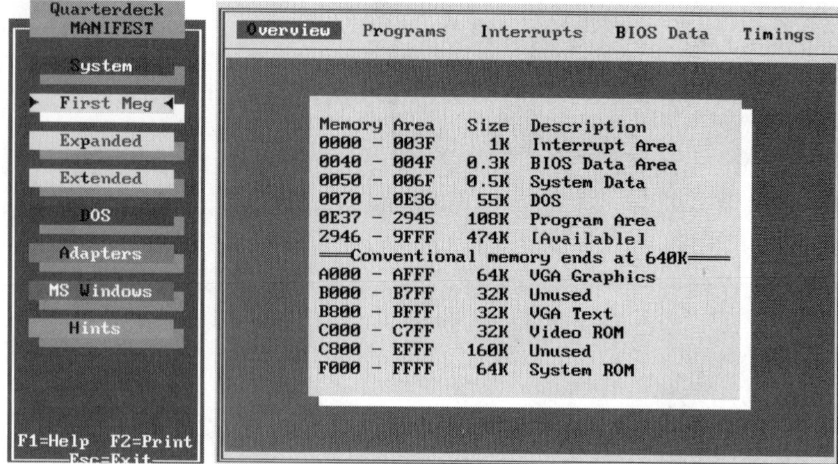

Figure 7-4 Manifest First Meg screen

pare a DOS 6.0 configuration to the same QEMM configuration. Listing 7-1 shows the DOS 6.0 configuration files. We are loading the ANSI.SYS driver in the CONFIG.SYS file and the DOSKEY TSR in the AUTOEXEC.BAT file.

Listing 7-1 DOS 6.0 Configuration

```
AUTOEXEC.BAT Contents
--------------------
C:\DOS\SMARTDRV.EXE
PROMPT $p$g
PATH C:\DOS
LOADHIGH C:\DOS\DOSKEY

CONFIG.SYS Contents
--------------------
FILES=21
BUFFERS=15
DEVICE=C:\DOS\HIMEM.SYS
DEVICE=C:\DOS\EMM386.EXE NOEMS
DOS=HIGH, UMB
DEVICEHIGH=C:\DOS\ANSI.SYS
```

Notice we are also using HIMEM.SYS, EMM386.EXE with the NOEMS option, and DOS=HIGH, UMB. This provides access to the upper memory blocks. We load the ANSI.SYS driver into upper memory using DEVICEHIGH and the DOSKEY TSR using LOADHIGH. Listing 7-2 shows the MEM/C output for this configuration. We'll use these values as a point of comparison with the configuration created by QEMM.

Listing 7-2 MEM/C Output—DOS 6.0 Configuration

```
Modules using memory below 1 MB:

  Name           Total        =   Conventional    +   Upper Memory
  --------  ----------------   ----------------   ----------------
  MSDOS        13885   (14K)      13885   (14K)          0    (0K)
  HIMEM         1168    (1K)       1168    (1K)          0    (0K)
  EMM386        3120    (3K)       3120    (3K)          0    (0K)
  COMMAND       2912    (3K)       2912    (3K)          0    (0K)
  ANSI          4240    (4K)          0    (0K)       4240    (4K)
  SMARTDRV     27280   (27K)          0    (0K)      27280   (27K)
  DOSKEY        4144    (4K)          0    (0K)       4144    (4K)
  Free        757360  (740K)     634192  (619K)     123168  (120K)

Memory Summary:

  Type of Memory       Total       =       Used        +       Free
  ----------------  -----------------   -----------------   -----------------
  Conventional        655360   (640K)      21168    (21K)     634192   (619K)
  Upper               158832   (155K)      35664    (35K)     123168   (120K)
  Adapter RAM/ROM     393216   (384K)     393216   (384K)          0     (0K)
  Extended (XMS)     2986896  (2917K)    1270672  (1241K)    1716224  (1676K)
  ----------------  -----------------   -----------------   -----------------
  Total memory       4194304  (4096K)    1720720  (1680K)    2473584  (2416K)

  Total under 1 MB    814192   (795K)      56832    (56K)     757360   (740K)

  Largest executable program size          634096   (619K)
  Largest free upper memory block          123072   (120K)
  MS-DOS is resident in the high memory area.
```

The figures to watch are those listed in boldface. For example, we are interested primarily in upper and conventional memory space. We'll also keep an eye on extended memory to see how it is affected by QEMM.

An Express Install with Express Optimize

We are using the suggestions of QEMM to reconfigure our system. After running the installation and OPTIMIZE, QEMM has come up with the configuration files shown in Listing 7-3.

Listing 7-3 QEMM Configuration

```
AUTOEXEC.BAT Contents
----------------
C:\QEMM\LOADHI /R:1 /LO C:\DOS\SMARTDRV.EXE
PROMPT $p$g
PATH C:\QEMM;C:\DOS
C:\QEMM\LOADHI /R:2 C:\DOS\DOSKEY
```

continued on next page

continued from previous page

```
CONFIG.SYS Contents
------------------
DEVICE=C:\QEMM\DOSDATA.SYS
DEVICE=C:\QEMM\QEMM386.SYS RAM R:1
DEVICE=C:\QEMM\DOS-UP.SYS @C:\QEMM\DOS-UP.DAT
DEVICE=C:\QEMM\LOADHI.SYS /R:1 C:\QEMM\QDPMI.SYS SWAPFILE=DPMI.SWP
SWAPSIZE=1024
FILES=21
BUFFERS=15
DOS=HIGH, UMB
SHELL=C:\QEMM\LOADHI.COM /R:2 /RES=2992 /SQF C:\COMMAND.COM C:\ /P
```

As you can see, QEMM has made several modifications to our configuration files. Starting in CONFIG.SYS, the first line loads QEMM's DOSDATA.SYS driver. Recall that this driver is necessary to run the DOS-Up feature. The second line loads the QEMM386.SYS driver. This is the replacement for EMM386.EXE and HIMEM.SYS, which have been removed.

The third line loads the DOS-UP.SYS driver and the fourth line loads the driver for the DOS Protected Mode Interface host. QEMM adds the last line, a SHELL statement to load the command interpreter (COMMAND.COM) into high memory.

There were three changes to the AUTOEXEC.BAT file. First, the SMARTDRV.EXE driver is now loaded using LOADHI instead of LOADHIGH. The switches (/R:1) direct the driver into a specific area of high memory. The next change is the addition of the QEMM directory to the PATH statement. The last change is using LOADHI to load DOSKEY into high memory.

Now let's compare results. Listing 7-4 shows the MEM/C output for this configuration.

Listing 7-4 MEM/C Output—QEMM Configuration

```
Modules using memory below 1 MB:

  Name          Total        =   Conventional    +   Upper Memory
  --------  ----------------   ----------------   ----------------
  QEMM386        928     (1K)        928    (1K)          0    (0K)
  LOADHI         112     (0K)        112    (0K)          0    (0K)
  COMMAND       2912     (3K)        272    (0K)       2640    (3K)
  QDPMI         2032     (2K)          0    (0K)       2032    (2K)
  SMARTDRV     27280    (27K)          0    (0K)      27280   (27K)
  DOS-UP         224     (0K)          0    (0K)        224    (0K)
  DOSDATA       5424     (5K)          0    (0K)       5424    (5K)
  DOSKEY        4144     (4K)          0    (0K)       4144    (4K)
  FILES          976     (1K)          0    (0K)        976    (1K)
  FCBS           272     (0K)          0    (0K)        272    (0K)
  WKBUFFER       528     (1K)          0    (0K)        528    (1K)
```

```
  LASTDRIV        464    (0K)          0    (0K)        464    (0K)
  STACKS         1872    (2K)          0    (0K)       1872    (2K)
  INSTALL         160    (0K)          0    (0K)        160    (0K)
  Free         752576  (735K)     649760  (635K)     102816  (100K)

Memory Summary:

  Type of Memory         Total        =        Used          +        Free
  ----------------  -----------------   -----------------   -----------------
  Conventional         655360    (640K)      5600      (5K)     649760    (635K)
  Upper                148048    (144K)     45232     (44K)     102816    (100K)
  Adapter RAM/ROM      393216    (384K)    393216    (384K)          0      (0K)
  Extended (XMS)      2997680   (2927K)   2239296   (2187K)     758384    (740K)
  ----------------  -----------------   -----------------   -----------------
  Total memory        4194304   (4096K)   2683344   (2620K)    1510960   (1476K)

  Total under 1 MB     809296    (790K)     56720     (55K)     752576    (735K)

  Total Expanded (EMS)                    3440640   (3360K)
  Free Expanded (EMS)                     1736704   (1696K)
  Largest executable program size          649744    (635K)
  Largest free upper memory block           68208     (67K)
  MS-DOS is resident in the high memory area.
```

You can see a number of differences between the DOS 6.0 and QEMM memory summaries. The most important difference is that 649,760 bytes are free in conventional memory compared to 634,096 in the DOS 6.0 configuration; a gain of 16K. The gain is primarily due to the size of QEMM386.SYS compared to EMM386.EXE. QEMM is also capable of loading more of DOS into high memory than DOS 6.0 (or 5.0).

QEMM does not report as much total upper memory as DOS 6.0. However, this is slightly deceiving. QEMM does not try for additional upper memory if it doesn't need it. Because we are not loading numerous large drivers in our configuration, QEMM detects this and does not try for additional upper memory space. If QEMM determines that additional upper memory space is required, it invokes the Stealth ROM option.

Also notice that there is a drop in free extended memory. This is also a bit deceiving. We are also simulating expanded memory; this is a default in QEMM. Don't worry though, QEMM can switch the amounts of free extended/expanded memory depending on the program requirements. For example, if you start Microsoft Windows, QEMM will make more extended memory available.

You can see that QEMM is a possible choice if you have to load a lot of drivers and TSRs into high memory, or if you need the maximum conventional memory possible.

Now let's look at another popular third-party memory manager: 386MAX.

386MAX—The Intelligent Memory Manager

386MAX by Qualitas is another popular third-party memory manager. Essentially, it uses techniques similar to QEMM. It does the job that EMM386.EXE did in DOS 5.0 and DOS 6.0. 386MAX is very aggressive in its pursuit of upper memory addresses, even with a default setup.

386MAX System Requirements

The following is a list of the minimum requirements to run 386MAX:

- 80386SX Processor or Higher
- 256K of Extended Memory
- MS-DOS (Version 3.3 and Up)
- Hard Disk

Features of 386MAX

Qualitas has introduced new features in version 7.0 including a Windows PIF editor and DOSMAX for Windows. Here is a brief look at the features of 386MAX with the purpose and function of each feature.

386MAX.SYS

This driver is the replacement for HIMEM.SYS and EMM386.EXE. It is the heart of 386MAX. It uses a fraction of the memory required by its two predecessors. A line for this driver is automatically added during installation.

386LOAD

386MAX has two versions of 386LOAD. The first version, 386LOAD.SYS, loads device drivers. The second version, 386LOAD.COM, loads TSRs in the AUTOEXEC.BAT file (or the command line). The installation program will automatically modify your configuration using 386LOAD to load your drivers and TSRs high (instead of DEVICEHIGH or LOADHIGH).

ROMSearch

ROMSearch is similar to Stealth ROM in QEMM. The ROMSearch program finds additional areas of high memory. ROMSearch is run automatically from the Maximize program. We'll discuss the Maximize program in a moment.

ExtraDOS

This loads the FILES, BUFFERS, FCBS, LASTDRIVE, COMMAND.COM, etc. into high memory for another increase in conventional memory. ExtraDOS must be manually added to your configuration files.

QCache

If you're using the DOS SMARTDrive disk caching program, the 386MAX install may ask you if you want to replace it with QCache. QCache is the 386MAX disk caching software. Qualitas suggests that you let the install program automatically make this change.

386DISK

This driver is the 386MAX equivalent to DOS' RAMDRIVE.SYS. Qualitas suggests you use this RAM disk utility if you require a RAM disk and are running 386MAX. You must add a line manually to use this feature.

Maximize

This is the program that determines the optimum configuration for your system. It uses a similar technique to QEMM's Optimize. The Maximize program is run automatically on install. It will reboot your system several times to make adjustments and select the proper configuration.

Let's see how Maximize fits into the installation sequence for 386MAX.

Installing 386MAX

The install program for 386MAX is more inquisitive than the QEMM install program. It does ask more questions, but it is more aggressive in getting upper memory addresses. Figure 7-5 shows the flow of the 386MAX installation process.

After copying the 386MAX files to your hard disk, the install program asks you if you want EMS support. The default answer to this question depends on your current configuration. If you are using expanded memory now, the default answer is YES. If you're not using expanded memory, the default answer is NO. You can override any of the default answers.

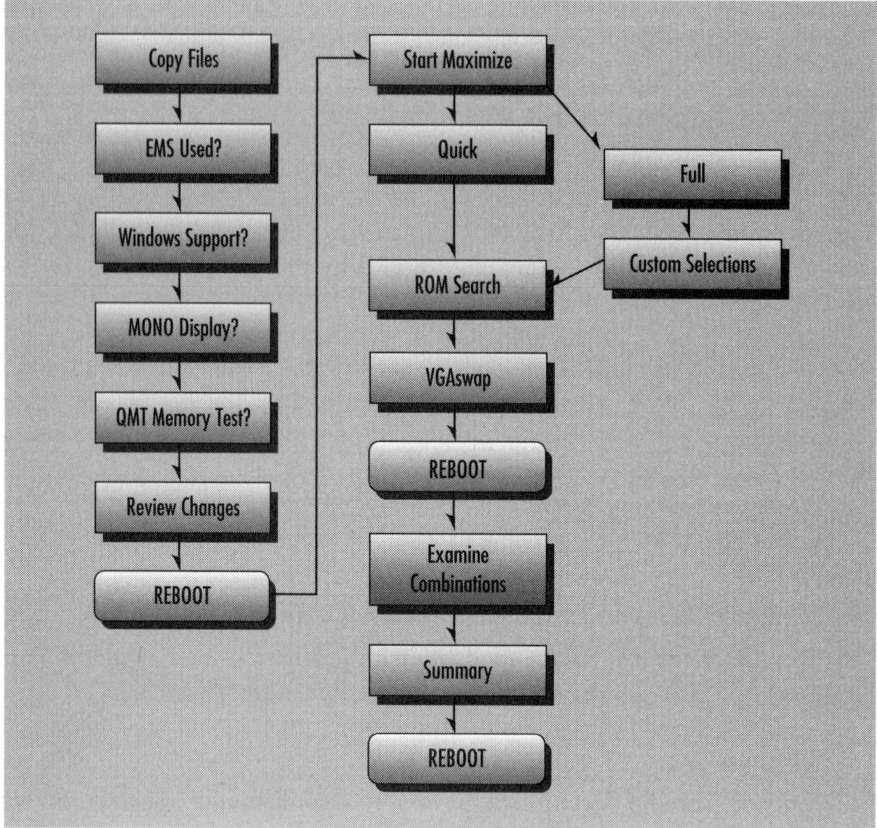

Figure 7-5 An overview of 386MAX installation

The next step asks if you want Windows support. Answering YES will increase the resident size of 386MAX, but it provides a better configuration for Windows users.

The install program asks if you are using the monochrome display region. If you are not, it uses the upper memory addresses (formerly the mono display RAM) for device drivers and TSRs. Most EGA/VGA cards do not use this region of upper memory.

The next question is whether or not you want to run the QMT memory tester. Answering YES to this question will test your computer's memory immediately. It will also test the memory when the installation program reboots your computer.

The 386MAX install program lets you examine all of the changes to your AUTOEXEC.BAT and CONFIG.SYS. You can also view online documentation at this point. After reviewing and accepting the changes, the install program reboots your computer.

As your computer restarts, the Maximize program starts. You can select the Quick or the Full optimize option. The Full option lets you customize the Maximize parameters. After making your selections, the next step is ROM Search. You can use this option to tell 386MAX to find additional upper memory address space.

Next you are asked if you want to run VGAswap. This program can create even more upper memory addresses by relocating your VGA BIOS. At this point, Maximize reboots your computer again.

As your computer restarts, the Maximize program examines the combinations, makes a configuration selection, and provides a summary on your display. Maximize reboots your system a final time; at this point you can use your computer again.

386MAX Utilities

386MAX has several utilities in addition to the memory management features. QEMM had the Manifest program that was a collection of utilities in one program. 386MAX offers stand-alone utilities that perform many of the same services.

Qualitas Memory Tester

The Qualitas Memory Tester, or QMT, is a comprehensive memory testing utility. You can run up to six different types of tests, either automatically in AUTOEXEC.BAT, or any time you want from the DOS command line. This tester tests to a low level that most users will never need.

The 386MAX Shell and ASQ

The 386MAX shell contains several utilities. Figure 7-6 shows a screen from the 386MAX shell. One of these utilities, ASQ, lets you examine your system in several ways: memory, hardware, configuration, installed ROM, etc. It performs many features including taking a snapshot of your configuration at a given time. You can compare snapshots of two configurations to compare results.

MAX Text Editor

Also built into the 386MAX shell is a text editor. You can directly modify any of your configuration files in this editor. You can also use DOS EDIT or any other DOS text editor.

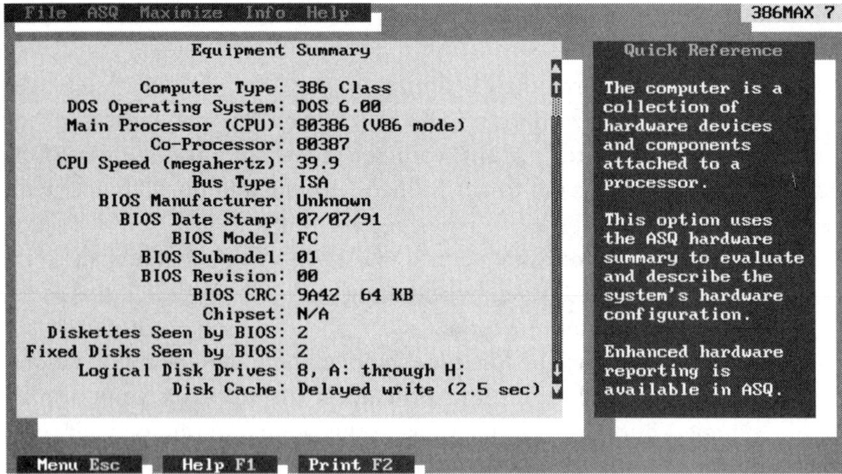

Figure 7-6 The 386MAX shell

386UTIL

This utility shows you how 386MAX is managing your memory in detail. It is a more powerful version of the DOS MEM command. You can run 386UTIL from the 386MAX shell. Figure 7-7 shows a memory summary from the 386MAX utilities. Figure 7-8 shows a detail of high DOS space (upper memory).

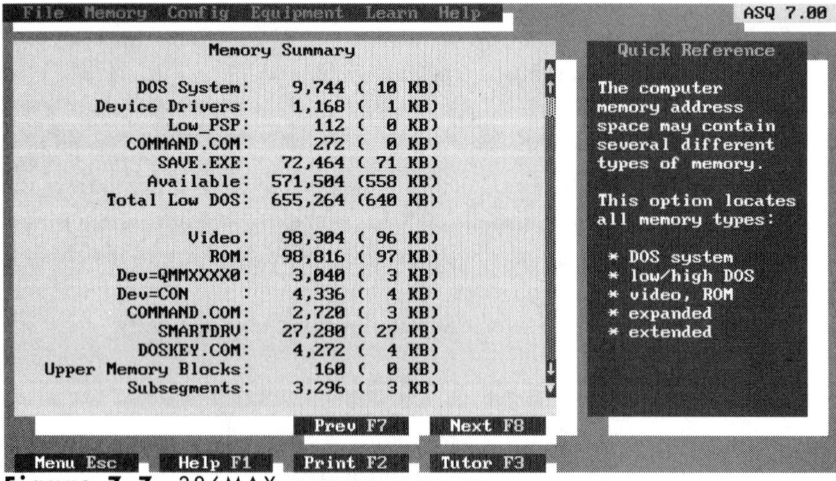

Figure 7-7 386MAX memory summary

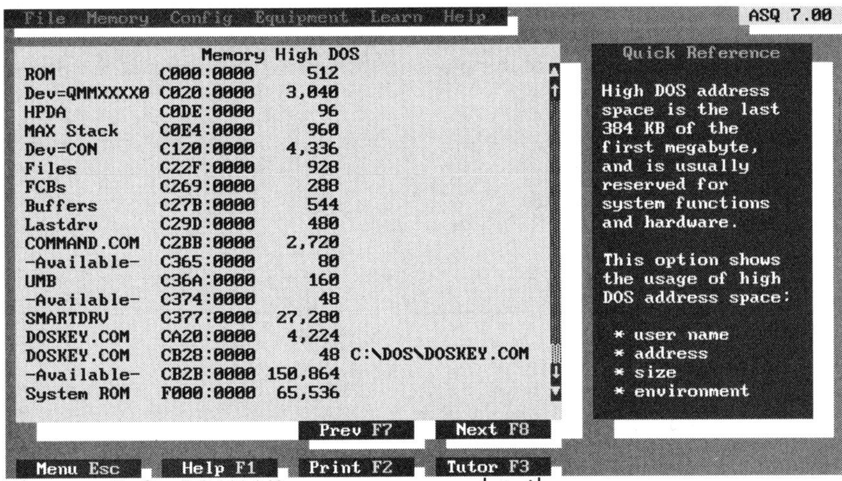

Figure 7-8 386MAX upper memory detail

DOSMAX for Windows

This utility helps you out if you are running memory hungry DOS programs inside of Microsoft Windows. It has one drawback, however. It cannot run DOS programs that use a graphics mode. It can only run DOS text mode programs. Given these conditions, DOSMAX can provide up to 736K of DOS memory for a DOS program running inside Windows.

Qualitas PIF Editor

The Qualitas PIF (program information file) editor is a replacement for the Microsoft Windows PIF editor. It has more features than the Windows version, including the ability to test applications on the spot. You can fine tune your PIFs much quicker with the Qualitas PIF editor.

Comparing 386MAX to DOS 6.0

Now we'll perform a comparison between 386MAX and DOS 6.0. We are using the same DOS 6.0 configuration files (shown in Listing 7-1) we used in the QEMM comparison. We can also use the MEM /C output in Listing 7-2 to compare the results with 386MAX.

A Default 386MAX Configuration

We are using the defaults for the 386MAX installation. After running the installation program and Maximize, 386MAX has produced the configuration files shown in Listing 7-5.

Listing 7-5 386MAX Configuration

```
AUTOEXEC.BAT Contents
---------------------
C:\386MAX\QMT /C QUICK=1
C:\DOS\SMARTDRV.EXE
PROMPT $p$g
PATH C:\DOS
C:\386MAX\386load size=6432 prog=C:\DOS\DOSKEY

CONFIG.SYS Contents
---------------------
FILES=21
BUFFERS=15
DOS=HIGH
Device=c:\386max\386max.sys pro=c:\386max\386max.pro
device=C:\386MAX\386load.sys size=9072 prog=C:\DOS\ANSI.SYS
REM MAXIMIZE: ExtraDOS must come at the end of CONFIG.SYS
Device=C:\386MAX\ExtraDOS.max pro=C:\386MAX\ExtraDOS.PRO
Install=C:\386MAX\ExtraDOS.max
```

The 386MAX installation and Maximize programs have made several modifications to the original DOS 6.0 configuration files. The new driver for 386MAX is in the fourth line of CONFIG.SYS. This is the replacement for HIMEM.SYS and EMM386.EXE. Note that they are removed from the file.

The fifth line in CONFIG.SYS uses 386LOAD to load ANSI.SYS into high memory. The sixth line is a remark line. This is a reminder not to manually add any lines after the ExtraDOS lines. The last two lines load and install the ExtraDOS driver.

The AUTOEXEC.BAT file contains two modifications. The first is the addition of QMT (Memory Tester) to the beginning of the file. This will run the memory tester (quick version) every time you restart you computer.

The other modification is to the last line in AUTOEXEC.BAT. This line loads the DOSKEY TSR into upper memory using the 386LOAD feature. Let's see the effects of this 386MAX configuration on memory. Listing 7-6 shows the MEM /C output for the 386MAX configuration.

Listing 7-6 MEM /C—386MAX Configuration

```
Modules using memory below 1 MB:

  Name           Total       =   Conventional   +   Upper Memory
  --------  ----------------   ----------------   ----------------
  MSDOS         9869   (10K)      9869   (10K)          0    (0K)
  386MAX        1072    (1K)      1072    (1K)          0    (0K)
  386LOAD         80    (0K)        80    (0K)          0    (0K)
  Low_PSP        112    (0K)       112    (0K)          0    (0K)
  COMMAND       2912    (3K)       272    (0K)       2640    (3K)
  640K)         7248    (7K)         0    (0K)       7248    (7K)
                3296    (3K)         0    (0K)       3296    (3K)
  --------       128    (0K)         0    (0K)        128    (0K)
  th : Jan       240    (0K)         0    (0K)        240    (0K)
  MSDOS          128    (0K)         0    (0K)        128    (0K)
  SMARTDRV     27280   (27K)         0    (0K)      27280   (27K)
  DOSKEY        4272    (4K)         0    (0K)       4272    (4K)
  Free        794736  (776K)    643872  (629K)     150864  (147K)

Memory Summary:

  Type of Memory         Total        =       Used        +       Free
  ----------------  -----------------   -----------------   -----------------
  Conventional        655360   (640K)      11488     (11K)    643872   (629K)
  Upper               196096   (192K)      45232     (44K)    150864   (147K)
  Adapter RAM/ROM     393216   (384K)     393216    (384K)         0     (0K)
  Extended (XMS)     2949632  (2881K)    1442304   (1409K)   1507328  (1472K)
  ----------------  -----------------   -----------------   -----------------
  Total memory       4194304  (4096K)    1892240   (1848K)   2302064  (2248K)

  Total under 1 MB    851456   (832K)      56720     (55K)    794736   (776K)

  Largest executable program size         643856    (629K)
  Largest free upper memory block         150864    (147K)
  MS-DOS is resident in the high memory area.
```

As with the QEMM example, you can see a number of differences between the DOS 6.0 and 386MAX memory summaries. Again, the amount of free conventional memory has increased to 643,856 bytes (compared to 634,096 in the DOS 6.0 configuration). The gain is primarily due to the size of 386MAX.SYS compared to EMM386.EXE. Like QEMM, 386MAX is capable of loading more of DOS into high memory than DOS 6.0 (or 5.0).

Note that the amount of total upper memory has increased dramatically due to 386MAX's aggressive approach. There are 196,096 bytes of upper memory in 386MAX and 158,832 bytes of upper memory in DOS 6.0. You can see where this would be desirable if you have several device drivers and TSRs.

Also notice that there is a slight drop in free extended memory. This is due to the use of extended memory to backfill the newly found upper memory areas. All in all, 386MAX improved the memory configuration for this example system. How much of an impact 386MAX has depends on the individual computer's configuration.

Now let's summarize our look at third-party memory management.

Summary

If you need a lot of conventional memory and you must load several device drivers, a third-party memory manager may be for you. We looked at an overview of two of the top memory managers: QEMM and 386MAX. Both of these products increase upper memory space, and as a result, free up conventional memory. The following is a summary of the QEMM memory manager:

- QEMM386.SYS replaces HIMEM.SYS and EMM386.EXE, saving conventional memory.
- The DOS-Up program relocates the majority of DOS into high memory.
- LOADHI.SYS is used in place of DEVICEHIGH in CONFIG.SYS. LOADHI (which calls LOADHI.COM) is used in place of LOADHIGH, or LH, in AUTOEXEC.BAT.
- DOS 6.0 users can use Stealth DoubleSpace to relocate the DoubleSpace driver.
- The Stealth ROM feature hides system ROMs and makes additional upper memory addresses available.
- The installation program for QEMM uses the Optimize program. Optimize examines all configuration possibilities and chooses the optimum.
- Manifest is a utility program shipped with QEMM. You can edit configuration files and obtain detailed information about your system hardware, memory, and configuration.

The following is a summary of the 386MAX memory manager:

- 386MAX.SYS replaces HIMEM.SYS and EMM386.EXE, saving conventional memory.
- 386LOAD.SYS is used in place of DEVICEHIGH. 386LOAD.COM is used in place of LOADHIGH, or LH.
- QCache is a disk caching program and is a replacement for SMARTDrive.
- The ROMSearch feature makes additional upper memory addresses available.
- The installation program for 386MAX uses the Maximize program. Maximize examines all configuration possibilities and chooses the optimum.
- 386MAX comes with several utilities. The 386MAX shell contains ASQ, a text editor, and 386UTIL. In ASQ you can take a snapshot of your configuration to compare with other configurations.

With the information from this chapter, you should be able to determine if you would benefit from one of these memory managers. If you find yourself using many different sets of configuration files for your computer, a third-party memory manager may be the solution. The next chapter contains several sets of configuration files to use as a starting point in memory management.

The Configuration Files

This chapter contains several configuration files for DOS 5.0 and DOS 6. Each set of configuration files provides a service (for example, using upper memory, simulating expanded memory, etc.). You can use these files as a starting point on which to build your own, fine-tuned configuration.

Each set of files is accompanied with a list of the goals for the configuration, along with notes describing possible pitfalls, special system requirements, and minor adjustments you can make.

Both the DOS 5.0 and DOS 6 sections have configurations with Windows 3.1. If you use Microsoft Windows and DOS applications, you can find the right combination for your needs.

Each example includes a marker that indicates the proper location to load your device drivers in your CONFIG.SYS file. It also indicates whether or not you can load device drivers and TSRs in upper memory. The amount of upper memory available to load device drivers and TSRs varies from computer to computer.

All configuration files in this chapter assume that DOS is installed to drive C: in the DOS directory. Also we assume that Windows is installed on driver C: in the WINDOWS directory. If you have installed DOS or Windows to any other drive or directory, make the necessary adjustments before using the files.

TOPICS COVERED

DOS 5.0 Configurations

DOS 5.0 with Windows 3.1 Configurations

DOS 6 Configurations

DOS 6 with Windows 3.1 Configurations

DOS 5.0 Configurations (Without Windows 3.1)

This section provides four different DOS 5.0 configurations that you can use as a starting point for your system. We have provided an overview, the purpose, and notes about each configuration. If you are using DOS 5.0 and Microsoft Windows 3.1, skip to the next section.

80286 Configuration

We're naming the first configuration after the 80286 because it is the configuration limit as far as this processor is concerned. You can load DOS in high memory (using HIMEM.SYS and DOS=HIGH); however, you cannot use EMM386.EXE or load device drivers and TSRs in upper memory.

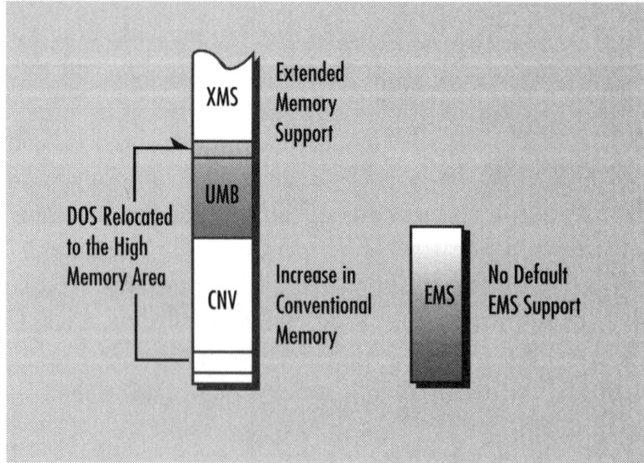

Figure 8-1 80286 configuration

The configuration files are shown in Listing 8-1. A graphical representation of the results from this configuration is shown in Figure 8-1.

Purpose of the Configuration

- Provides extended memory support (HIMEM.SYS).
- Relocates DOS into high memory (DOS=HIGH).
- Maximizes memory configuration for the 80286.

Listing 8-1 80286 Configuration Files

```
Contents of AUTOEXEC.BAT
------------------------
@ECHO OFF
CLS
PROMPT $p$g
PATH=C:\DOS;
<load TSRs here--do not use LOADHIGH>

Contents of CONFIG.SYS
------------------------
FILES=21
BUFFERS=15
DEVICE=C:\DOS\HIMEM.SYS
DOS=HIGH
<load device drivers here>
```

Notes

- EMS support with external LIM drivers only (EMS on an expansion board).
- You can use SMARTDrive with this configuration (and load it into extended memory, if enough extended memory is available).
- Windows and other applications requiring extended memory can use this configuration.

Maximum Extended Memory with Upper Memory Support

This configuration provides maximum extended memory while providing upper memory support as depicted in Figure 8-2. As with the 80286 configuration, these files (shown in Listing 8-2) provide extended memory support and access to the high memory area with HIMEM.SYS. The DOS=HIGH, UMB line in

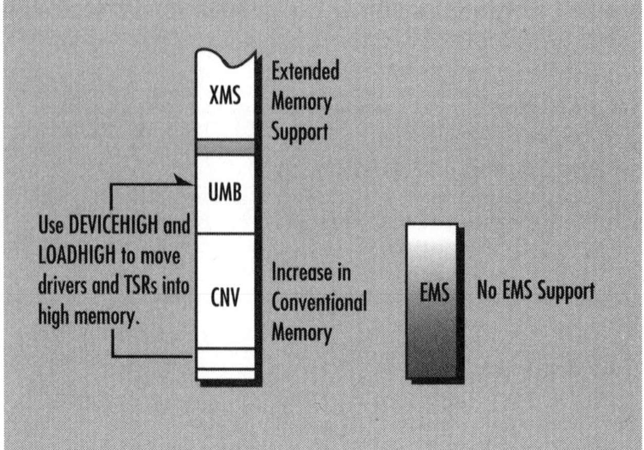

Figure 8-2 Maximum extended memory with upper memory support

the CONFIG.SYS file relocates DOS into the high memory area and enables the upper memory blocks. Note that this line appears after the EMM386.EXE line. This is required if you use the DOS UMB option.

In addition, we've added the EMM386.EXE driver with the NOEMS option to the configuration. This provides access to upper memory, but does not simulate any expanded memory.

Purpose of the Configuration

- Provides extended memory support (HIMEM.SYS).
- Relocates DOS into high memory (DOS=HIGH).
- Provides access to upper memory with EMM386.EXE NOEMS and the DOS=UMB command.
- Combines the DOS=HIGH and DOS=UMB into one line.

Listing 8-2 Maximum Extended Memory with Upper Memory Support

```
Contents of AUTOEXEC.BAT
------------------------
@ECHO OFF
CLS
PROMPT $p$g
PATH=C:\DOS;
<load TSRs here--you can optionally use LOADHIGH before the filename>
```

```
Contents of CONFIG.SYS
------------------------
FILES=21
BUFFERS=15
DEVICE=C:\DOS\HIMEM.SYS
DEVICE=C:\DOS\EMM386.EXE NOEMS
DOS=HIGH, UMB
<load device drivers here with DEVICE or DEVICEHIGH>
```

Notes

- You can load device drivers and TSRs into high memory. The amount of free high memory varies from computer to computer. Observe the startup message from EMM386.EXE to find out how much upper memory is available.
- No expanded memory support.
- You can use SMARTDrive with this configuration (and load it into extended memory, if enough extended memory is available).
- Windows and other applications requiring extended memory can use this configuration.

Expanded and Extended Memory with Upper Memory Support

This configuration provides extended and expanded memory while providing upper memory support. Figure 8-3 shows the layout of this configuration. This configuration relocates DOS to the high memory area. The DOS=HIGH, UMB line in the CONFIG.SYS file relocates DOS into the high memory area and enables the upper memory blocks. Note that this line appears after the EMM386.EXE line. This is required if you use the DOS UMB option.

In addition, we've added the EMM386.EXE driver with the RAM option to the configuration. This provides access to upper memory and simulates 256K of expanded memory by default. Optionally, you can add a number that represents the specific amount (in kilobytes) of expanded memory to simulate. For example, EMM386.EXE 1024 RAM would simulate 1 megabyte of expanded memory. This would require at least 1,408K of extended memory (1,024K for the expanded memory and 384K to backfill upper memory).

Purpose of the Configuration

- Provides extended memory support (HIMEM.SYS).
- Relocates DOS into high memory (DOS=HIGH).

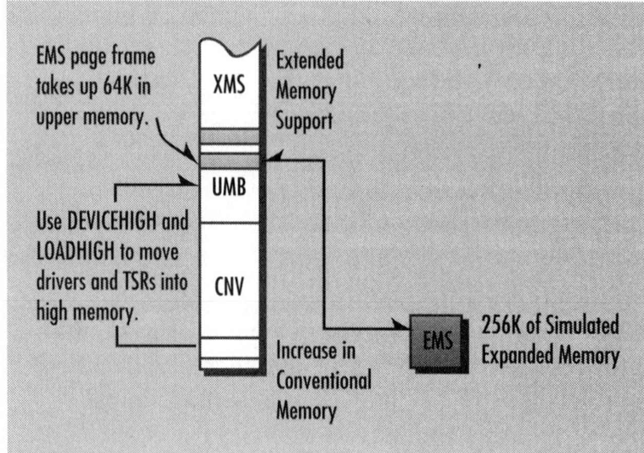

Figure 8-3 Expanded and extended memory with upper memory support

- Simulates 256K of expanded memory with EMM386.EXE RAM.
- Provides access to upper memory with EMM386.EXE NOEMS and the DOS=UMB command.

Listing 8-3 shows the CONFIG.SYS and AUTOEXEC.BAT file for this configuration.

Listing 8-3 Expanded and Extended Memory with Upper Memory Support

```
Contents of AUTOEXEC.BAT
------------------------
@ECHO OFF
CLS
PROMPT $p$g
PATH=C:\DOS;
<load TSRs here--you can optionally use LOADHIGH before the filename>

Contents of CONFIG.SYS
------------------------
FILES=21
BUFFERS=15
DEVICE=C:\DOS\HIMEM.SYS
DEVICE=C:\DOS\EMM386.EXE RAM
DOS=HIGH, UMB
<load device drivers here with DEVICE or DEVICEHIGH>
```

Notes

- You can load device drivers and TSRs into high memory. The amount of free high memory varies from computer to computer. Observe the startup message from EMM386.EXE to find out how much upper memory is available.
- The amount of free upper memory will decrease by 64K because of the EMS page frame (required to simulate expanded memory).
- The amount of free extended memory will decrease as you simulate expanded memory.
- You can use SMARTDrive with this configuration (and load it into extended or expanded memory).
- Windows and other applications requiring extended memory can use this configuration.

SMARTDrive in Extended Memory

The configuration depicted in Figure 8-4 builds on the maximum extended memory example. We've added the DOS 5.0 SMARTDRV.SYS driver to the CONFIG.SYS file. Notice that we are loading the SMARTDrive driver into upper memory with the DEVICEHIGH command. The SMARTDrive disk cache is located in extended memory by default.

In this example, we've created a disk cache with a 2,048K maximum size and a 1,024K minimum size. If you have less RAM, you should use values that stay within the capacity of your system.

Purpose of the Configuration

- Places the SMARTDRV.SYS driver in upper memory.
- Creates a disk cache in extended memory.
- Provides extended memory support (HIMEM.SYS).
- Relocates DOS into high memory (DOS=HIGH).
- Provides access to upper memory with EMM386.EXE NOEMS and the DOS=UMB command.

Listing 8-4 shows the configuration files for this example.

Listing 8-4 SMARTDrive in Extended Memory

```
Contents of AUTOEXEC.BAT
------------------------
@ECHO OFF
CLS
PROMPT $p$g
PATH=C:\DOS;
<load TSRs here--you can optionally use LOADHIGH before the filename>

Contents of CONFIG.SYS
------------------------
FILES=21
BUFFERS=15
DEVICE=C:\DOS\HIMEM.SYS
DEVICE=C:\DOS\EMM386.EXE NOEMS
DOS=HIGH, UMB
DEVICEHIGH=C:\DOS\SMARTDRV.SYS 2048 1024
<load other device drivers here with DEVICE or DEVICEHIGH>
```

Notes

- You must have enough free extended memory to create the SMARTDrive disk cache.
- You can load device drivers and TSRs into high memory. The amount of free high memory varies from computer to computer. Observe the startup message from EMM386.EXE to find out how much upper memory is available.

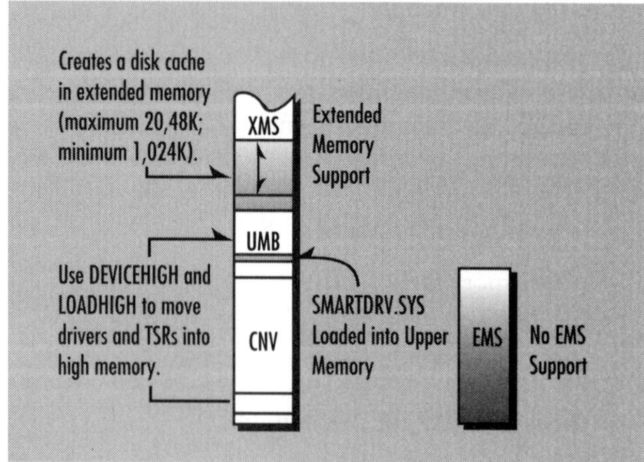

Figure 8-4 SMARTDrive in extended memory

- No expanded memory support.
- Windows and other applications requiring extended memory can use this configuration. See the following configurations for the Windows 3.1 updated SMARTDrive driver.

DOS 5.0 with Windows 3.1 Configurations

This section provides two different DOS 5.0 configurations that you can use as a starting point for your system. We have provided an overview, the purpose, and notes about each configuration. If you are using DOS 6, skip to the next section. If you are using DOS 6 and Microsoft Windows 3.1, skip to the last section.

Windows 3.1—No Expanded Memory Support

The configuration shown in Figure 8-5 provides a starting point for a DOS 5.0 system running Microsoft Windows 3.1. Because the Windows system and Windows applications require extended memory, we are using the HIMEM.SYS driver.

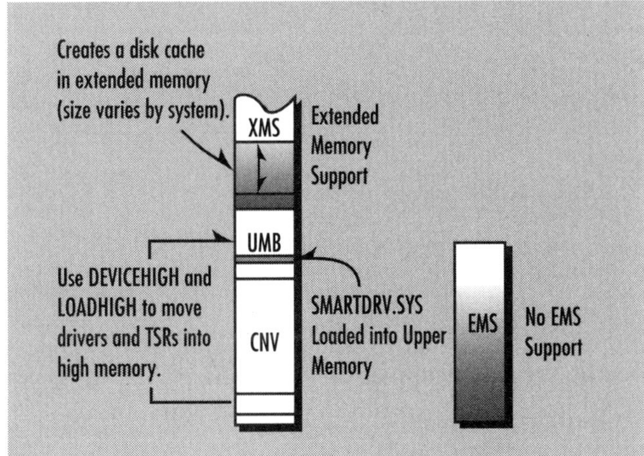

Figure 8-5 Windows 3.1—no expanded memory support

Note that we are also using the SMARTDRV.EXE driver (provided with Windows) instead of the SMARTDRV.SYS driver (provided with DOS 6). Always remember to use the most updated driver.

Purpose of the Configuration

- Acts as a starting configuration for DOS 5.0 and Windows 3.1.
- Creates a disk cache in extended memory by default.
- Uses LOADHIGH to load the SMARTDRV.EXE driver into upper memory.
- Provides extended memory support (HIMEM.SYS).
- Relocates DOS into high memory (DOS=HIGH).
- Provides access to upper memory with EMM386.EXE NOEMS and the DOS=UMB command.

Listing 8-5 shows a starting configuration for DOS 5.0 and Windows 3.1.

Listing 8-5 Windows 3.1—No Expanded Memory Support

```
Contents of AUTOEXEC.BAT
------------------------
@ECHO OFF
CLS
LOADHIGH C:\WINDOWS\SMARTDRV.EXE
PROMPT $p$g
PATH=C:\DOS;C:\WINDOWS;
<load TSRs here--you can optionally use LOADHIGH before the filename>

Contents of CONFIG.SYS
------------------------
FILES=21
BUFFERS=15
DEVICE=C:\WINDOWS\HIMEM.SYS
DEVICE=C:\WINDOWS\EMM386.EXE NOEMS
DOS=HIGH, UMB
<load other device drivers here with DEVICE or DEVICEHIGH>
```

Notes

- The Windows 3.1 Setup program automatically adds the HIMEM.SYS and SMARTDRV.EXE lines (if they are not in your configuration already).

- SMARTDRV.EXE automatically sizes the disk cache based on your system's RAM capacity.
- You can load device drivers and TSRs into high memory. The amount of free high memory varies from computer to computer. Observe the startup message from EMM386.EXE to find out how much upper memory is available.
- No expanded memory support.

Windows 3.1—with Expanded Memory Support

Figure 8-6 shows a configuration similar to the previous one, except we are simulating expanded memory. This is a good starting configuration if you are running Windows with DOS applications that require expanded memory.

Once again, we are using the SMARTDRV.EXE driver (provided with Windows) instead of the SMARTDRV.SYS driver (provided with DOS 6). Always remember to use the latest driver.

Purpose of the Configuration

- Acts as a starting configuration for DOS and Windows 3.1.
- Provides 256K of simulated expanded memory using the RAM option of EMM386.EXE.
- Creates a disk cache in extended memory by default.
- Uses LOADHIGH to load the SMARTDRV.EXE driver into upper memory using LOADHIGH.
- Provides extended memory support (HIMEM.SYS).
- Relocates DOS into high memory (DOS=HIGH).
- Provides access to upper memory with EMM386.EXE RAM and the DOS=UMB command.

Listing 8-6 shows the files for this configuration.

Listing 8-6 Windows 3.1—With Expanded Memory Support

```
Contents of AUTOEXEC.BAT
------------------------
@ECHO OFF
CLS
```

continued on next page

continued from previous page

```
LOADHIGH C:\WINDOWS\SMARTDRV.EXE
PROMPT $p$g
PATH=C:\DOS;C:\WINDOWS;
<load TSRs here--you can optionally use LOADHIGH before the filename>

Contents of CONFIG.SYS
------------------------
FILES=21
BUFFERS=15
DEVICE=C:\WINDOWS\HIMEM.SYS
DEVICE=C:\WINDOWS\EMM386.EXE RAM
DOS=HIGH, UMB
<load other device drivers here with DEVICE or DEVICEHIGH>
```

Notes

- The Windows 3.1 Setup program automatically adds the HIMEM.SYS and SMARTDRV.EXE lines (if they are not in your configuration already).
- SMARTDRV.EXE automatically sizes the disk cache based on your system's RAM capacity.
- You can load device drivers and TSRs into high memory. The amount of free high memory varies from computer to computer. Observe the startup message from EMM386.EXE to find out how much upper memory is available.

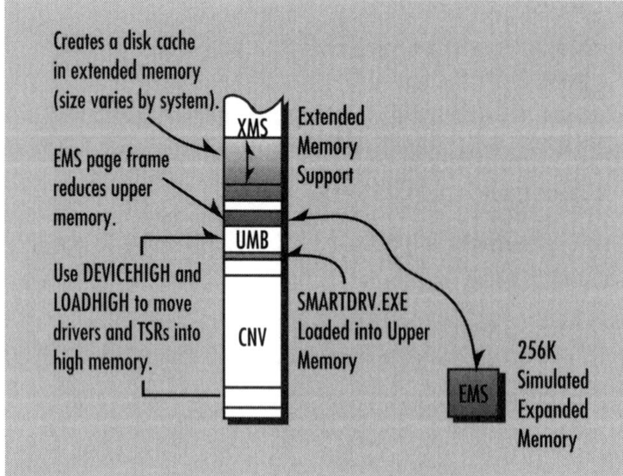

Figure 8-6 Windows 3.1—with expanded memory support

- The amount of free upper memory will decrease by 64K because of the EMS page frame (required to simulate expanded memory).
- The amount of free extended memory will decrease as you simulate expanded memory.

DOS 6 Configurations (Without Windows 3.1)

This section provides five different DOS 6 configurations that you can use as a starting point for your system. We have provided an overview, the purpose, and notes about each configuration. If you are using DOS 6 and Microsoft Windows 3.1, skip to the next section.

80286 Configuration

This is the equivalent configuration for 80286 processors in DOS 6; it is depicted in Figure 8-7. You can load DOS in high memory (using HIMEM.SYS and DOS=HIGH); however, you cannot use EMM386.EXE or load device drivers and TSRs in upper memory.

Purpose of the Configuration

- Provides extended memory support (HIMEM.SYS).
- Relocates DOS into high memory (DOS=HIGH).
- Maximizes memory configuration for the 80286.

Listing 8-7 shows an example set of files for an 80286 processor.

Listing 8-7 80286 Configuration Files

```
Contents of AUTOEXEC.BAT
------------------------
@ECHO OFF
CLS
PROMPT $p$g
PATH=C:\DOS;
<load TSRs here--do not use LOADHIGH>
```

continued on next page

continued from previous page

```
Contents of CONFIG.SYS
-------------------------
FILES=21
BUFFERS=15
DEVICE=C:\DOS\HIMEM.SYS
DOS=HIGH
<load device drivers here>
```

Notes

- EMS support with external LIM drivers only (EMS on an expansion board).
- You can use SMARTDrive with this configuration (and load it into extended memory, if enough extended memory is available).
- Windows and other applications requiring extended memory can use this configuration.

Maximum Extended with Upper Memory Support

Figure 8-8 shows the layout of a configuration that provides maximum extended memory as well as upper memory support. As with the 80286 configuration, these files (shown in Listing 8-2) provide extended memory support access to the high memory area with HIMEM.SYS. The DOS=HIGH, UMB line in the CONFIG.SYS file relocates DOS into the high memory area and enables the upper memory blocks. Note that this line appears after the EMM386.EXE line. This is required if you use the DOS UMB option.

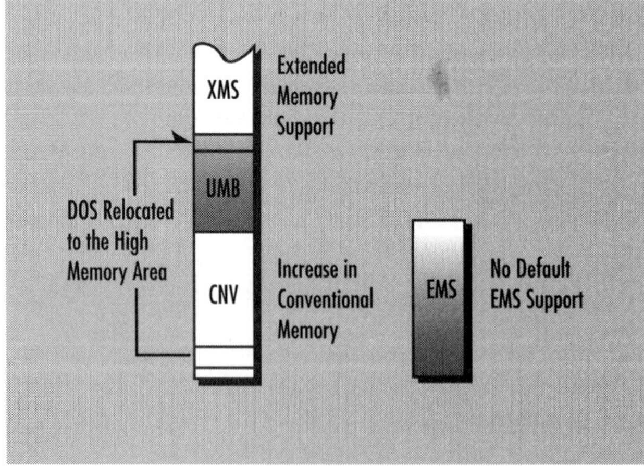

Figure 8-7 80286 configuration

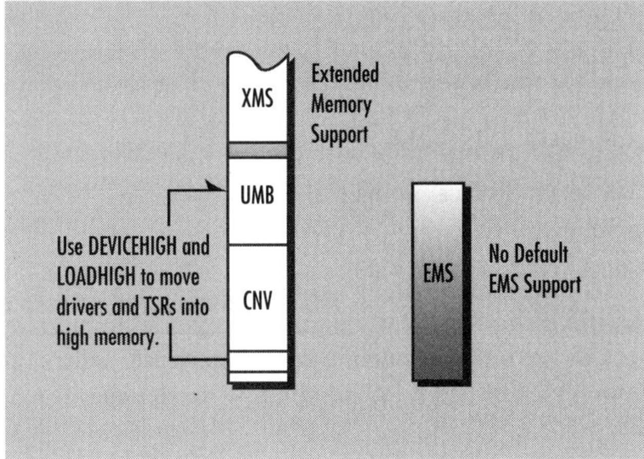

Figure 8-8 Maximum extended memory with upper memory support

In addition, we've added the EMM386.EXE driver with the NOEMS option to the configuration. This provides access to upper memory, but does not simulate any expanded memory.

Purpose of the Configuration

- Provides extended memory support (HIMEM.SYS).
- Relocates DOS into high memory (DOS=HIGH).
- Provides access to upper memory with EMM386.EXE NOEMS and the DOS=UMB command.
- Combines DOS=HIGH and DOS=UMB into one line.

Listing 8-8 shows the files for this configuration.

Listing 8-8 Maximum Extended Memory with Upper Memory Support

```
Contents of AUTOEXEC.BAT
------------------------
@ECHO OFF
CLS
PROMPT $p$g
PATH=C:\DOS;
<load TSRs here--you can optionally use LOADHIGH before the filename>
```

continued on next page

continued from previous page

```
Contents of CONFIG.SYS
-----------------------
FILES=21
BUFFERS=15
DEVICE=C:\DOS\HIMEM.SYS
DEVICE=C:\DOS\EMM386.EXE NOEMS
DOS=HIGH, UMB
<load device drivers here with DEVICE or DEVICEHIGH>
```

Notes

- You can load device drivers and TSRs into high memory. The amount of free high memory varies from computer to computer. Observe the startup message from EMM386.EXE to find out how much upper memory is available.
- No expanded memory support.
- You can use SMARTDrive with this configuration (and load it into extended memory, if enough extended memory is available).
- Windows and other applications requiring extended memory can use this configuration.

Expanded Plus Upper Memory Support

The configuration type depicted in Figure 8-9 provides extended and expanded memory while providing upper memory support. This configuration relocates DOS to the high memory area. The DOS=HIGH, UMB line in the CONFIG.SYS file relocates DOS into the high memory area and enables the upper memory blocks. Note that this line appears after the EMM386.EXE line. This is required if you use the DOS UMB option.

In addition, we've added the EMM386.EXE driver with the RAM option to the configuration. This provides access to upper memory and simulates expanded memory. The DOS 6 version of EMM386.EXE can switch the amounts of free extended and expanded memory depending on the demands of your applications.

Purpose of the Configuration

- Provides extended memory support (HIMEM.SYS).
- Relocates DOS into high memory (DOS=HIGH).
- Simulates expanded memory with EMM386.EXE RAM.
- Provides access to upper memory with EMM386.EXE NOEMS and the DOS=UMB command.

Listing 8-9 shows the files for this configuration.

Listing 8-9 Expanded and Extended Memory with Upper Memory Support

```
Contents of AUTOEXEC.BAT
------------------------
@ECHO OFF
CLS
PROMPT $p$g
PATH=C:\DOS;
<load TSRs here--you can optionally use LOADHIGH before the filename>

Contents of CONFIG.SYS
------------------------
FILES=21
BUFFERS=15
DEVICE=C:\DOS\HIMEM.SYS
DEVICE=C:\DOS\EMM386.EXE RAM
DOS=HIGH, UMB
<load device drivers here with DEVICE or DEVICEHIGH>
```

Notes

- You can load device drivers and TSRs into high memory. The amount of free high memory varies from computer to computer. Observe the startup message from EMM386.EXE to find out how much upper memory is available.
- The amount of free upper memory will decrease by 64K because of the EMS page frame (required to simulate expanded memory).

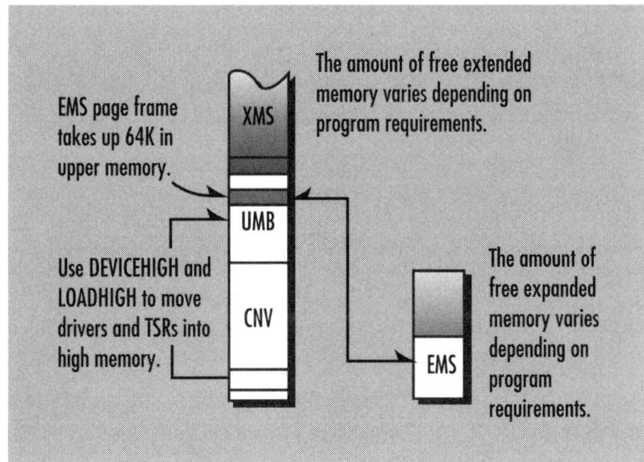

Figure 8-9 Expanded and extended memory with upper memory support

- EMM386.EXE will change the amount of free expanded/extended memory depending on the requirements of your programs.
- You can use SMARTDrive with this configuration.
- Windows and other applications requiring extended memory can use this configuration.
- DOS applications requiring expanded memory can use this configuration.

SMARTDrive in Extended Memory

The configuration type shown in Figure 8-10 builds on the maximum extended memory example. We've added the DOS 6 SMARTDRV.EXE driver to the AUTOEXEC.BAT file. Notice that we are loading the SMARTDrive driver into upper memory with the LOADHIGH command. The SMARTDrive disk cache is located in extended memory by default. You cannot load the SMARTDrive disk cache in expanded memory with the DOS 6 EMM386.EXE driver.

As with the Windows 3.1 version of SMARTDRV.EXE driver, the size of the disk cache depends on the amount of memory installed in your computer.

Purpose of the Configuration

- Places the SMARTDRV.SYS driver in upper memory.
- Creates a disk cache in extended memory. Its size depends on your system's memory capacity.
- Provides extended memory support (HIMEM.SYS).
- Relocates DOS into high memory (DOS=HIGH).
- Provides access to upper memory with EMM386.EXE NOEMS and the DOS=UMB command.

Listing 8-10 shows the configuration files for this example.

Listing 8-10 SMARTDrive in Extended Memory

```
Contents of AUTOEXEC.BAT
------------------------
@ECHO OFF
CLS
LOADHIGH C:\DOS\SMARTDRV.EXE
PROMPT $p$g
```

```
PATH=C:\DOS;
<load TSRs here--you can optionally use LOADHIGH before the filename>

Contents of CONFIG.SYS
------------------------
FILES=21
BUFFERS=15
DEVICE=C:\DOS\HIMEM.SYS
DEVICE=C:\DOS\EMM386.EXE NOEMS
DOS=HIGH, UMB
<load other device drivers here with DEVICE or DEVICEHIGH>
```

Notes

- The size of the disk cache depends on the amount of free extended memory installed in your system. Refer to Chapter 6, *Windows Memory Management,* for specific cache sizes.
- You can load device drivers and TSRs into high memory. The amount of free high memory varies from computer to computer. Observe the startup message from EMM386.EXE to find out how much upper memory is available.
- No expanded memory support.
- Windows and other applications requiring extended memory can use this configuration. Remember to use the DOS 6 version of EMM386.EXE and SMARTDRV.EXE. DOS 6 drivers are newer than those provided with Windows 3.1.

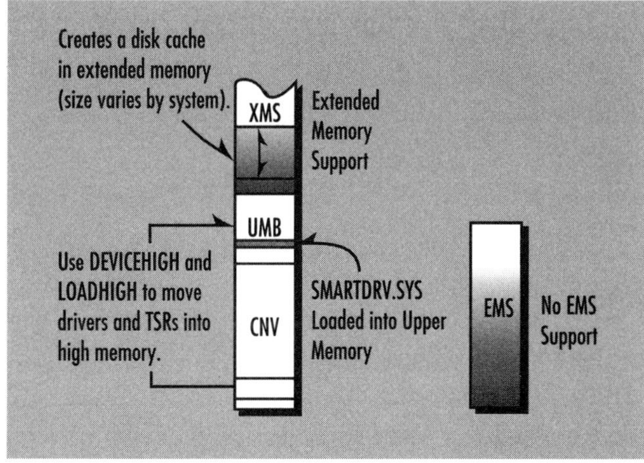

Figure 8-10 SMARTDrive in extended memory

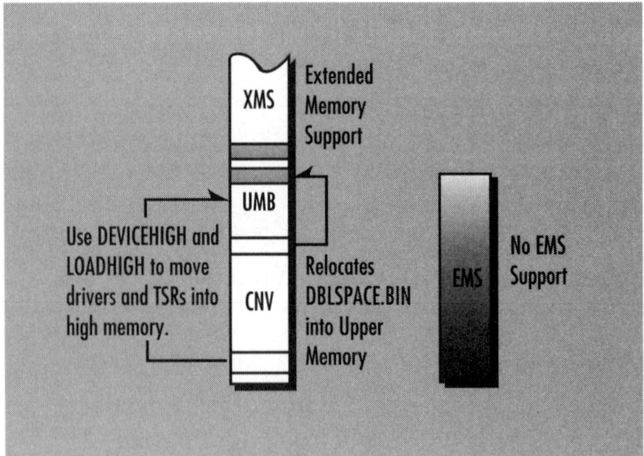

Figure 8-11 DoubleSpace in upper memory

DoubleSpace in Upper Memory

DoubleSpace is a great way to get more space out of your disk drive; however, it does have one drawback: a large device driver. This configuration (shown in Figure 8-11) moves the driver into upper memory, freeing valuable conventional memory. Keep in mind that you must have enough free upper memory available to store this driver.

The DBLSPACE.SYS driver actually loads a file named DBLSPACE.BIN into the upper section of conventional memory. This configuration attempts to relocate this file into upper memory. The DEVICEHIGH command in this example will fail if you do not have enough upper memory to store DBLSPACE.BIN.

Purpose of the Configuration

- Places the DBLSPACE.BIN file in upper memory (via DBLSPACE.SYS).
- Provides extended memory support (HIMEM.SYS).
- Relocates DOS into high memory (DOS=HIGH).
- Provides access to upper memory with EMM386.EXE NOEMS and the DOS=UMB command.

Listing 8-11 shows the CONFIG.SYS and AUTOEXEC.BAT file for this configuration.

Listing 8-11 DoubleSpace in Upper Memory

```
Contents of AUTOEXEC.BAT
------------------------
@ECHO OFF
CLS
PROMPT $p$g
PATH=C:\DOS;
<load TSRs here--you can optionally use LOADHIGH before the filename>

Contents of CONFIG.SYS
------------------------
FILES=21
BUFFERS=15
DEVICE=C:\DOS\HIMEM.SYS
DEVICE=C:\DOS\EMM386.EXE NOEMS
DOS=HIGH, UMB
DEVICEHIGH=C:\DOS\DBLSPACE.SYS
<load other device drivers here with DEVICE or DEVICEHIGH>
```

Notes

- Relocates the DBLSPACE.BIN file into upper memory (if enough upper memory is available).
- No expanded memory support.
- Windows and other applications requiring extended memory can use this configuration. Remember to use the DOS 6 version of EMM386.EXE. DOS 6 drivers are newer than those provided with Windows 3.1.

DOS 6 with Windows 3.1 Configurations

This section provides a starting DOS 6 and Windows 3.1 configuration. We have provided an overview, the purpose, and notes about this configuration. You can also change the EMM386.EXE switch to RAM to simulate expanded memory in this example.

DOS 6 and Windows 3.1

The configuration depicted in Figure 8-12 provides a starting point for a DOS 6 system running Microsoft Windows 3.1. Because the Windows system and Windows applications require extended memory, we are using the HIMEM.SYS driver.

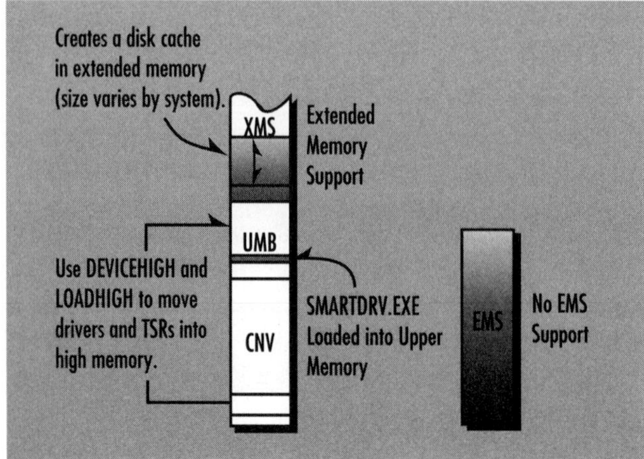

Figure 8-12 DOS 6 and Windows 3.1

Note that we are also using the SMARTDRV.EXE driver (provided with DOS 6) instead of the SMARTDRV.EXE driver (provided with Windows 3.1). Always remember to use the latest driver.

Purpose of the Configuration

- Acts as starting configuration for DOS 6 and Windows 3.1.
- Creates a disk cache in extended memory by default.
- Uses LOADHIGH to load the SMARTDRV.EXE driver into upper memory.
- Provides extended memory support (HIMEM.SYS).
- Relocates DOS into high memory (DOS=HIGH).
- Provides access to upper memory with EMM386.EXE NOEMS and the DOS=UMB command.

Listing 8-12 shows a starting configuration for DOS 6 and Windows 3.1.

Listing 8-12 DOS 6 and Windows 3.1

```
Contents of AUTOEXEC.BAT
------------------------
@ECHO OFF
CLS
LOADHIGH C:\DOS\SMARTDRV.EXE
```

```
PROMPT $p$g
PATH=C:\DOS;C:\WINDOWS;
<load TSRs here--you can optionally use LOADHIGH before the filename>

Contents of CONFIG.SYS
-----------------------
FILES=21
BUFFERS=15
DEVICE=C:\DOS\HIMEM.SYS
DEVICE=C:\DOS\EMM386.EXE NOEMS
DOS=HIGH, UMB
<load other device drivers here with DEVICE or DEVICEHIGH>
```

Notes

- The Windows 3.1 Setup program automatically adds the HIMEM.SYS and SMARTDRV.EXE lines; however, you should use the drivers in the DOS directory because the DOS 6 versions are newer.
- SMARTDRV.EXE automatically sizes the disk cache based on your system's RAM capacity.
- You can load device drivers and TSRs into high memory. The amount of free high memory varies from computer to computer. Observe the startup message from EMM386.EXE to find out how much upper memory is available.
- There is no expanded memory support in this configuration. Change the EMM386.EXE NOEMS option to RAM to simulate expanded memory.

Summary

This chapter provided several sets of configuration files that you can use as a starting point for your system. The key to selecting the correct configuration depends on how you use your system. For example, which DOS version are you using, or are you running Windows?

Once you have these questions answered, select a configuration that best suits your collection of programs. For example, if you never use a program that requires expanded memory, do not use a configuration that simulates it.

Another key to getting the most of your configuration is to use the latest set of drivers (HIMEM.SYS, EMM386.EXE, SMARTDRV.EXE, and so on). For example, Windows 3.1 drivers are newer than DOS 5.0 drivers and DOS 6 drivers are newer than Windows 3.1 drivers.

Up to this point, you've seen several memory management techniques and have a solid starting point on which to build your custom configurations. Now let's look at some hardware issues that arise when using multimedia devices. The next chapter covers software and hardware conflicts.

IRQs, DMA, and Other Mysteries

With our memory problems hopefully behind us, let's look at the hardware and software conflicts that frequently occur in today's computers. You shouldn't have too many problems if you purchased a full-blown multimedia-ready computer recently. Such systems have already been properly configured by the manufacturer or dealer. However, if you add a new device or upgrade an existing device, you may introduce different types of conflicts in your machine. Of course, you may be adding multimedia capability to an existing system. This involves adding drivers for the CD ROM drive, sound card, etc.

It would be impossible to list every possible conflict you may run into in this book. Although there are standards that computer and peripheral manufacturers follow, each company approaches configuration somewhat differently. Even if we were to place a stake in the ground today and list the many combinations of computer and related hardware, such a list would be outdated in a matter of months.

The best defense to conflicts is a good offense. If you understand the principles behind interrupt requests (IRQs), direct memory access (DMA), and input/output addressing, you will have the ability to solve problems on your own, regardless of the new hardware or software you may purchase.

After reading this chapter, you will understand the causes of IRQ, DMA, and I/O conflicts. Knowing the causes, you should be able to configure your system and avoid potential problems. Let's look at the topics covered in this chapter.

TOPICS COVERED

Understanding Interrupt Requests (IRQs)

Interrupt requests, or IRQs, are the way devices such as serial ports, SCSI cards, sound cards, and others communicate with the microprocessor. For example, when your sound card needs to get your microprocessor's attention, it uses an interrupt request to do it. Figure 9-1 shows a peripheral card sending an IRQ to an 80386 processor.

Each device must have an IRQ line to the processor. It is important not to assign two devices to the same IRQ line. Doing so can cause unpredictable results.

To find out which IRQ setting to use, we must first examine the system's current usage of IRQs.

IRQs and Your Computer

Table 9-1 shows IRQ0 through IRQ15. The IRQs that are available on a base system are highlighted in boldface. Your system already may have other devices using some of the IRQs marked available.

Note that the system uses some of the IRQs for the system timer, the keyboard, two serial ports, a parallel port, the floppy disk, hard disk, and others. If you are not using a second serial port, you can use IRQ3 for your device.

Not all hardware allows all possible IRQ settings. For example, some peripheral devices allow you to select only from IRQ2, 3, 4, 5, and 7. Consult your documentation for possible IRQ settings for your hardware.

If you have DOS 6 or Windows, you can use MSD Microsoft Diagnostics to view IRQs. QEMM and 386MAX have similar utilities. Figure 9-2 shows the MSD screen for IRQs.

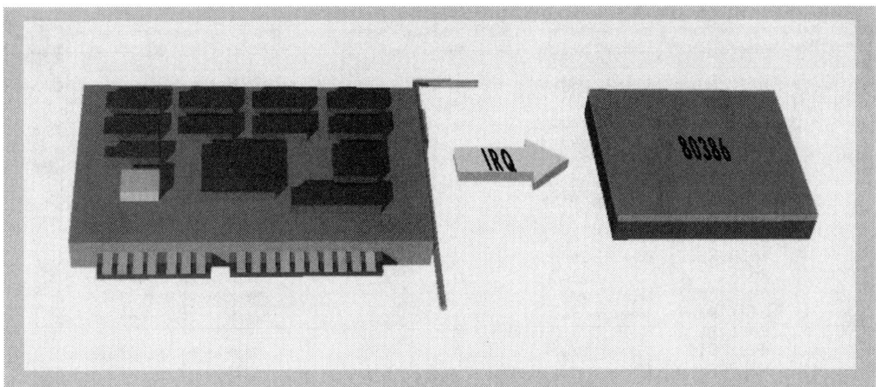

Figure 9-1 A Peripheral device interrupts the microprocessor

IRQ#	Assignment
IRQ0	System Timer
IRQ1	Keyboard
IRQ2	**Available**
IRQ3	COM2: or COM4: Serial Port
IRQ4	COM1: or COM3: Serial Port
IRQ5	**Available**
IRQ6	Floppy Disk
IRQ7	LPT1: Parallel Port
IRQ8	Real Time Clock
IRQ9	BIOS
IRQ10	**Available**
IRQ11	**Available**
IRQ12	**Available**
IRQ13	Math Coprocessor
IRQ14	Hard Disk
IRQ15	**Available**

Table 9-1 Standard IRQ assignments

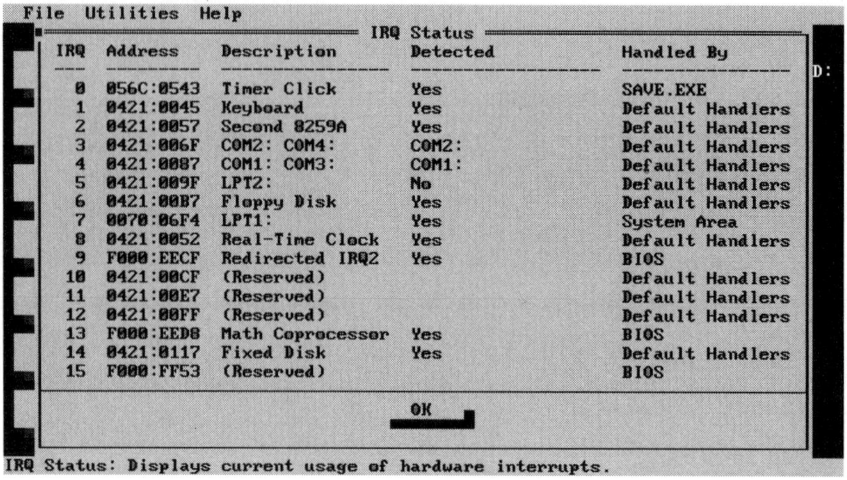

File Utilities Help

IRQ Status

IRQ	Address	Description	Detected	Handled By
0	056C:0543	Timer Click	Yes	SAVE.EXE
1	0421:0045	Keyboard	Yes	Default Handlers
2	0421:0057	Second 8259A	Yes	Default Handlers
3	0421:006F	COM2: COM4:	COM2:	Default Handlers
4	0421:0087	COM1: COM3:	COM1:	Default Handlers
5	0421:009F	LPT2:	No	Default Handlers
6	0421:00B7	Floppy Disk	Yes	Default Handlers
7	0070:06F4	LPT1:	Yes	System Area
8	0421:0052	Real-Time Clock	Yes	Default Handlers
9	F000:EECF	Redirected IRQ2	Yes	BIOS
10	0421:00CF	(Reserved)		Default Handlers
11	0421:00E7	(Reserved)		Default Handlers
12	0421:00FF	(Reserved)		Default Handlers
13	F000:EED0	Math Coprocessor	Yes	BIOS
14	0421:0117	Fixed Disk	Yes	Default Handlers
15	F000:FF53	(Reserved)		BIOS

OK

IRQ Status: Displays current usage of hardware interrupts.

Figure 9-2 Microsoft Diagnostics IRQ screen

Setting the IRQ on Your Hardware

When you install a new sound card, or other device requiring an IRQ setting, you must first determine the current state of your system. Do this by examining the IRQ settings of the existing hardware. This way you can determine a free IRQ for the new device.

Once you have determined the desired IRQ setting, you must configure your device. This is done by using one of two methods. The first, most popular, method is setting the IRQ using a jumper on the expansion board. The second method is setting the IRQ using software, usually by an installation program.

Many devices have programs that test the configuration of IRQs as well as DMA and I/O port settings. We'll discuss DMA and I/O ports later in this chapter.

IRQs and Your Software

The IRQ setting is not just for your hardware. The software that controls the device must also know the IRQ setting. This software may be a device driver for a SCSI (small computer systems interface) controller. It can also be software, such as a multimedia application or game that uses a sound card. In order for the software to properly access the sound card, it must know the IRQ setting of the card.

How software is configured for the proper IRQ depends on the wishes of the software developer. Device drivers usually use switches on the command line. For example, the switch may be /I5 indicating IRQ5, or Q:3 indicating IRQ3. Programs that use sound cards usually have configuration within the program, or command line switches.

Symptoms of IRQ Conflicts and Mismatches

The symptoms for IRQ conflicts and mismatches are very different. A conflict occurs when more than one device is set to the same IRQ. A mismatch occurs when the device IRQ doesn't match that of the supporting software.

IRQ conflicts can cause different types of symptoms. It can range from your computer locking up while its booting to a lockup when the device is accessed. You should always test the software you plan to use with any device before closing and securing the cover.

Direct Memory Access Channels (DMA)

Some devices use direct memory access channels for rapid data exchange between the device and memory. Examples of devices that use DMA are sound cards, scanner cards, network cards, SCSI controllers, and tape backup controllers. It is important that two devices never use the same DMA channel at the same time.

The Advantage of DMA

Figure 9-3 shows a comparison of a device that doesn't use DMA to a device using DMA. A device that does not use a DMA channel must route all data through the processor. This not only takes time, but more importantly, it's the microprocessor's time. System performance is affected because the microprocessor is busy handling the transfer of data.

The second example in Figure 9-3 shows a device using a DMA channel. Instead of the data being routed through the processor, it is routed by a DMA controller. The device essentially can exchange data directly with RAM. This frees up the processor for more important tasks.

DMA Channels and Your Computer

If you have an 80286 machine or above, you have six possible DMA channels available. Table 9-2 shows a list of the DMA channels in a base system. The available channels are in boldface. Note that the floppy disk and memory refresh use DMA channels 2 and 4 respectively.

If your device uses DMA, it may not support all possible channels. For example, some devices support two channels, such as 1 and 3. Like IRQ settings, the DMA channel selection is either made by jumper or software configuration.

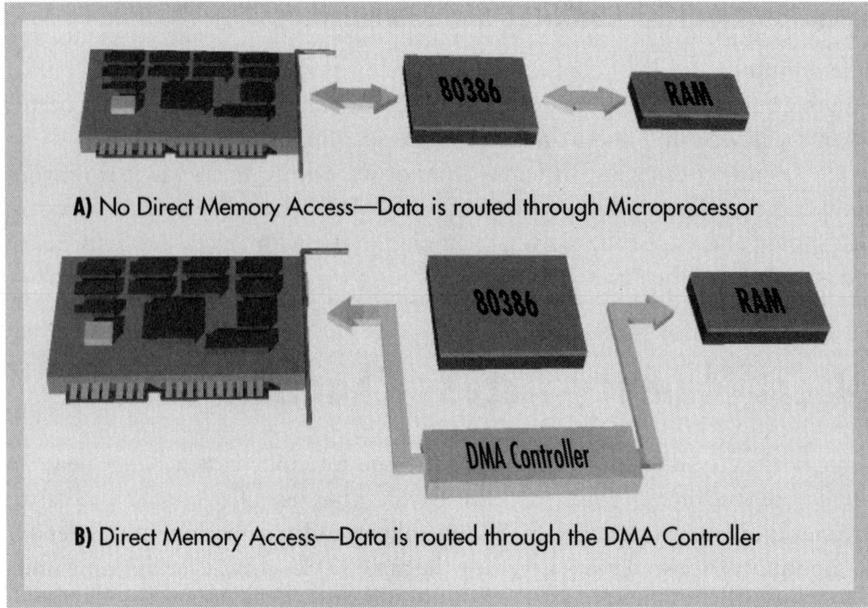

Figure 9-3 Direct memory access

DMA Channel	Used by
0	**Available**
1	**Available**
2	Floppy Disk
3	**Available**
4	Memory Refresh
5	**Available**
6	**Available**
7	**Available**

Table 9-2 DMA channels

Sharing DMA Channels

Although you should not configure two devices with the same IRQ setting, you can possibly share a DMA channel between devices. However, you must be certain that both devices will not be active at the same time. For example, if you have a sound card and a tape backup controller using DMA channel 1, you will not have a problem unless you activate both simultaneously.

Symptoms of DMA Conflicts

DMA conflicts usually cause your system to lock up or behave erratically. This will only occur when two devices access the same DMA channel simultaneously. It's usually fairly easy to determine the conflict by observing which devices are active at the time of the symptom. With this information, you can adjust the configuration to solve the problem or avoid using the devices simultaneously.

Input/Output Ports (I/O)

Another possible configuration problem you can encounter is I/O port conflict. Each peripheral device in your system has one or more I/O ports. The device communicates through these I/O ports. Each port has a specific address, usually expressed as a four-digit hexadecimal number.

Your device may or may not have a configurable I/O port. If it does, it is important to examine your system for a possible I/O port conflict. This will usually only occur if you have two devices with configurable I/O ports.

You should never have two devices configured with the same I/O port. Most devices that allow the configuration of an I/O port offer alternate addresses. This should resolve the problem in most cases.

Examples of I/O Addresses

To provide an example of I/O addresses, you can examine your serial and parallel ports. If you have Windows 3.1 or DOS 6 you can use Microsoft Diagnostics (MSD.EXE) to examine your serial and parallel I/O addresses. Figure 9-4 shows the I/O ports for two serial and two parallel ports. Each port is assigned a specific address, in this case 03F8h, 02F8h, 0378h, and 0278h. If any other device were to use these addresses, an I/O conflict would occur.

If you have DOS 6 or Windows you can use MSD Microsoft Diagnostics to view port addresses. QEMM and 386MAX have similar utilities. Figures 9-5 and

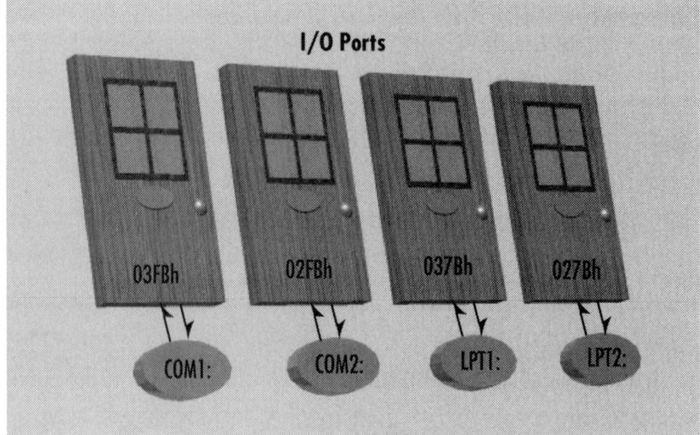

Figure 9-4 Popular I/O addresses—serial (COM1: and COM2:) and parallel (LPT1: and LPT2:) ports

9-6 show the serial and parallel I/O port address screens for QEMM (Manifest) and 386MAX (ASQ).

Symptoms of I/O Mismatch

When an I/O conflict occurs, the result varies. Usually one or both of the devices involved in the conflict does not behave properly. In some cases, the computer

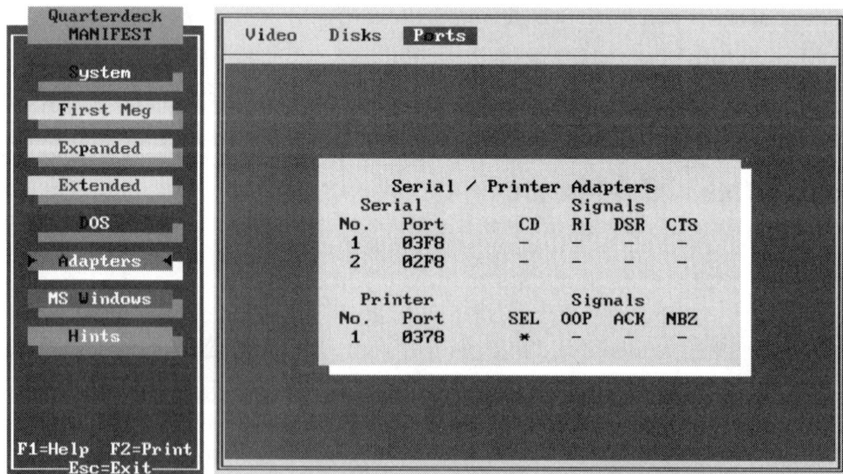

Figure 9-5 QEMM (Manifest) reports serial/parallel I/O port addresses

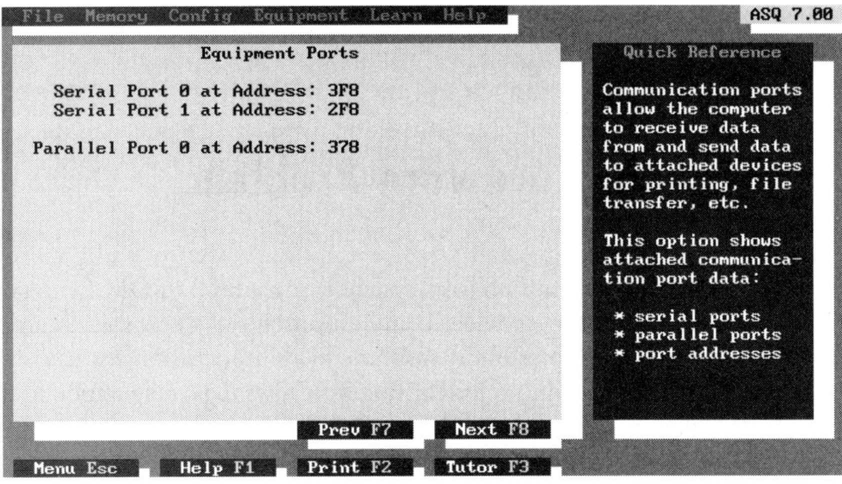

Figure 9-6 386MAX (ASQ) reports serial/parallel I/O port addresses

may lock up. As with DMA conflict, it's usually simple to track down I/O conflicts by observing which two devices are active at the same time.

Troubleshooting Problems

As mentioned in the introduction to this chapter, the best defense to resolving IRQ, DMA, and I/O problems is a good offense. This simply means knowing your current system configuration before attempting to install a new device.

The following tips should help you avoid, locate, and resolve conflicts:

- Make a chart of IRQ and DMA settings used in your system. The tables in this chapter and your system documentation will help you find the information. The Microsoft Diagnostics program (supplied with DOS 6 and Windows 3.1) is also useful in examining your system's IRQ usage.
- Set your new device to avoid potential conflicts. You may need to set IRQ, DMA, or I/O port addresses (or any combination of the three).
- If you install a device and a conflict occurs, try other settings to resolve the problem. Some devices may not be able to coexist in your system, especially if you have several expansion boards.

- If your system locks up, make a note of what devices were active when the lockup occurred.

A Multimedia Hardware Problem

Here is an example of how hardware conflicts can occur when you add multimedia software to your system. Bob has a system that has a CD-ROM (with an SCSI adapter) and a custom video board. He just purchased a new sound card. After installing the new adapter, Bob's machine locks up occasionally, usually when he tries to activate the sound card. Listing 9-1 shows the configuration files that are causing the problem.

Listing 9-1 Problem Configuration Files (IRQ Conflict)

```
AUTOEXEC.BAT contents
---------------------
&ECHO OFF
CLS
PATH C:\DOS;C:\GAMES;C:\MEDIA;
C:\SCSI\MSCDEX /e
LOADHIGH C:\MOUSE\MOUSE
LOADHIGH C:\DOS\DOSKEY

CONFIG.SYS contents
---------------------
FILES=20
BUFFERS=10
DEVICE=C:\DOS\HIMEM.SYS
DEVICE=C:\DOS\EMM386.EXE NOEMS
DOS=HIGH,UMB
DEVICEHIGH=C:\SOUND\SOUNDMAN.SYS /i:5
DEVICEHIGH=C:\SCSI\ADAPTER.SYS
DEVICEHIGH=C:\VIDEO\VESA.SYS
```

These files don't show anything unusual on the surface so Bob consults his adapter documentation for the video card and SCSI card. He finds that the SCSI adapter uses IRQ5 as a default. This is the IRQ that is conflicting with the sound card. To solve the problem, Bob reassigns the IRQ on the new sound card to IRQ7 using a jumper. He also must modify the CONFIG.SYS file to reflect the change. Note that some devices, but not all, have setup programs that do this for you. Listing 9-2 shows the final configuration files for Bob's system. The change is shown in boldface.

Listing 9-2 Solution Configuration Files (IRQ Conflict)

```
AUTOEXEC.BAT contents
---------------------
&ECHO OFF
CLS
PATH C:\DOS;C:\GAMES;C:\MEDIA;
C:\SCSI\MSCDEX /e
LOADHIGH C:\MOUSE\MOUSE
LOADHIGH C:\DOS\DOSKEY

CONFIG.SYS contents
---------------------
FILES=20
BUFFERS=10
DEVICE=C:\DOS\HIMEM.SYS
DEVICE=C:\DOS\EMM386.EXE NOEMS
DOS=HIGH,UMB
DEVICEHIGH=C:\SOUND\SOUNDMAN.SYS /i:7
DEVICEHIGH=C:\SCSI\ADAPTER.SYS
DEVICEHIGH=C:\VIDEO\VESA.SYS
```

Bob must keep in mind that there may still be a conflict with IRQ7. Recall that this interrupt is also used by the printer. If Bob has a printer he must not print and use the sound card at the same time. However, this is a better combination than the original files. The possibility of the CD-ROM and sound card being active simultaneously is greater than the printer and sound card being activated simultaneously.

That completes our discussion of IRQ, DMA, and I/O conflicts. Let's review the topics covered in this chapter.

Summary

One of the great benefits of personal computers is they are expandable. There are literally hundreds of devices that you can install to enhance and extend the capabilities of your system. The only potential downside to these devices comes in the form of conflicts. Knowing why conflicts occur can help you prevent them in your system. Here is a review of the topics covered in this chapter.

- Interrupt requests, or IRQs, are used by devices to get the attention of the microprocessor.
- Two devices should not be set to the same IRQ. Doing so may cause an IRQ conflict.

- IRQ conflicts can occur during startup or during operation when one of the conflicting devices is active.
- How you set the IRQ for a device depends on the device itself. Some devices use jumper settings, others uses programs to configure the device.
- Software cannot access a device unless it knows the IRQ setting of the device.
- Direct memory access (DMA) channels are used to rapidly exchange data between devices and memory.
- Devices can share a DMA channel providing they are not active at the same time.
- Each device (including many devices controlled by the operating system) has one or more I/O ports.
- Two devices cannot use the same I/O port at the same time.
- I/O port conflicts are usually caused by two I/O configurable devices being set to the same address.

Armed with this information, you should be able to prepare for conflicts within your system. The more familiar you are with your system's configuration, the less likely you are to run into problems in the future.

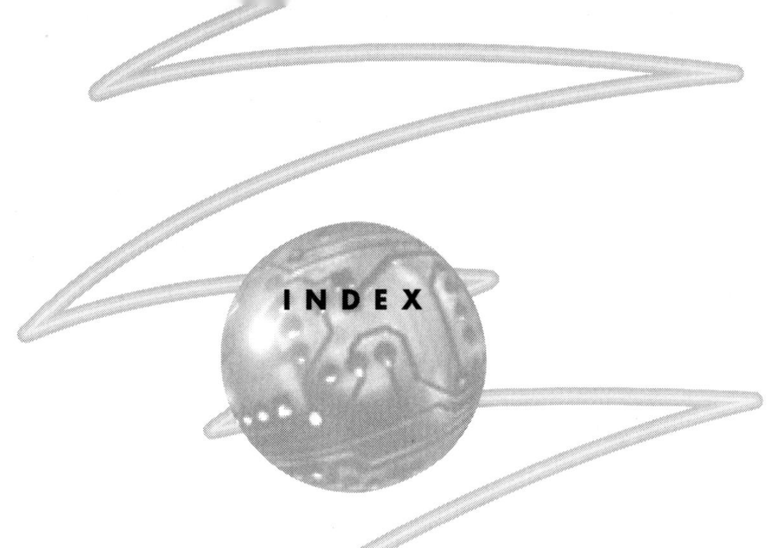
INDEX

D

E

N

P

Q

R

S

T

U

W

Books have a substantial influence on the destruction of the forests of the Earth. For example, it takes 17 trees to produce one ton of paper. A first printing of 30,000 copies of a typical 480 page book consumes 108,000 pounds of paper which will require 918 trees!

Waite Group Press™ is against the clear-cutting of forests and supports reforestation of the Pacific Northwest of the United States and Canada, where most of this paper comes from. As a publisher with several hundred thousand books sold each year, we feel an obligation to give back to the planet. We will therefore support and contribute a percentage of our proceeds to organizations which seek to preserve the forests of planet Earth.

WAITE GROUP PRESS™

WALKTHROUGHS AND FLYBYS CD

Phil Shatz

Fly around buildings before they exist, tour the inner workings of imaginary machines, and play electronic music while watching the motion of atoms. Welcome to the world of animated PC demos, a new area of technology and design that relies on high-powered PCs, an assortment of graphics animation software, a Sound Blaster board, and some special tricks. The *Walkthroughs and Flybys CD* presents breathtaking computer animation and music including over 300 megabytes of Autodesk 3D studio movies.

ISBN: 1-878739-40-9, 128 pages, 1-CD-ROM, $29.95, Available now

MULTIMEDIA CREATIONS Hands-On Workshop for Exploring Animation

Phillip Shaddock

Contemplating the jump into multimedia? Do it with *Multimedia Creations* and its powerful bundled GRASP program. Whether novice or programmer, you can create your own animated interactive audio-visual programs: from concept through post production, renderings to video tape. After a brief primer on PC video systems and animation fundamentals, you can start working with GRASP, creating everything from educational programs to your own multimedia cartoons. Work through the entire book/disk package to learn tricks like windowing, color cycling, sprite animation, delta compression techniques, and classical flip-book-style animation. And there are advanced chapters with in-depth coverage and reference sources for power users. Accompanying shareware programs provide you with the basic tools for creating complete multimedia presentations on the PC. For MS/PC DOS machines.

ISBN: 1-878739-26-3, 450 pages, 2-5.25" disks, $44.95, Available now

FRACTALS FOR WINDOWS

Tim Wegner, Mark Peterson, Bert Tyler, Pieter Branderhorst

Create new fractals and control over 85 different fractal types with a zoom box, menus, and a mouse! Bundled with WINFRACT, a powerful Windows version of FRACTINT for DOS, this package is faster than lightning at computing mind-bending fractals. Novices and experienced programmers alike will love this rich resource of spectacular images that you can use with other Windows programs. Create fractal wallpaper for your desktop or copy them to the clipboard and paste them into other applications. The book includes 3-D glasses, world-class fractal recipes, and source code for WINFRACT, as well as stunning color photos.

ISBN 1-878739-25-5, 358 pages, 1-3.5" disk and 3-D glasses, $34.95, Available now

Send for our unique catalog to get more information about these books, as well as our outstanding and award-winning titles, including:

Virtual Reality Creations: Use this book, along with the included REND386 software and Fresnel viewers, to build virtual worlds—limited only by your imagination.

Master C: Let the PC Teach You C and **Master C++: Let the PC Teach You Object-Oriented Programming:** Both book/disk software packages turn your computer into an infinitely patient C and C++ professor.

Image Lab: This unique book/disk set is a complete PC-based "digital darkroom" that covers virtually all areas of graphic processing and manipulation.

Nanotechnology Playhouse: This book and disk set is an accessible introduction to nanotechnology (the science of making devices, materials, objects of all kinds, one atom at a time). It includes multimedia demos to give you a taste of tomorrow.

Sound Effects Playhouse: An easy-to-use, hands-on workshop for creating, editing, and playing sounds under DOS and Windows. Includes 5MB of digitized sound files and utilities.

Virtual Reality Playhouse: Jack-in to the world of Virtual Reality with this playful book/disk package. Eight demos with VR simulations let you create your own personal digital dimension.

Artificial Life Playhouse: Turn your PC into an experimenter's lab to find out more about this exciting new area of scientific exploration. Eight demo programs are included.

PDA PLayhouse: Test drive the office of the future with this guide. Mac and PC simulations of the Apple Newton, Sharp Wizard, and AT&T EO, and others are included.

MULTITASK WINDOWS NT

Joel Powell

Multitask Windows NT makes programming for Microsoft's new 32-bit operating system quick and easy. You'll see how to master the tools and coding concepts of the new Win32 subsystem while getting a comprehensive overview of Windows NT API additions. Learn how to write programs that benefit from preemptive multitasking, and threads that take full advantage of NT. The extensive tutorials level that lofty NT learning curve. A disk with source code is included.

ISBN 1-878739-57-3, 562 pages, 1-3.5" disk, $34.95, Available now

FALCON 3: THE COMPLETE HANDBOOK

Joel Powell and Tom Basham

In step-by-step lessons you'll go from ground school up to mastery of the skies. You'll get plenty of hands-on training, feedback, and airspace adventure! The disk gives you the thrill of flying with over 30 custom control missions, a full-featured demo, and two hot utilities, FALCONR and F3MAPS.

ISBN: 1-878739-29-8, 652 pages, disk included, $34.95, Available now

WAITE GROUP PRESS™

TO ORDER TOLL FREE CALL 1-800-368-9369

TELEPHONE 415-924-2575 • FAX 415-924-2576

OR SEND ORDER FORM TO: WAITE GROUP PRESS, 200 TAMAL PLAZA, CORTE MADERA, CA 94925

Qty	Book	US/Can Price	Total
____	Artificial Life Playhouse	$34.95/44.95	______
____	Falcon 3: The Complete Handbook	$34.95/44.95	______
____	Fractals for Windows	$34.95/44.95	______
____	Image Lab	$39.95/49.95	______
____	Master C ☐ 3.5" ☐ 5.25" disks	$44.95/62.95	______
____	Master C++ ☐ 3.5" ☐ 5.25" disks	$39.95/49.95	______
____	Multimedia Creations	$44.95/56.95	______
____	Multitask Windows NT	$34.95/48.95	______
____	Nanotechnology Playhouse	$23.95/33.95	______
____	PDA Playhouse	$24.95/34.95	______
____	Sound Effects Playhouse	$24.95/34.95	______
____	Virtual Reality Creations	$34.95/48.95	______
____	Virtual Reality Playhouse	$22.95/29.95	______
____	Walkthroughs & Flybys CD	$29.95/41.95	______

alif. residents add 7.25% Sales Tax ______

hipping

SPS ($5 first book/$1 each add'l) ______
PS Two Day ($10/$2) ______
anada ($10/$4) ______

TOTAL ______

Ship to

Name ____________________

Company ____________________

Address ____________________

City, State, Zip ____________________

Phone ____________________

All orders must be prepaid
Payment Method

☐ Check Enclosed ☐ VISA ☐ MasterCard

Card # ____________________ Exp. Date ________

Signature ____________________

SATISFACTION GUARANTEED
OR YOUR MONEY BACK.
NO QUESTIONS ASKED.

SATISFACTION REPORT CARD

Please fill out this card if you want to know of future updates to *Memory Management in a Multimedia World* or to receive our catalog.

WAITE GROUP PRESS™

Company Name: ____________________

Division/Department: ____________ **Mail Stop:** ____________

Last Name: ____________ **First Name:** ____________ **Middle Initial:** ______

Street Address: ____________________

City: ____________ **State:** ____________ **Zip:** ______

Daytime telephone: ( ) ____________________

Date product was acquired: **Month** ______ **Day** ______ **Year** ______ **Your Occupation:** ____________

Overall, how would you rate *Memory Management in a Multimedia World*?

☐ Excellent ☐ Very good ☐ Good
☐ Fair ☐ Below average ☐ Poor

What did you like MOST about this book? ____________________

What did you like LEAST about this book? ____________________

How did you use this book (problem-solver, tutorial, reference...)? ____________________

Did you enjoy the approach of this book? ____________________

Is there any program or subject you would like to see The Waite Group cover in a similar approach? ____________________

What is your level of computer expertise?

☐ New ☐ Dabbler ☐ Hacker
☐ Power user ☐ Programmer ☐ Experienced professional

Please describe your computer hardware:

Computer ____________ Hard disk ____________
Video card ____________ Monitor ____________
Printer ____________ Peripherals ____________
Sound board ____________ CD ROM ____________

What is the primary use for your computer? ____________________

Where did you buy this book?

☐ Bookstore (name): ____________
☐ Discount store (name): ____________
☐ Computer store (name): ____________
☐ Catalog (name): ____________
☐ Direct from WGP ☐ Other ____________

What price did you pay for this book? ____________

What influenced your purchase of this book?

☐ Recommendation ☐ Advertisement
☐ Magazine review ☐ Store display
☐ Mailing ☐ Book's format
☐ Reputation of Waite Group Press
☐ Other ____________

How many computer books do you buy each year? ______
How many other Waite Group books do you own? ______
What is your favorite Waite Group book? ____________

Additional comments? ____________________

Please send to: **Waite Group Press**
Attn: Memory Management
200 Tamal Plaza
Corte Madera, CA 94925

☐ **Check here for a free Waite Group catalog**

Companion Disk Order Form

A 3.5-inch, 720KB companion disk is available for this book. The companion disk for *Memory Management in a Multimedia World* includes all the configuration batch files presented in this book. The companion disk ensures that you spend more time using your computer and less time setting it up.

To order by phone call 800-368-9369 or Fax 415-924-2576

or send to Waite Group Press, 200 Tamal Plaza, Corte Madera, CA 94925

Name

Company

Address

Street Address Only, No P.O. Box

City State ZIP –

Daytime Phone

Quantity

Name	Item #	Disk Size	Quantity	Price	
Memory Management in a Multimedia World companion disk	CD018	3.5"		x $15.00	
				Sales Tax	
				Shipping	
				Total Due	

Sales Tax—California addresses add 7.25% sales tax.

Shipping—Price includes First Class shipping within the Continental U.S. Add $10 Canada, or $15 Foreign for shipping and handling. Allow 4 to 6 weeks. Prices subject to change. Purchase orders subject to credit approval, and verbal purchase orders will not be accepted.

Method of Payment

Please make checks or money orders payable to The Waite Group. To pay by credit card, please complete the following:

Visa MasterCard Card Number Exp. Date ________

Cardholder's Name ________

Cardholder's Signature ________

Daytime Phone Number ________

Send to:
Waite Group Press, Inc.
Attn: *Memory Management in a Multimedia World* Companion Disk Offer
200 Tamal Plaza
Corte Madera, CA 94925